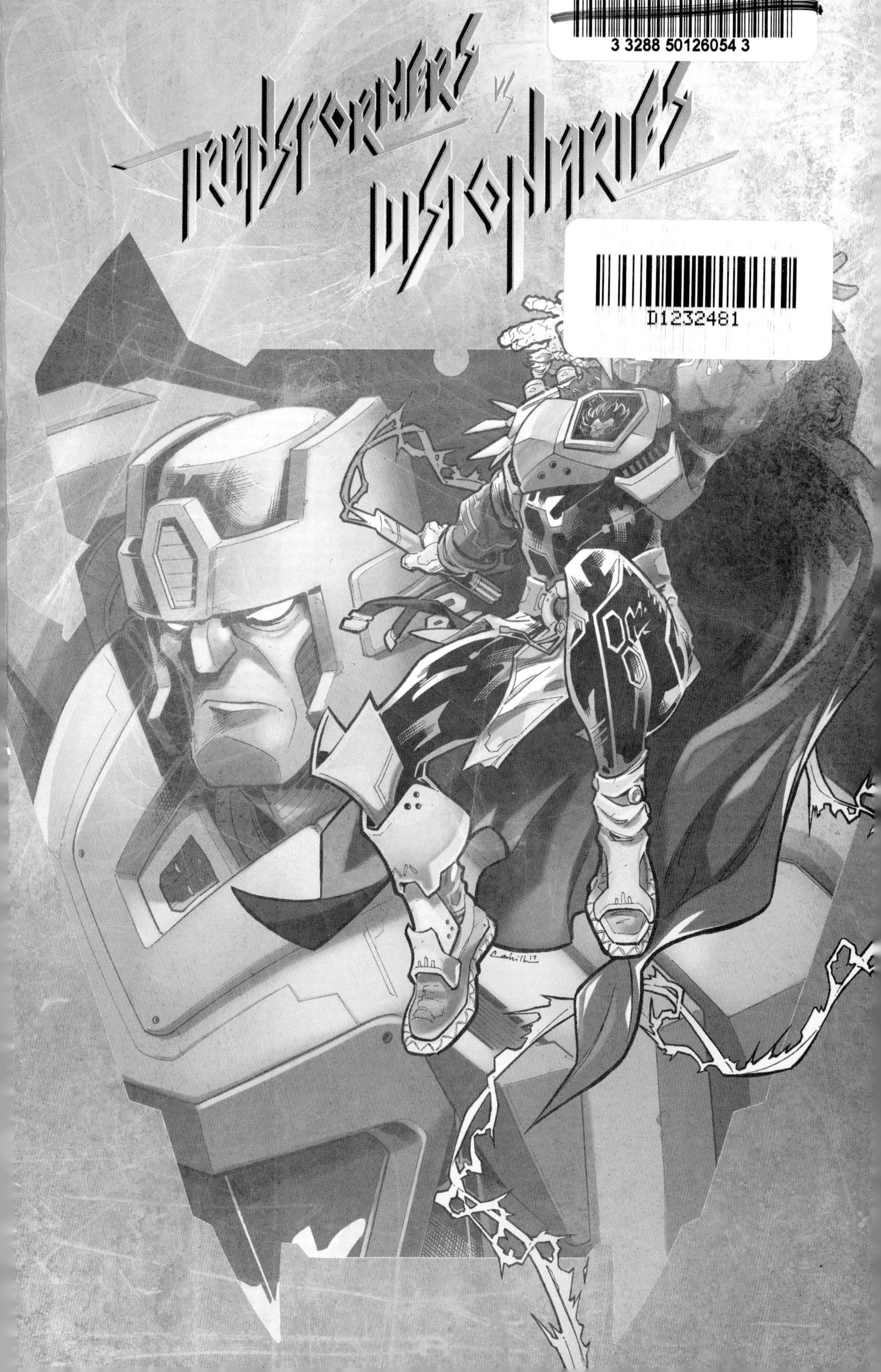
TRANSFORMERS vs. VISIONARIES

Become our fan on Facebook **facebook.com/idwpublishing**
Follow us on Twitter **@idwpublishing**
Subscribe to us on YouTube **youtube.com/idwpublishing**
See what's new on Tumblr **tumblr.idwpublishing.com**
Check us out on Instagram **instagram.com/idwpublishing**

Licensed By:

Greg Goldstein, President & Publisher
Robbie Robbins, EVP & Sr. Art Director
Matthew Ruzicka, CPA, Chief Financial Officer
David Hedgecock, Associate Publisher
Lorelei Bunjes, VP of Digital Services
Jerry Bennington, VP of New Product Development
Eric Moss, Sr. Director, Licensing & Business Development

Ted Adams, Founder & CEO of IDW Media Holdings

ISBN: 978-1-68405-283-7   21 20 19 18   1 2 3 4

Originally published as TRANSFORMERS VS. VISIONARIES issues #1–5..

Special thanks to Ben Montano, Josh Feldman, Ed Lane, Beth Artale,
Derryl DePriest, and Michael Kelly for their invaluable assistance.

For international rights, contact licensing@idwpublishing.com

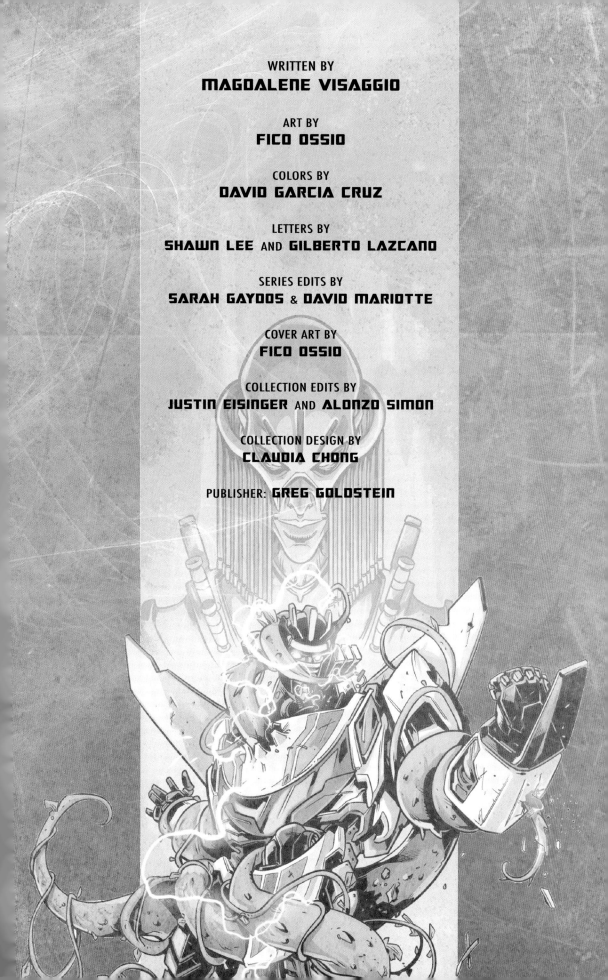

WRITTEN BY
MAGDALENE VISAGGIO

ART BY
FICO OSSIO

COLORS BY
DAVID GARCIA CRUZ

LETTERS BY
SHAWN LEE AND **GILBERTO LAZCANO**

SERIES EDITS BY
SARAH GAYDOS & **DAVID MARIOTTE**

COVER ART BY
FICO OSSIO

COLLECTION EDITS BY
JUSTIN EISINGER AND **ALONZO SIMON**

COLLECTION DESIGN BY
CLAUDIA CHONG

PUBLISHER: **GREG GOLDSTEIN**

PREVIOUSLY...

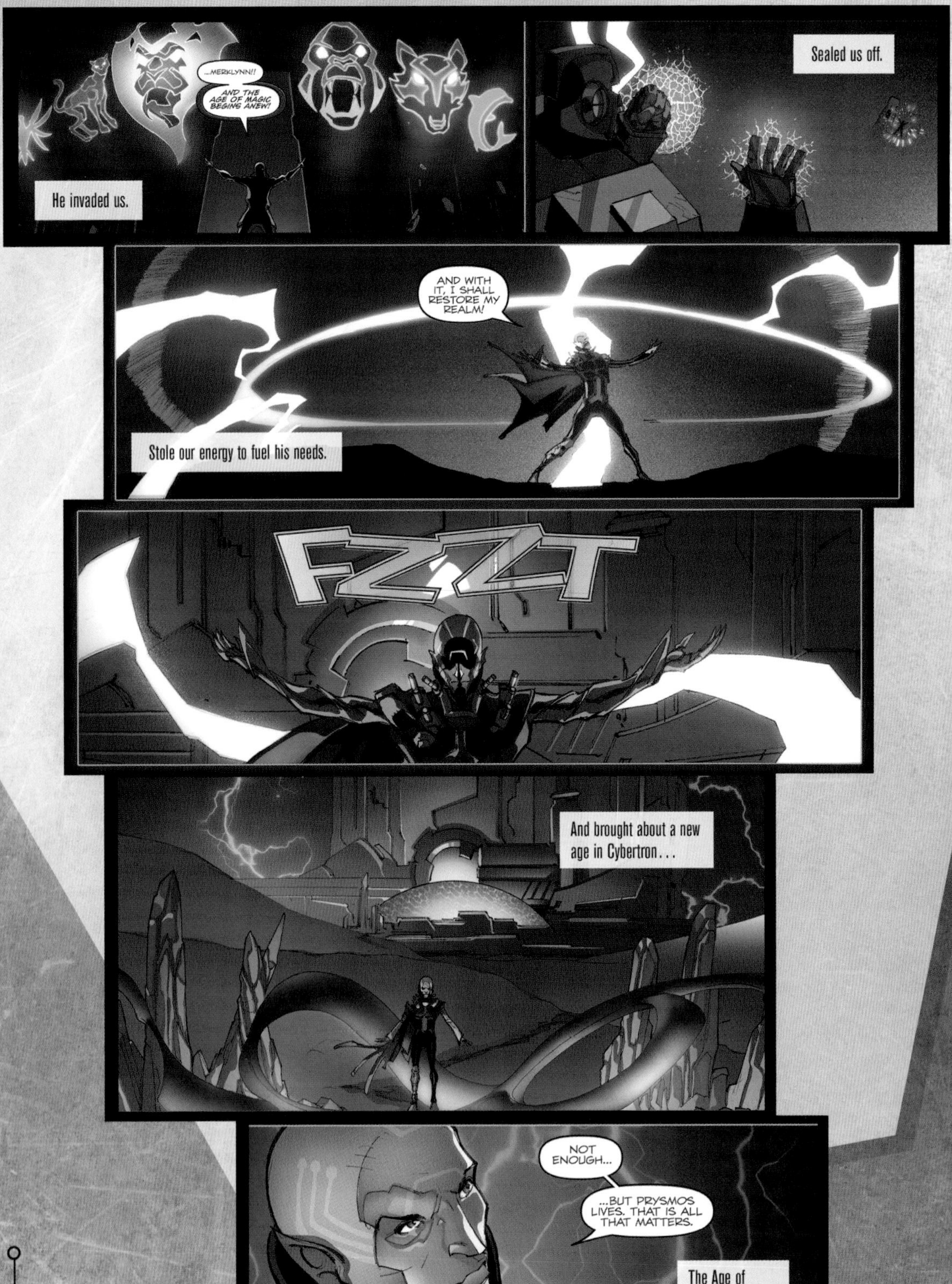
...MERKLYNN!!
AND THE AGE OF MAGIC BEGINS ANEW!
He invaded us.
Sealed us off.
AND WITH IT, I SHALL RESTORE MY REALM!
Stole our energy to fuel his needs.
FZZT
And brought about a new age in Cybertron...
NOT ENOUGH...
...BUT PRYSMOS LIVES. THAT IS ALL THAT MATTERS.
The Age of Magic begins...

ROLL CALL...

REPRESENTING
CYBERTRON

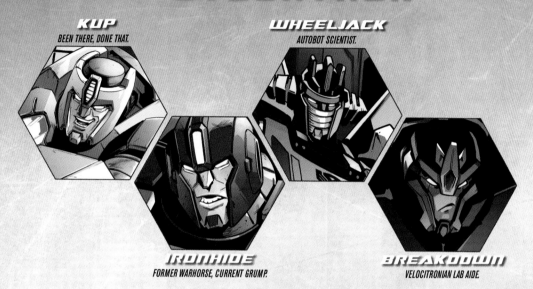

KUP
BEEN THERE, DONE THAT.

WHEELJACK
AUTOBOT SCIENTIST.

IRONHIDE
FORMER WARHORSE, CURRENT GRUMP.

BREAKDOWN
VELOCITRONIAN LAB AIDE.

REPRESENTING
NEW PRYSMOS

MERKLYNN
IMPRISONED PRYSMOSIAN MAGICIAN.

VIRULINA
DARKLING LORD. DONE WITH CYBERTRON.

LEORIC
SPECTRAL KNIGHT. MEOW.

CINDARR
DARKLING THINKER.

WITTERQUICK
SUPERFAST KNIGHT.

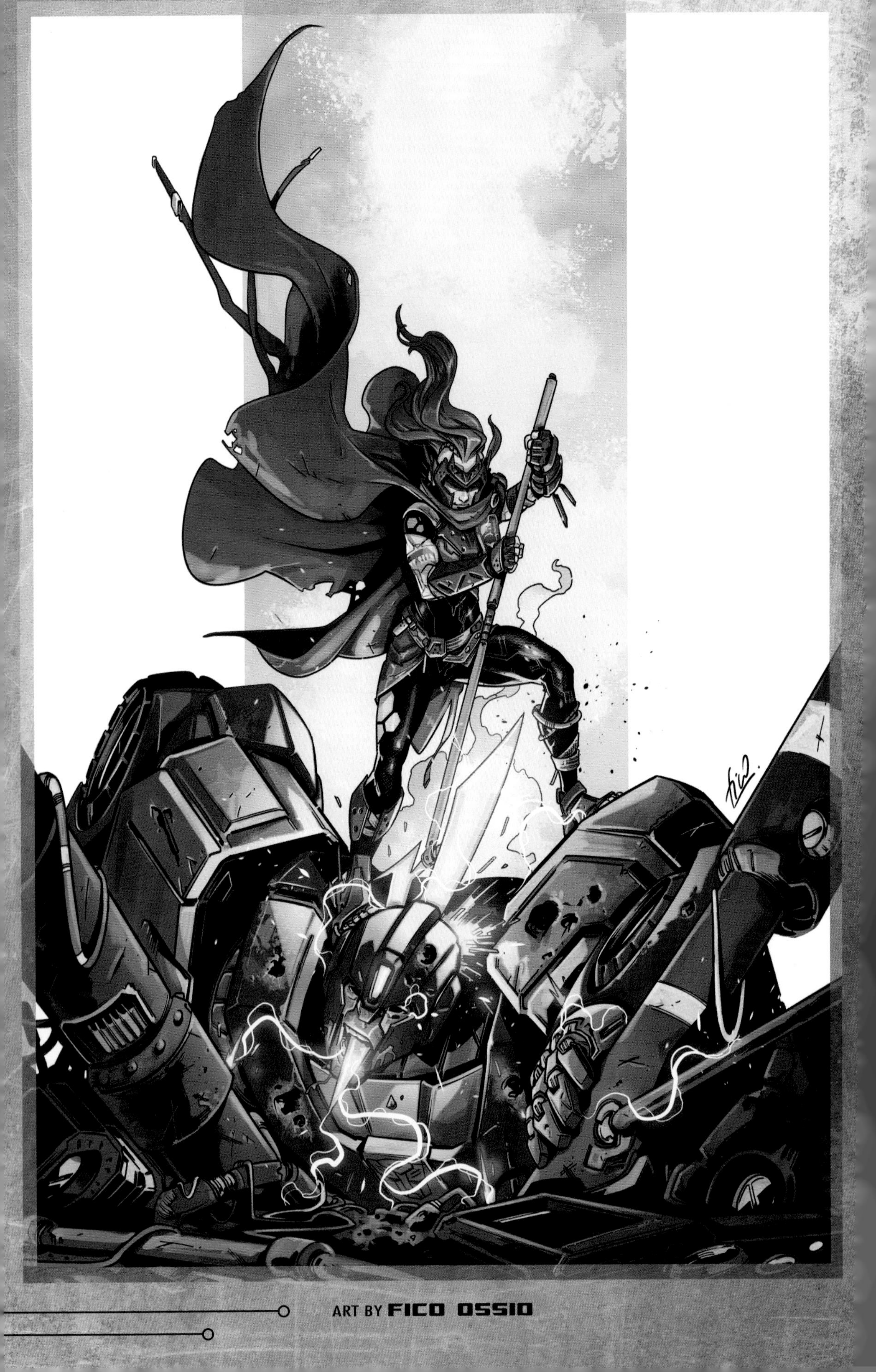

ART BY **FICO OSSIO**

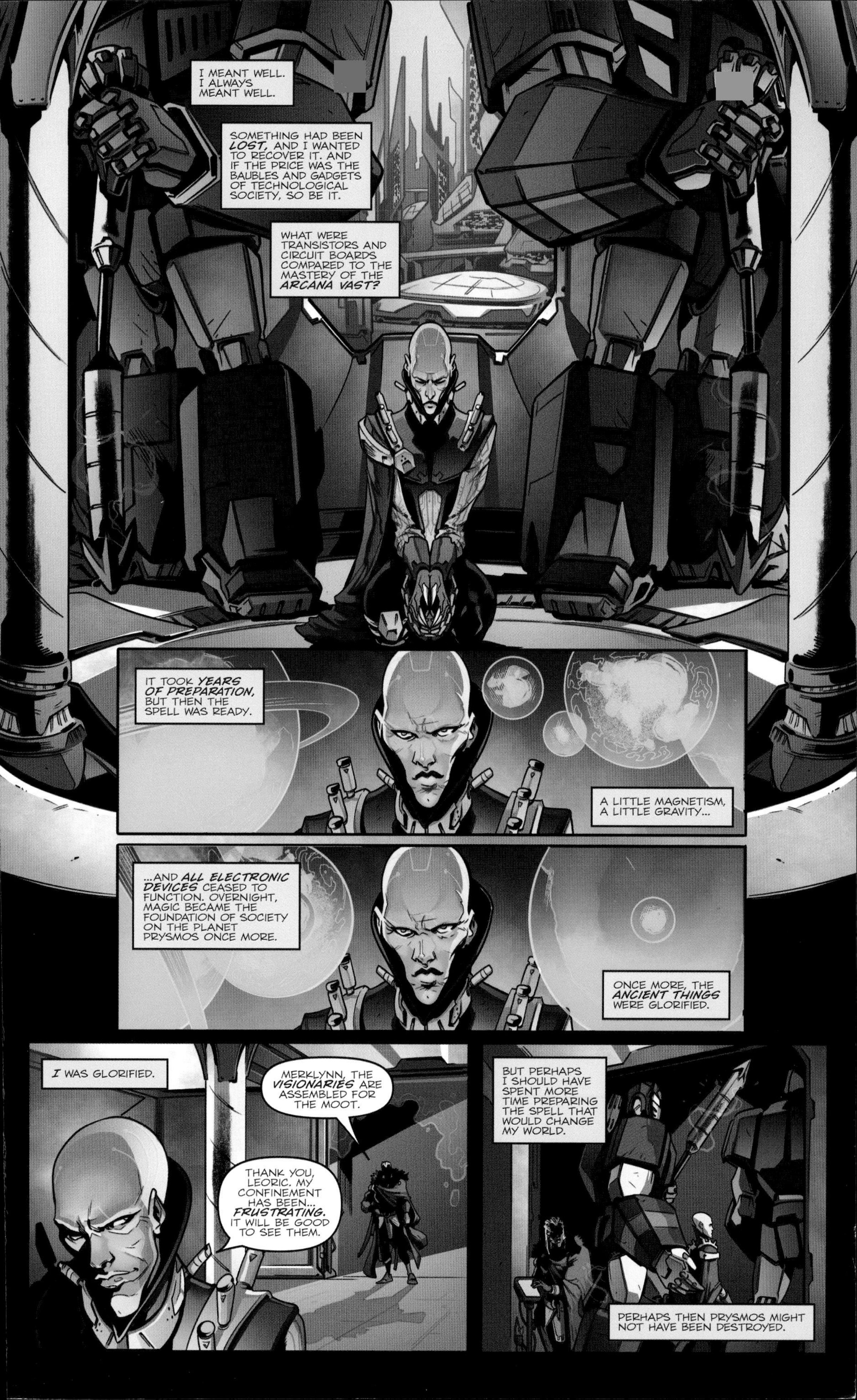
I MEANT WELL. I ALWAYS MEANT WELL.
SOMETHING HAD BEEN LOST, AND I WANTED TO RECOVER IT. AND IF THE PRICE WAS THE BAUBLES AND GADGETS OF TECHNOLOGICAL SOCIETY, SO BE IT.
WHAT WERE TRANSISTORS AND CIRCUIT BOARDS COMPARED TO THE MASTERY OF THE ARCANA VAST?
IT TOOK YEARS OF PREPARATION, BUT THEN THE SPELL WAS READY.
A LITTLE MAGNETISM, A LITTLE GRAVITY...
...AND ALL ELECTRONIC DEVICES CEASED TO FUNCTION. OVERNIGHT, MAGIC BECAME THE FOUNDATION OF SOCIETY ON THE PLANET PRYSMOS ONCE MORE.
ONCE MORE, THE ANCIENT THINGS WERE GLORIFIED.
I WAS GLORIFIED.
MERKLYNN, THE VISIONARIES ARE ASSEMBLED FOR THE MOOT.
THANK YOU, LEORIC. MY CONFINEMENT HAS BEEN... FRUSTRATING. IT WILL BE GOOD TO SEE THEM.
BUT PERHAPS I SHOULD HAVE SPENT MORE TIME PREPARING THE SPELL THAT WOULD CHANGE MY WORLD.
PERHAPS THEN PRYSMOS MIGHT NOT HAVE BEEN DESTROYED.

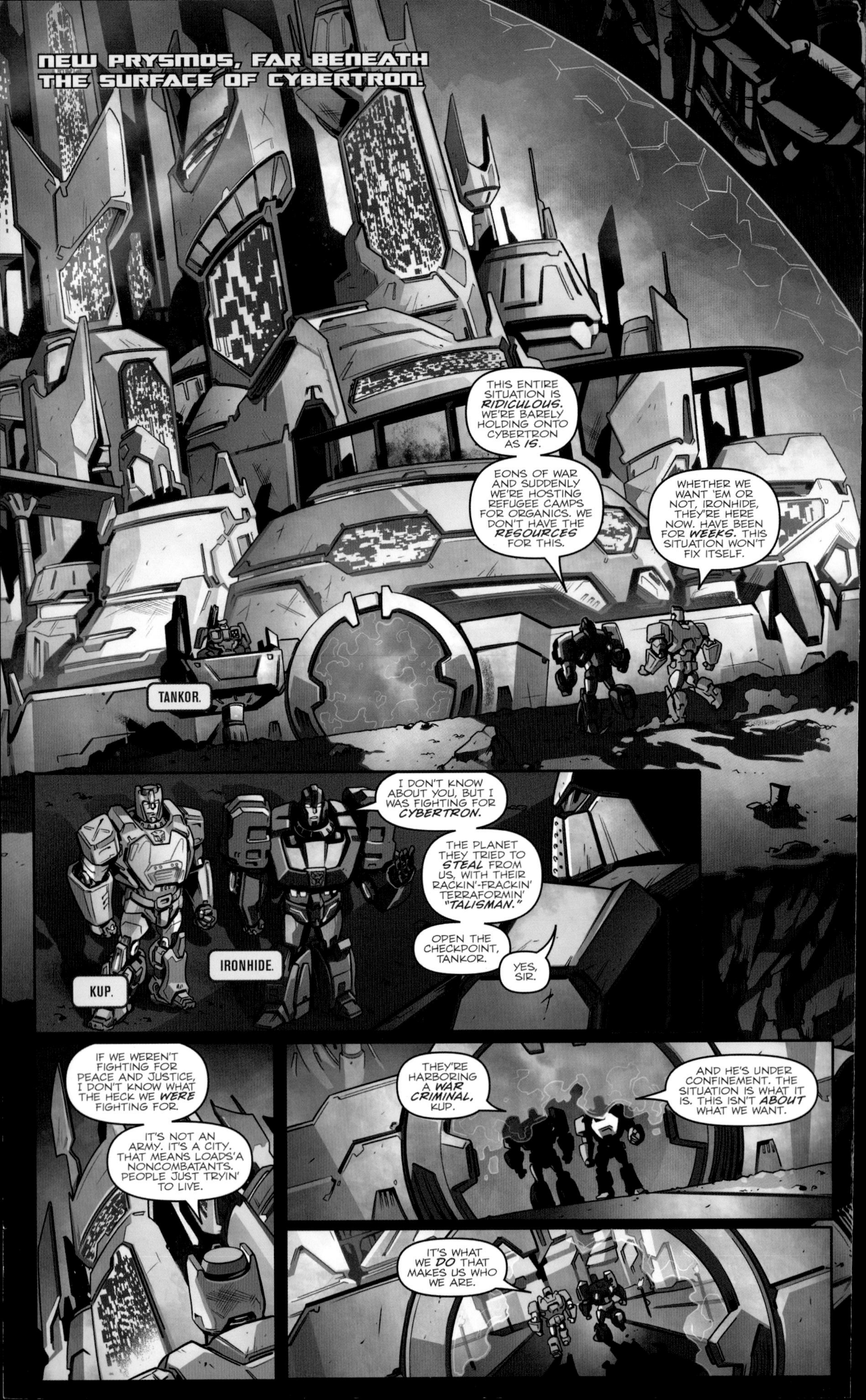
NEW PRYSMOS, FAR BENEATH THE SURFACE OF CYBERTRON.
THIS ENTIRE SITUATION IS RIDICULOUS. WE'RE BARELY HOLDING ONTO CYBERTRON AS IS.
EONS OF WAR AND SUDDENLY WE'RE HOSTING REFUGEE CAMPS FOR ORGANICS. WE DON'T HAVE THE RESOURCES FOR THIS.
WHETHER WE WANT 'EM OR NOT, IRONHIDE, THEY'RE HERE NOW. HAVE BEEN FOR WEEKS. THIS SITUATION WON'T FIX ITSELF.
TANKOR.
I DON'T KNOW ABOUT YOU, BUT I WAS FIGHTING FOR CYBERTRON.
THE PLANET THEY TRIED TO STEAL FROM US, WITH THEIR RACKIN'-FRACKIN' TERRAFORMIN' "TALISMAN."
OPEN THE CHECKPOINT, TANKOR.
YES, SIR.
IRONHIDE.
KUP.
IF WE WEREN'T FIGHTING FOR PEACE AND JUSTICE, I DON'T KNOW WHAT THE HECK WE WERE FIGHTING FOR.
IT'S NOT AN ARMY. IT'S A CITY. THAT MEANS LOADS'A NONCOMBATANTS. PEOPLE JUST TRYIN' TO LIVE.
THEY'RE HARBORING A WAR CRIMINAL, KUP.
AND HE'S UNDER CONFINEMENT. THE SITUATION IS WHAT IT IS. THIS ISN'T ABOUT WHAT WE WANT.
IT'S WHAT WE DO THAT MAKES US WHO WE ARE.

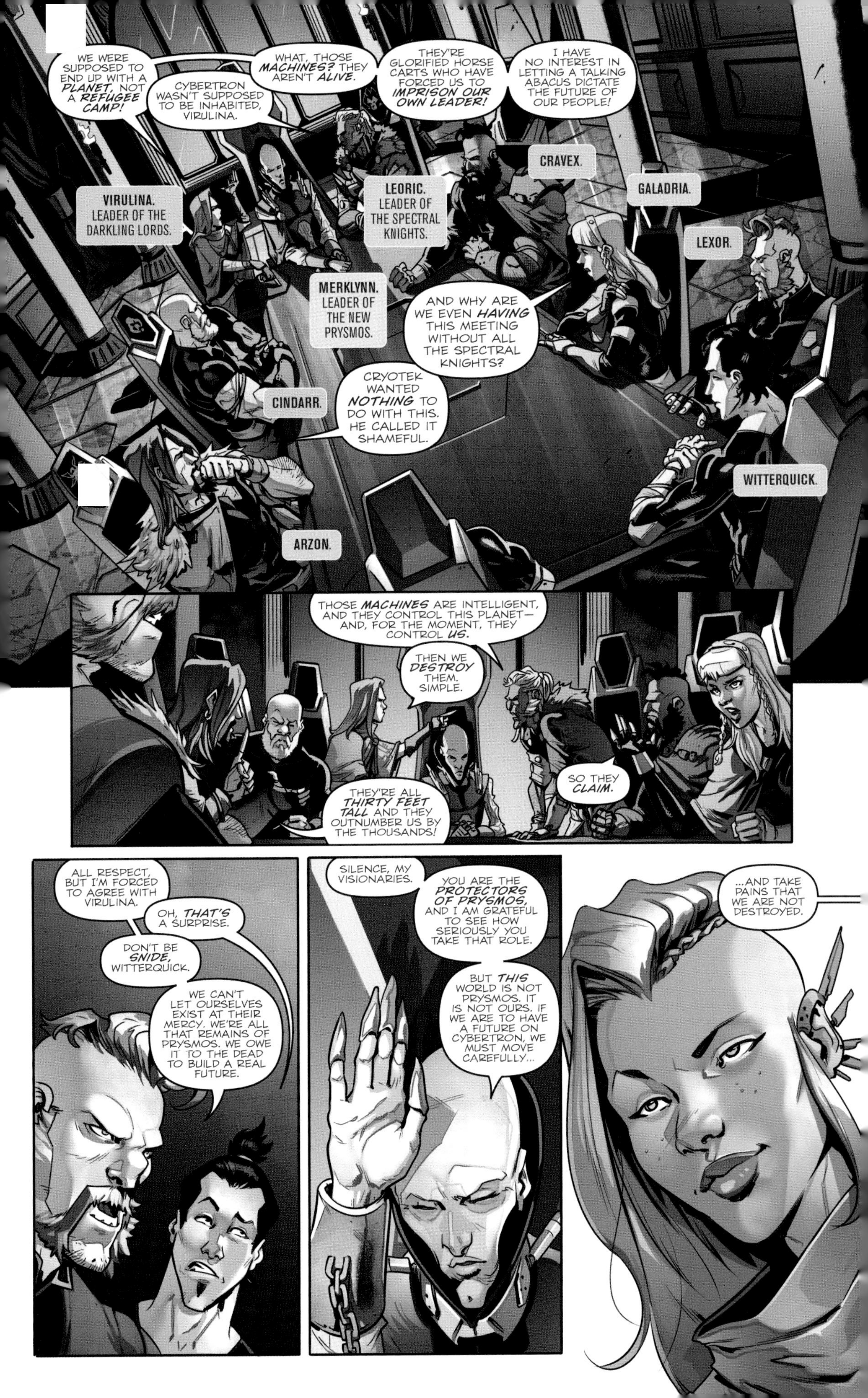

WE WERE SUPPOSED TO END UP WITH A *PLANET*, NOT A *REFUGEE CAMP!*
CYBERTRON WASN'T SUPPOSED TO BE INHABITED, VIRULINA.
WHAT, THOSE *MACHINES?* THEY AREN'T *ALIVE*.
THEY'RE GLORIFIED HORSE CARTS WHO HAVE FORCED US TO *IMPRISON OUR OWN LEADER!*
I HAVE NO INTEREST IN LETTING A TALKING ABACUS DICTATE THE FUTURE OF OUR PEOPLE!
VIRULINA. LEADER OF THE DARKLING LORDS.
LEORIC. LEADER OF THE SPECTRAL KNIGHTS.
CRAVEX.
GALADRIA.
LEXOR.
MERKLYNN. LEADER OF THE NEW PRYSMOS.
AND WHY ARE WE EVEN *HAVING* THIS MEETING WITHOUT ALL THE SPECTRAL KNIGHTS?
CRYOTEK WANTED *NOTHING* TO DO WITH THIS. HE CALLED IT SHAMEFUL.
CINDARR.
WITTERQUICK.
ARZON.
THOSE *MACHINES* ARE INTELLIGENT, AND THEY CONTROL THIS PLANET— AND, FOR THE MOMENT, THEY CONTROL *US*.
THEN WE *DESTROY* THEM. SIMPLE.
THEY'RE ALL *THIRTY FEET TALL* AND THEY OUTNUMBER US BY THE THOUSANDS!
SO THEY *CLAIM*.
ALL RESPECT, BUT I'M FORCED TO AGREE WITH VIRULINA.
OH, *THAT'S* A SURPRISE.
DON'T BE *SNIDE*, WITTERQUICK.
WE CAN'T LET OURSELVES EXIST AT THEIR MERCY. WE'RE ALL THAT REMAINS OF PRYSMOS. WE OWE IT TO THE DEAD TO BUILD A REAL FUTURE.
SILENCE, MY VISIONARIES.
YOU ARE THE *PROTECTORS OF PRYSMOS*, AND I AM GRATEFUL TO SEE HOW SERIOUSLY YOU TAKE THAT ROLE.
BUT *THIS* WORLD IS NOT PRYSMOS. IT IS NOT OURS. IF WE ARE TO HAVE A FUTURE ON CYBERTRON, WE MUST MOVE CAREFULLY...
...AND TAKE PAINS THAT WE ARE NOT DESTROYED.

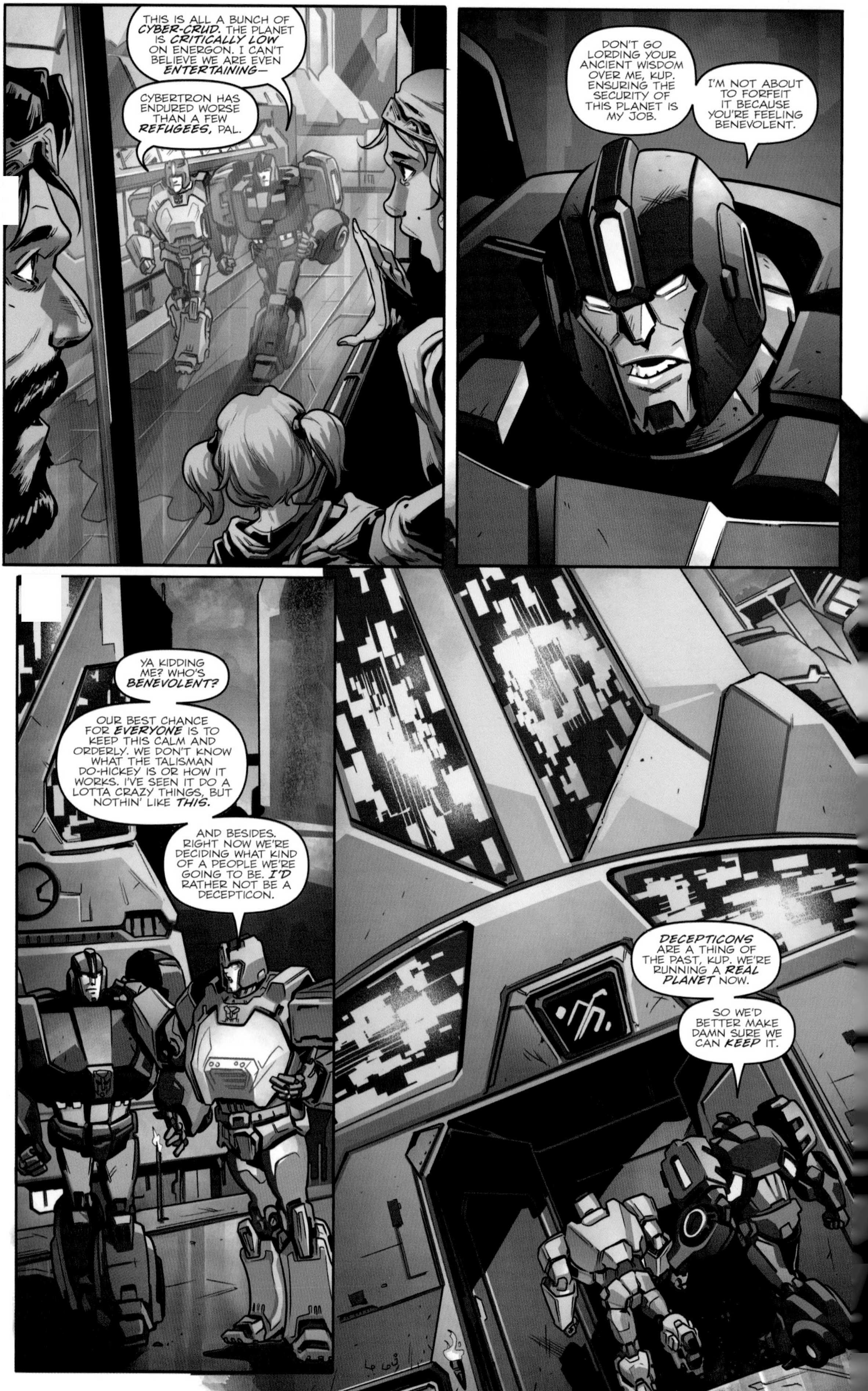
THIS IS ALL A BUNCH OF CYBER-CRUD. THE PLANET IS CRITICALLY LOW ON ENERGON. I CAN'T BELIEVE WE ARE EVEN ENTERTAINING—
CYBERTRON HAS ENDURED WORSE THAN A FEW REFUGEES, PAL.
DON'T GO LORDING YOUR ANCIENT WISDOM OVER ME, KUP. ENSURING THE SECURITY OF THIS PLANET IS MY JOB.
I'M NOT ABOUT TO FORFEIT IT BECAUSE YOU'RE FEELING BENEVOLENT.
YA KIDDING ME? WHO'S BENEVOLENT?
OUR BEST CHANCE FOR EVERYONE IS TO KEEP THIS CALM AND ORDERLY. WE DON'T KNOW WHAT THE TALISMAN DO-HICKEY IS OR HOW IT WORKS. I'VE SEEN IT DO A LOTTA CRAZY THINGS, BUT NOTHIN' LIKE THIS.
AND BESIDES. RIGHT NOW WE'RE DECIDING WHAT KIND OF A PEOPLE WE'RE GOING TO BE. I'D RATHER NOT BE A DECEPTICON.
DECEPTICONS ARE A THING OF THE PAST, KUP. WE'RE RUNNING A REAL PLANET NOW.
SO WE'D BETTER MAKE DAMN SURE WE CAN KEEP IT.

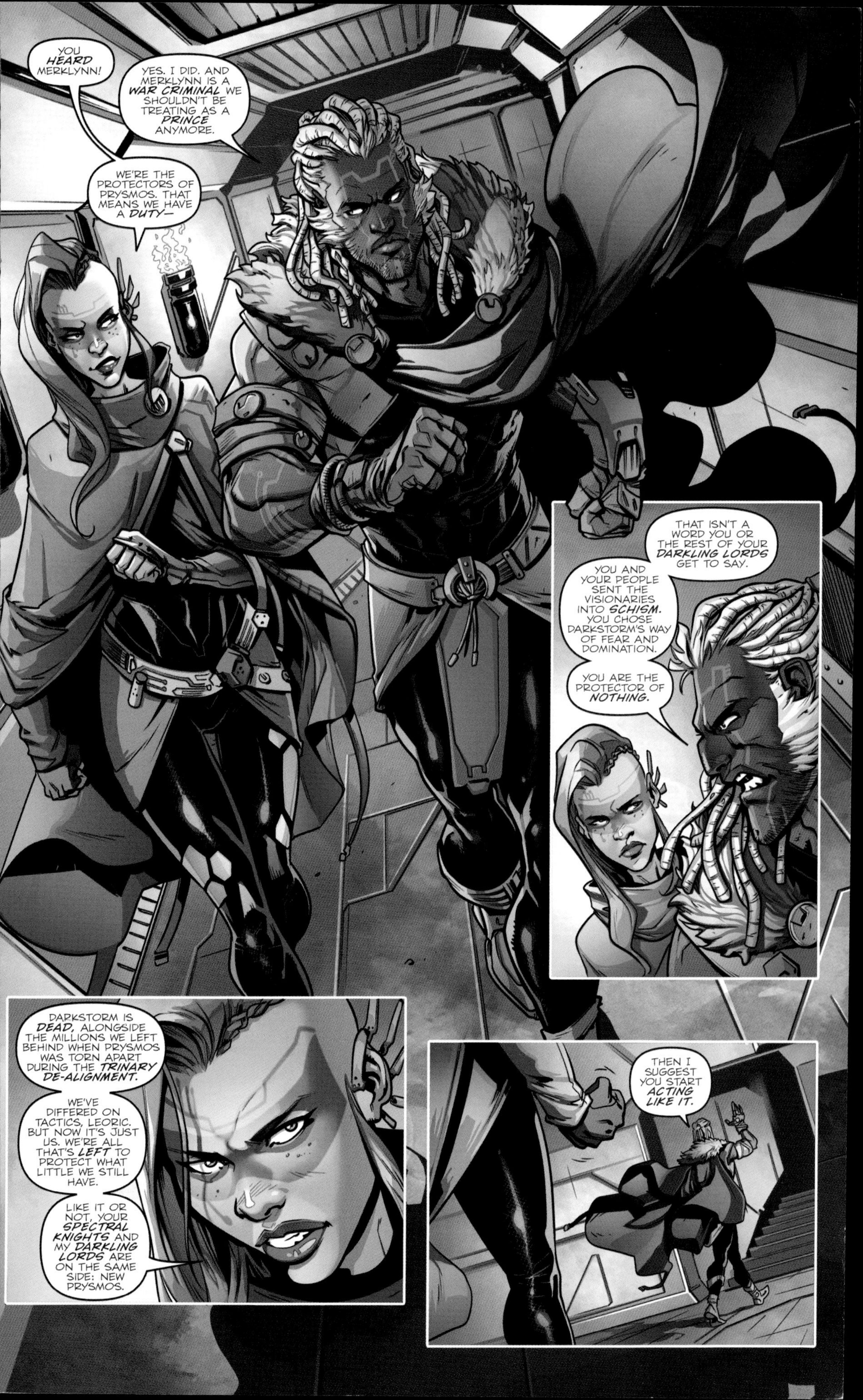

YOU HEARD MERKLYNN!
YES. I DID. AND MERKLYNN IS A WAR CRIMINAL WE SHOULDN'T BE TREATING AS A PRINCE ANYMORE.
WE'RE THE PROTECTORS OF PRYSMOS. THAT MEANS WE HAVE A DUTY—
THAT ISN'T A WORD YOU OR THE REST OF YOUR DARKLING LORDS GET TO SAY.
YOU AND YOUR PEOPLE SENT THE VISIONARIES INTO SCHISM. YOU CHOSE DARKSTORM'S WAY OF FEAR AND DOMINATION.
YOU ARE THE PROTECTOR OF NOTHING.
DARKSTORM IS DEAD, ALONGSIDE THE MILLIONS WE LEFT BEHIND WHEN PRYSMOS WAS TORN APART DURING THE TRINARY DE-ALIGNMENT.
WE'VE DIFFERED ON TACTICS, LEORIC. BUT NOW IT'S JUST US. WE'RE ALL THAT'S LEFT TO PROTECT WHAT LITTLE WE STILL HAVE.
LIKE IT OR NOT, YOUR SPECTRAL KNIGHTS AND MY DARKLING LORDS ARE ON THE SAME SIDE: NEW PRYSMOS.
THEN I SUGGEST YOU START ACTING LIKE IT.

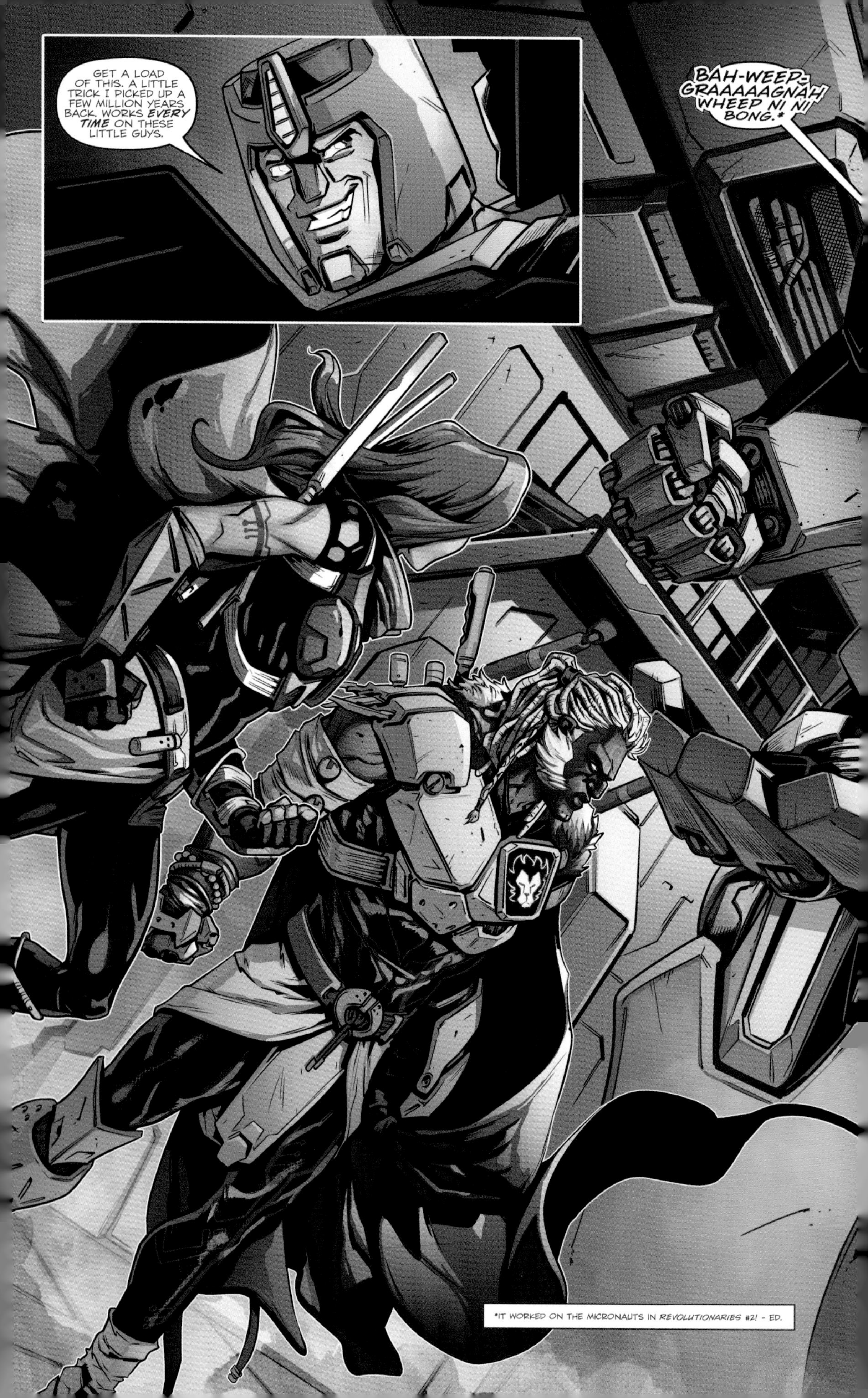
GET A LOAD OF THIS. A LITTLE TRICK I PICKED UP A FEW MILLION YEARS BACK. WORKS **EVERY TIME** ON THESE LITTLE GUYS.
BAH-WEEP-GRAAAAAGNAH WHEEP NI NI BONG.*
*IT WORKED ON THE MICRONAUTS IN *REVOLUTIONARIES* #2! - ED.

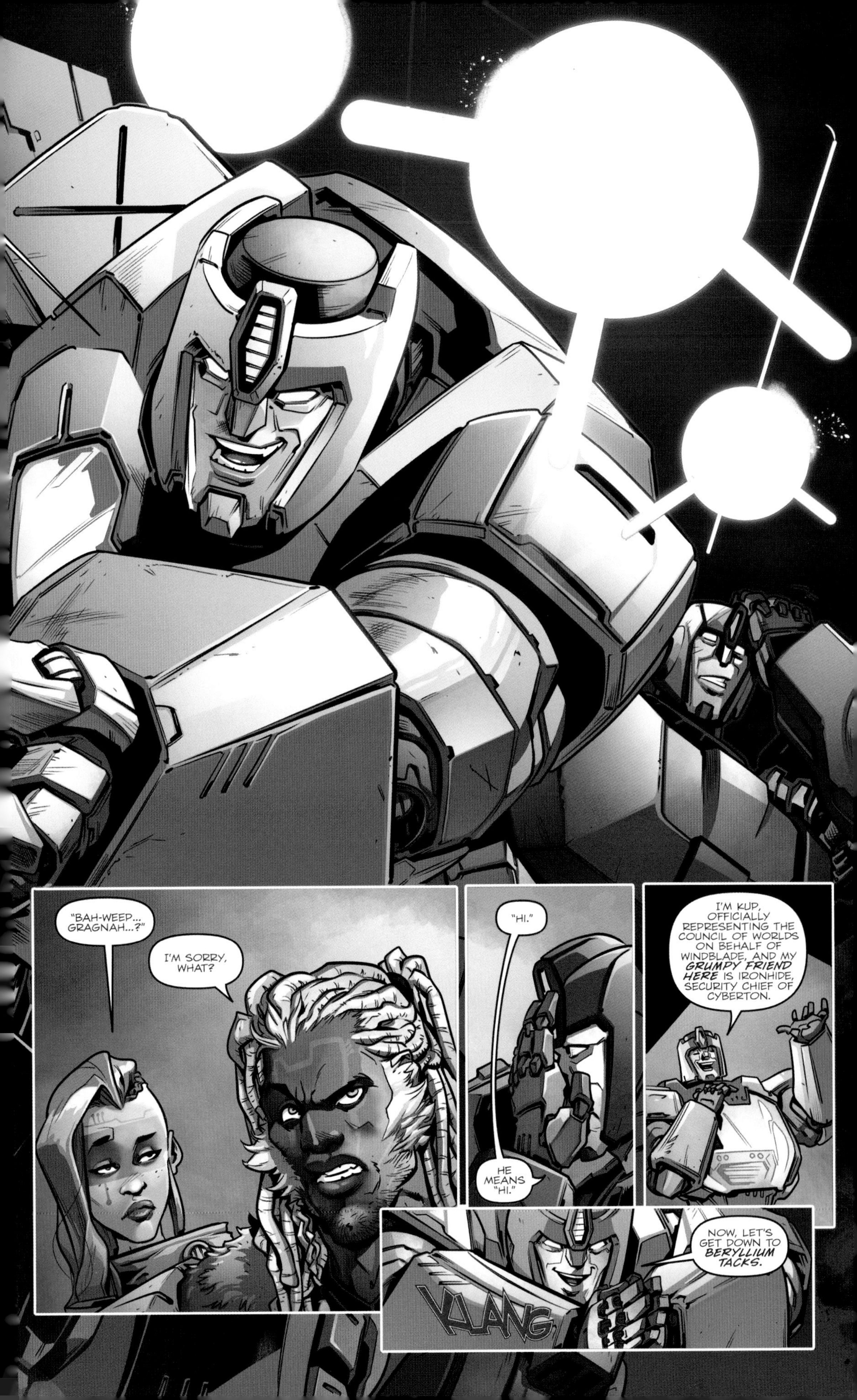

"BAH-WEEP... GRAGNAH...?"
I'M SORRY, WHAT?
"HI."
HE MEANS "HI."
I'M KUP, OFFICIALLY REPRESENTING THE COUNCIL OF WORLDS ON BEHALF OF WINDBLADE, AND MY GRUMPY FRIEND HERE IS IRONHIDE, SECURITY CHIEF OF CYBERTON.
NOW, LET'S GET DOWN TO BERYLLIUM TACKS.
KLANG

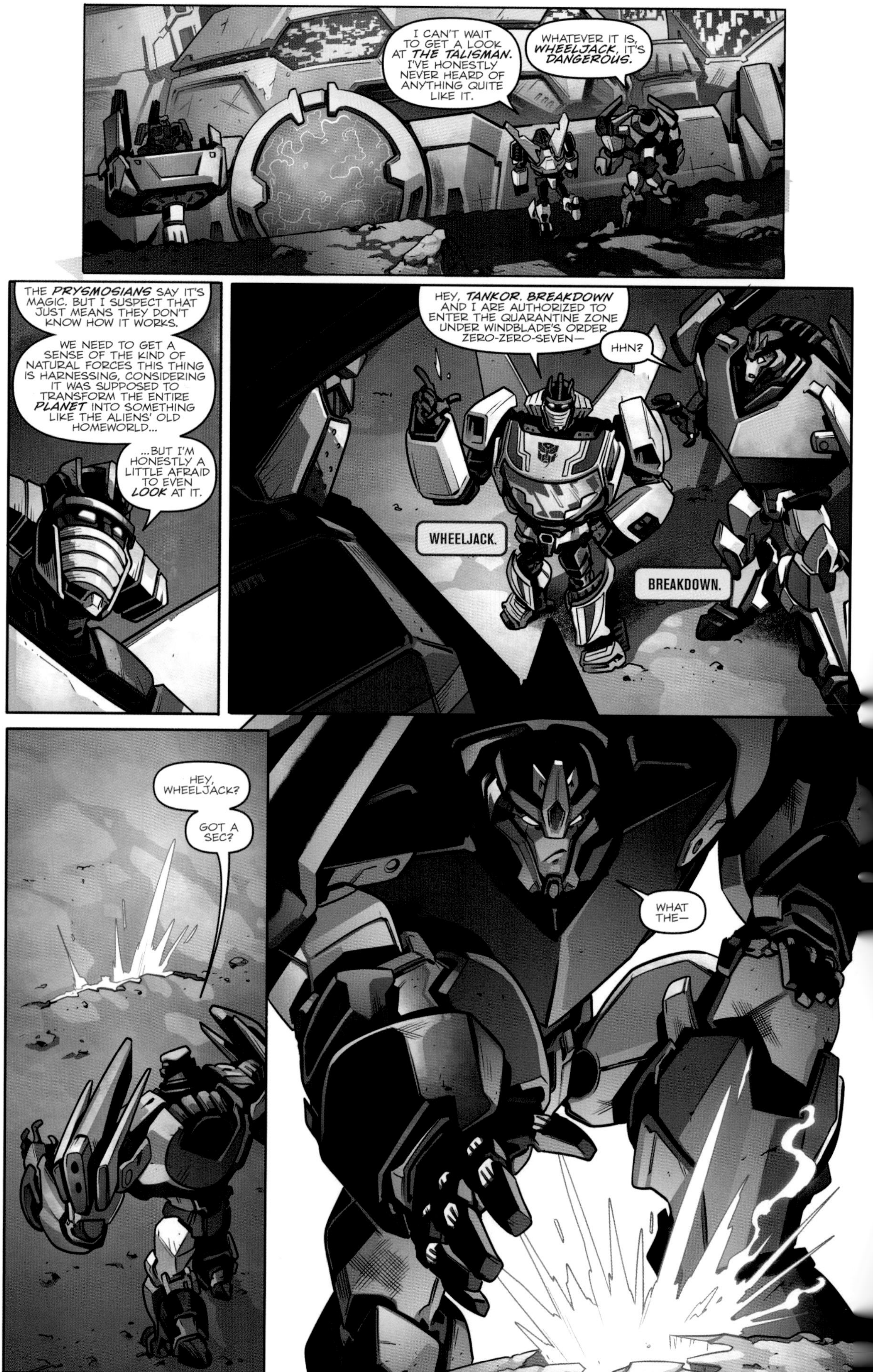
I CAN'T WAIT TO GET A LOOK AT THE TALISMAN. I'VE HONESTLY NEVER HEARD OF ANYTHING QUITE LIKE IT.
WHATEVER IT IS, WHEELJACK, IT'S DANGEROUS.
THE PRYSMOSIANS SAY IT'S MAGIC. BUT I SUSPECT THAT JUST MEANS THEY DON'T KNOW HOW IT WORKS.
WE NEED TO GET A SENSE OF THE KIND OF NATURAL FORCES THIS THING IS HARNESSING, CONSIDERING IT WAS SUPPOSED TO TRANSFORM THE ENTIRE PLANET INTO SOMETHING LIKE THE ALIENS' OLD HOMEWORLD...
...BUT I'M HONESTLY A LITTLE AFRAID TO EVEN LOOK AT IT.
HEY, TANKOR. BREAKDOWN AND I ARE AUTHORIZED TO ENTER THE QUARANTINE ZONE UNDER WINDBLADE'S ORDER ZERO-ZERO-SEVEN—
HHN?
WHEELJACK.
BREAKDOWN.
HEY, WHEELJACK?
GOT A SEC?
WHAT THE—

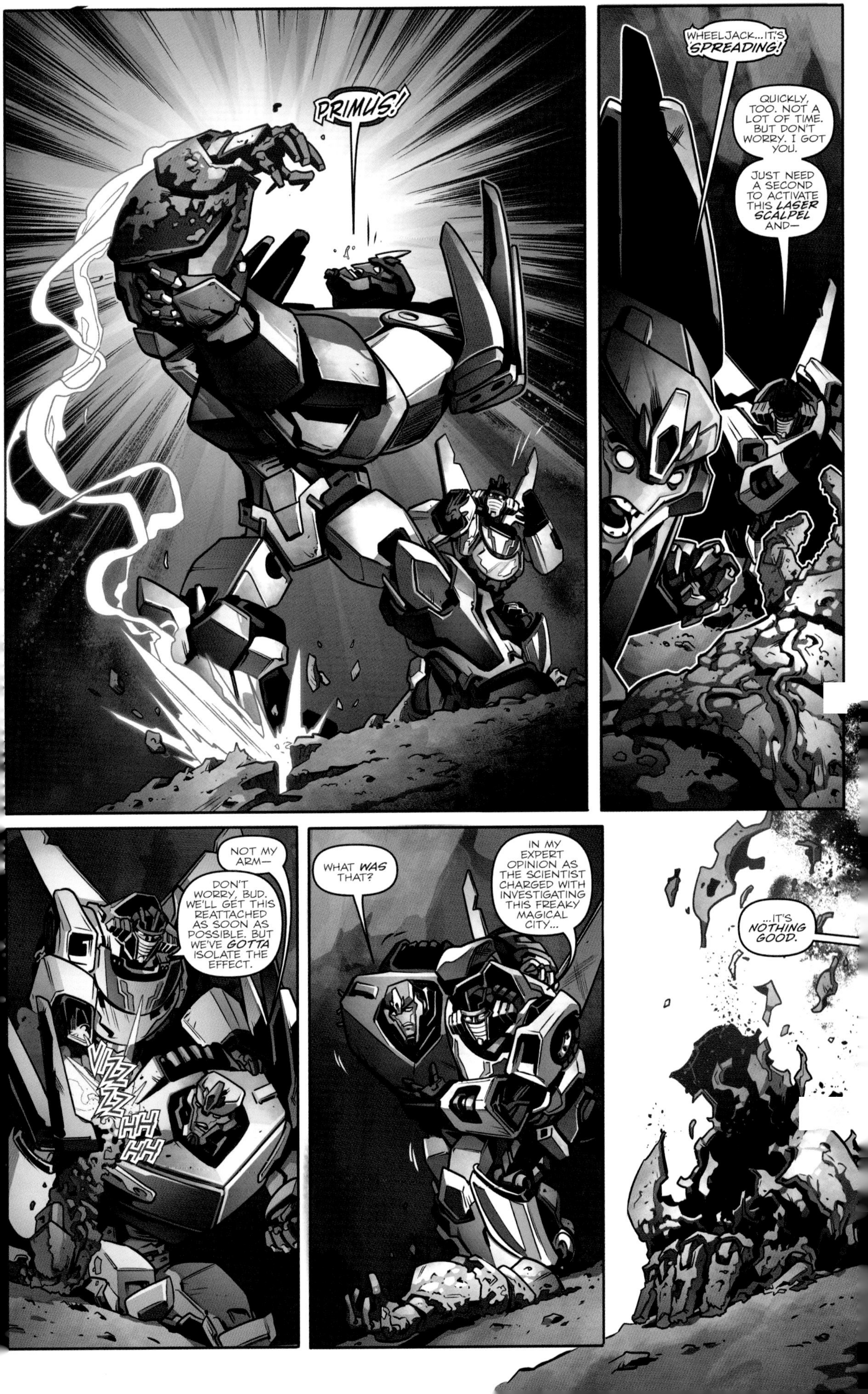
PRIMUS!
WHEELJACK...IT'S SPREADING!
QUICKLY, TOO. NOT A LOT OF TIME. BUT DON'T WORRY. I GOT YOU.
JUST NEED A SECOND TO ACTIVATE THIS LASER SCALPEL AND—
NOT MY ARM—
DON'T WORRY, BUD. WE'LL GET THIS REATTACHED AS SOON AS POSSIBLE. BUT WE'VE GOTTA ISOLATE THE EFFECT.
VZZZZZHHHH
WHAT WAS THAT?
IN MY EXPERT OPINION AS THE SCIENTIST CHARGED WITH INVESTIGATING THIS FREAKY MAGICAL CITY...
...IT'S NOTHING GOOD.

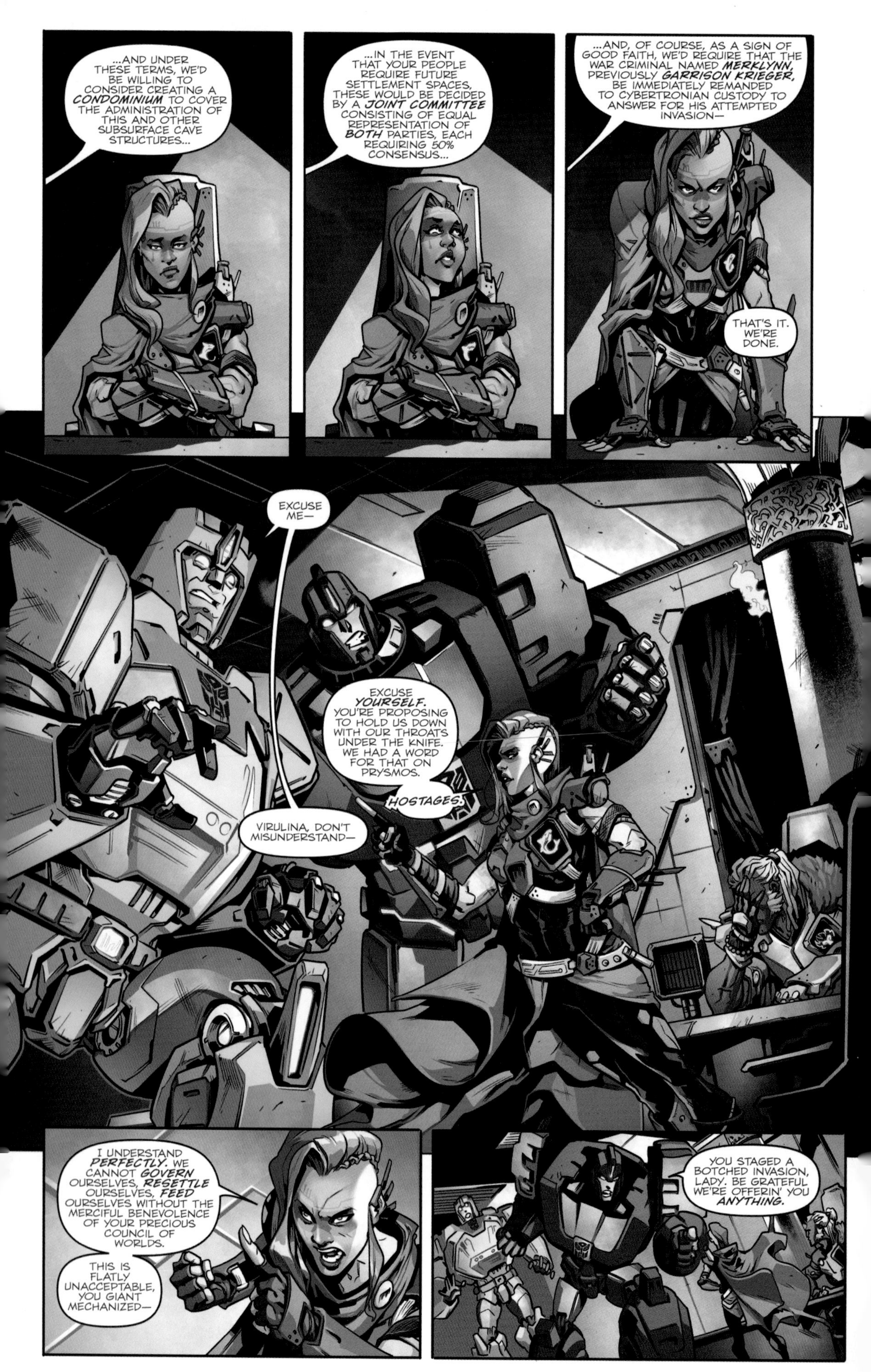
...AND UNDER THESE TERMS, WE'D BE WILLING TO CONSIDER CREATING A CONDOMINIUM TO COVER THE ADMINISTRATION OF THIS AND OTHER SUBSURFACE CAVE STRUCTURES...
...IN THE EVENT THAT YOUR PEOPLE REQUIRE FUTURE SETTLEMENT SPACES, THESE WOULD BE DECIDED BY A JOINT COMMITTEE CONSISTING OF EQUAL REPRESENTATION OF BOTH PARTIES, EACH REQUIRING 50% CONSENSUS...
...AND, OF COURSE, AS A SIGN OF GOOD FAITH, WE'D REQUIRE THAT THE WAR CRIMINAL NAMED MERKLYNN, PREVIOUSLY GARRISON KRIEGER, BE IMMEDIATELY REMANDED TO CYBERTRONIAN CUSTODY TO ANSWER FOR HIS ATTEMPTED INVASION—
THAT'S IT. WE'RE DONE.
EXCUSE ME—
EXCUSE YOURSELF. YOU'RE PROPOSING TO HOLD US DOWN WITH OUR THROATS UNDER THE KNIFE. WE HAD A WORD FOR THAT ON PRYSMOS.
HOSTAGES.
VIRULINA, DON'T MISUNDERSTAND—
I UNDERSTAND PERFECTLY. WE CANNOT GOVERN OURSELVES, RESETTLE OURSELVES, FEED OURSELVES WITHOUT THE MERCIFUL BENEVOLENCE OF YOUR PRECIOUS COUNCIL OF WORLDS.
THIS IS FLATLY UNACCEPTABLE, YOU GIANT MECHANIZED—
YOU STAGED A BOTCHED INVASION, LADY. BE GRATEFUL WE'RE OFFERIN' YOU ANYTHING.

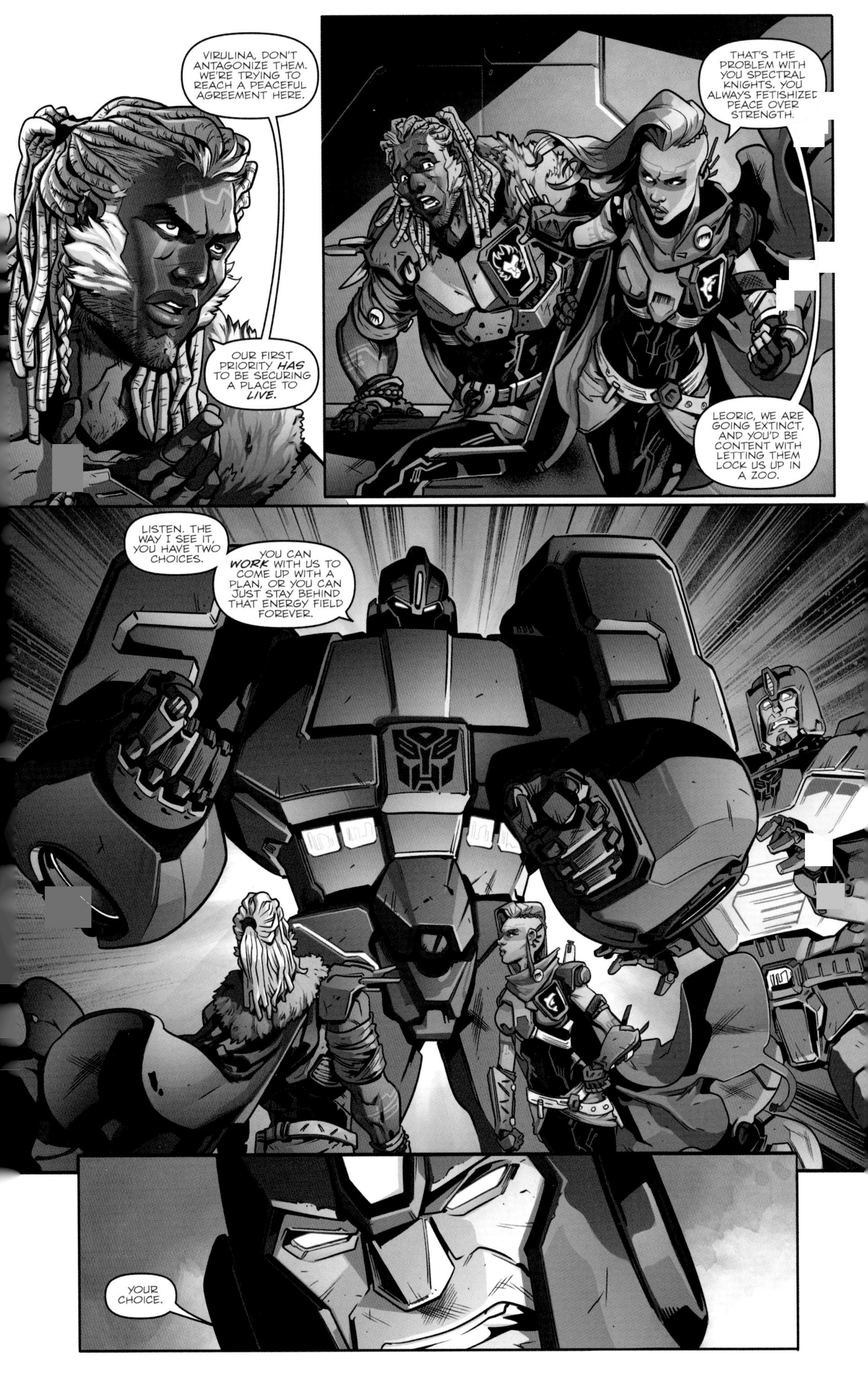
VIRULINA, DON'T ANTAGONIZE THEM. WE'RE TRYING TO REACH A PEACEFUL AGREEMENT HERE.
OUR FIRST PRIORITY HAS TO BE SECURING A PLACE TO LIVE.
THAT'S THE PROBLEM WITH YOU SPECTRAL KNIGHTS. YOU ALWAYS FETISHIZED PEACE OVER STRENGTH.
LEORIC, WE ARE GOING EXTINCT, AND YOU'D BE CONTENT WITH LETTING THEM LOCK US UP IN A ZOO.
LISTEN. THE WAY I SEE IT, YOU HAVE TWO CHOICES.
YOU CAN WORK WITH US TO COME UP WITH A PLAN, OR YOU CAN JUST STAY BEHIND THAT ENERGY FIELD FOREVER.
YOUR CHOICE.

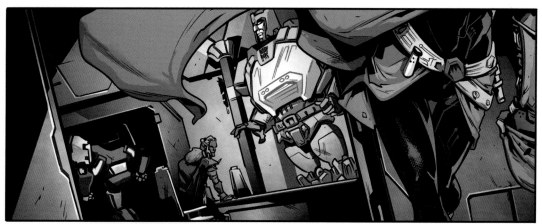

I'M SORRY ABOUT THAT. I *PROMISE* YOU THE VISIONARIES ARE COMMITTED TO THIS PROCESS. THE FUTURE OF OUR PEOPLE DEPENDS ON IT.

VIRULINA IS JUST... *PASSIONATE*, IS ALL.

I WANT TO BELIEVE *WE'RE* COMMITTED, TOO. BUT IT'S HARD TO STOP FIGHTING WHEN YOU FEEL YOU'VE GOT SOMETHING TO *LOSE*.

I KNOW. THE *SPECTRAL KNIGHTS* AND *DARKLING LORDS* HAVE BEEN AT EACH OTHER'S THROATS FOR AGES. IT'S TURNED VIOLENT MORE THAN ONCE.

I HAD HOPED OUR... *DIMINISHED PROSPECTS*... WOULD HELP HER SEE REASON. BUT SHE'S JUST AS INTRANSIGENT AS EVER.

LEORIC, I THINK WE'RE KIND OF IN THE SAME BOAT. YOU GUYS HAVE BOATS, RIGHT?

CYBERTRON SPENT MILLIONS OF YEARS IN CIVIL WAR. WE NEARLY WIPED OURSELVES OUT. BUT WE CAME BACK FROM THE *BRINK*. WE MADE PEACE WITH OUR ENEMIES.

MEGATRON, THE LEADER OF THE FOLKS MY SIDE WAS FIGHTING, EVEN *SWITCHED TEAMS*.

VIRULINA'S AFRAID. I GET THAT. PEOPLE GET RASH WHEN THEY'RE UP AGAINST THE WALL, AND HOO BOY, YOU GUYS ARE UP AGAINST A REAL *DOOZY* OF ONE.

BUT SHE'LL COME AROUND. SHE *HAS* TO.

FOR BOTH OUR SAKES, I HOPE THAT'S TRUE.

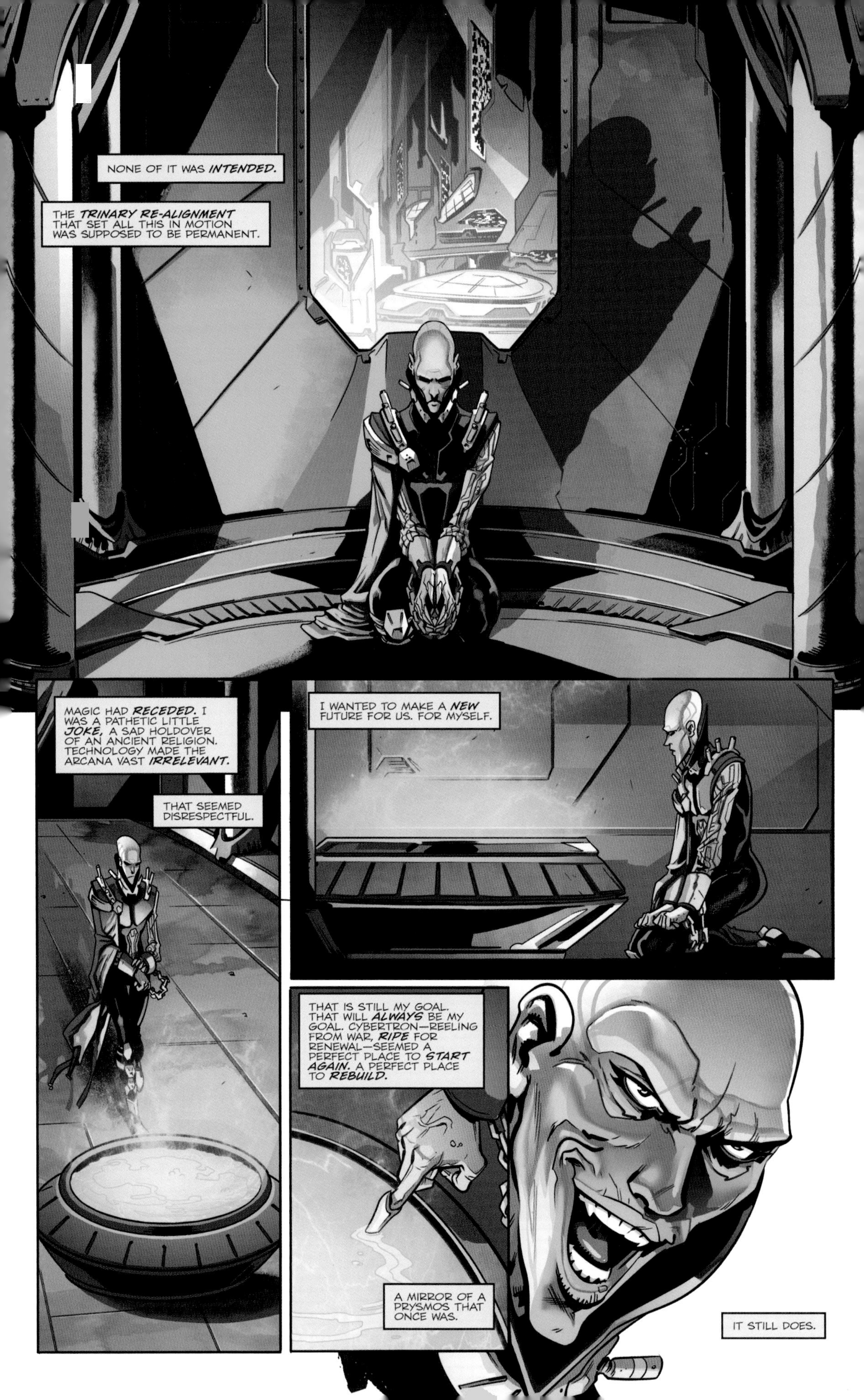
NONE OF IT WAS INTENDED.
THE TRINARY RE-ALIGNMENT THAT SET ALL THIS IN MOTION WAS SUPPOSED TO BE PERMANENT.
MAGIC HAD RECEDED. I WAS A PATHETIC LITTLE JOKE, A SAD HOLDOVER OF AN ANCIENT RELIGION. TECHNOLOGY MADE THE ARCANA VAST IRRELEVANT.
THAT SEEMED DISRESPECTFUL.
I WANTED TO MAKE A NEW FUTURE FOR US. FOR MYSELF.
THAT IS STILL MY GOAL. THAT WILL ALWAYS BE MY GOAL. CYBERTRON—REELING FROM WAR, RIPE FOR RENEWAL—SEEMED A PERFECT PLACE TO START AGAIN. A PERFECT PLACE TO REBUILD.
A MIRROR OF A PRYSMOS THAT ONCE WAS.
IT STILL DOES.

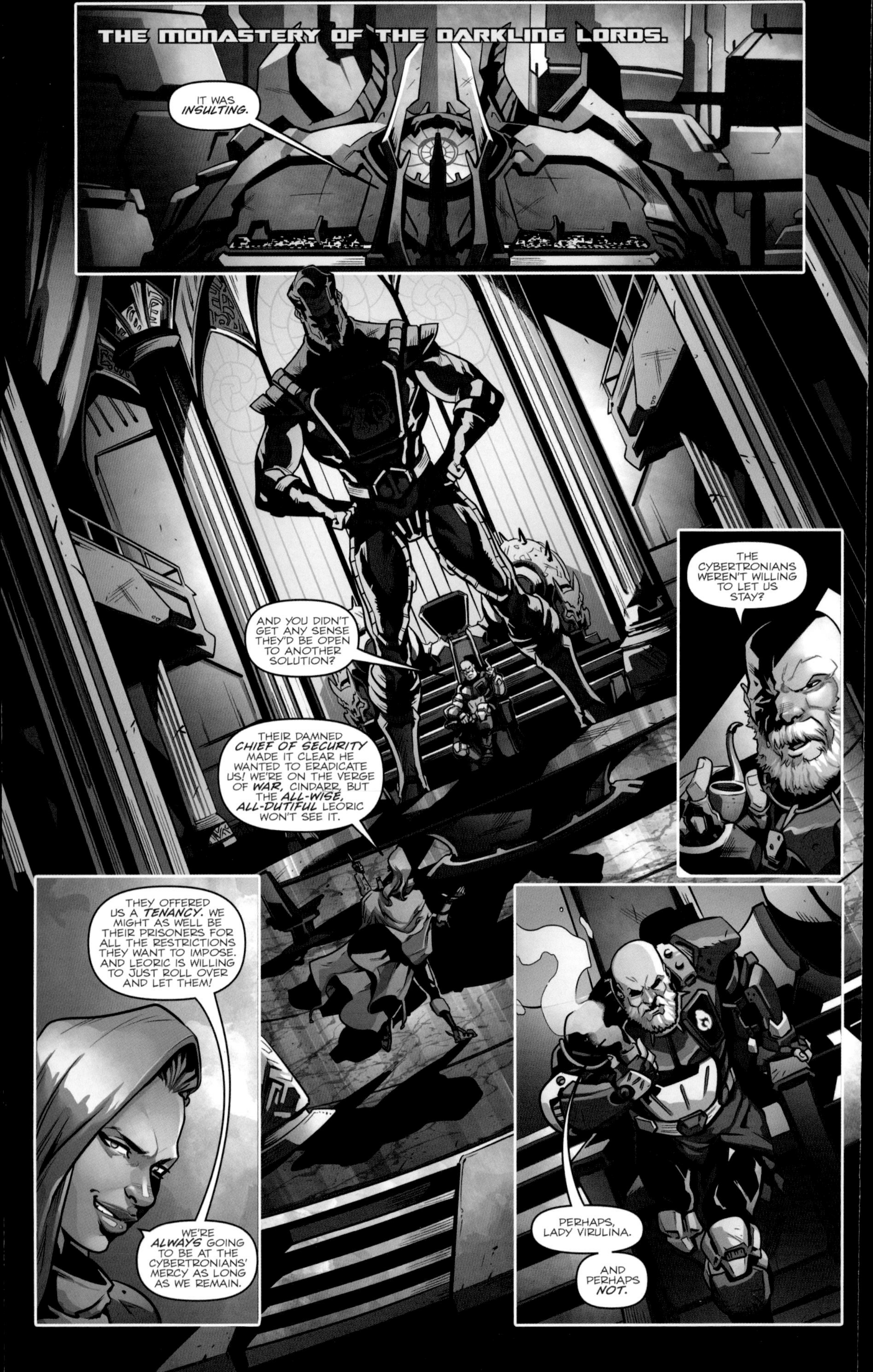

THE MONASTERY OF THE DARKLING LORDS.
IT WAS INSULTING.
AND YOU DIDN'T GET ANY SENSE THEY'D BE OPEN TO ANOTHER SOLUTION?
THEIR DAMNED CHIEF OF SECURITY MADE IT CLEAR HE WANTED TO ERADICATE US! WE'RE ON THE VERGE OF WAR, CINDARR, BUT THE ALL-WISE, ALL-DUTIFUL LEORIC WON'T SEE IT.
THE CYBERTRONIANS WEREN'T WILLING TO LET US STAY?
THEY OFFERED US A TENANCY. WE MIGHT AS WELL BE THEIR PRISONERS FOR ALL THE RESTRICTIONS THEY WANT TO IMPOSE. AND LEORIC IS WILLING TO JUST ROLL OVER AND LET THEM!
WE'RE ALWAYS GOING TO BE AT THE CYBERTRONIANS' MERCY AS LONG AS WE REMAIN.
PERHAPS, LADY VIRULINA.
AND PERHAPS NOT.

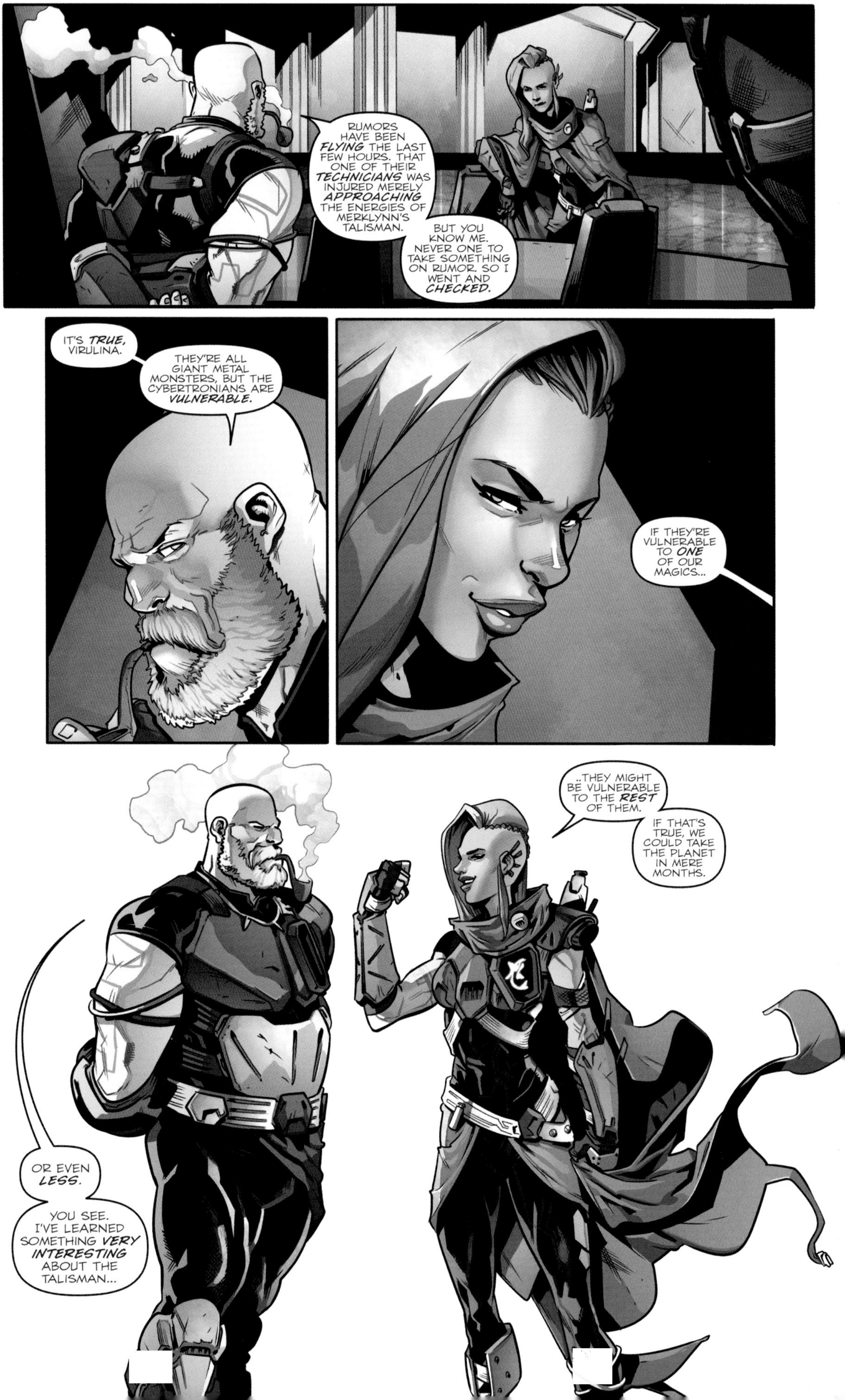
RUMORS HAVE BEEN FLYING THE LAST FEW HOURS. THAT ONE OF THEIR TECHNICIANS WAS INJURED MERELY APPROACHING THE ENERGIES OF MERKLYNN'S TALISMAN.
BUT YOU KNOW ME. NEVER ONE TO TAKE SOMETHING ON RUMOR. SO I WENT AND CHECKED.
IT'S TRUE, VIRULINA.
THEY'RE ALL GIANT METAL MONSTERS, BUT THE CYBERTRONIANS ARE VULNERABLE.
IF THEY'RE VULNERABLE TO ONE OF OUR MAGICS...
..THEY MIGHT BE VULNERABLE TO THE REST OF THEM.
IF THAT'S TRUE, WE COULD TAKE THE PLANET IN MERE MONTHS.
OR EVEN LESS.
YOU SEE. I'VE LEARNED SOMETHING VERY INTERESTING ABOUT THE TALISMAN...

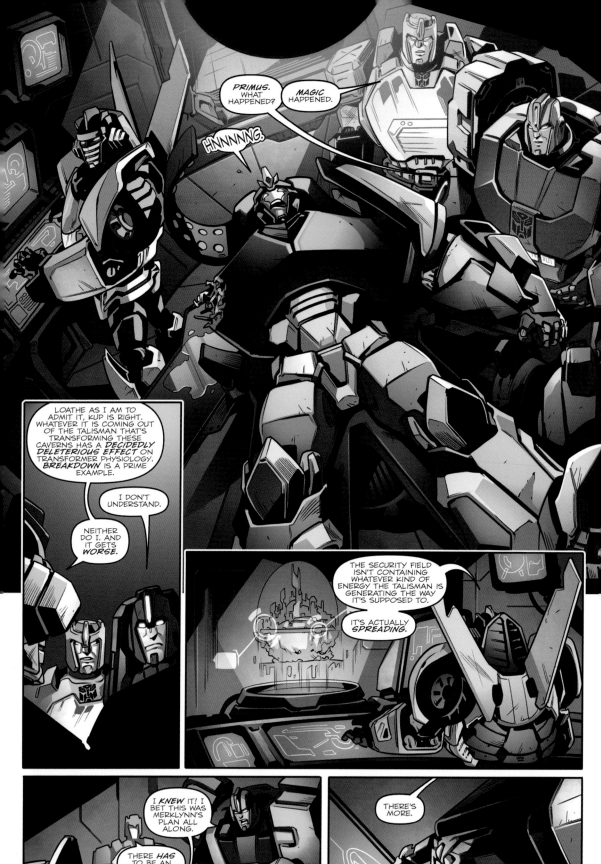

PRIMUS. WHAT HAPPENED?

MAGIC HAPPENED.

HNNNNNG.

LOATHE AS I AM TO ADMIT IT, KUP IS RIGHT. WHATEVER IT IS COMING OUT OF THE TALISMAN THAT'S TRANSFORMING THESE CAVERNS HAS A *DECIDEDLY DELETERIOUS EFFECT* ON TRANSFORMER PHYSIOLOGY. *BREAKDOWN* IS A PRIME EXAMPLE.

I DON'T UNDERSTAND.

NEITHER DO I. AND IT GETS *WORSE*.

THE SECURITY FIELD ISN'T CONTAINING WHATEVER KIND OF ENERGY THE TALISMAN IS GENERATING THE WAY IT'S SUPPOSED TO.

IT'S ACTUALLY *SPREADING*.

I *KNEW* IT! I BET THIS WAS MERKLYNN'S PLAN ALL ALONG.

THERE *HAS* TO BE AN EXPLANATION.

THAT *IS* THE EXPLANATION! THEY'VE BEEN PLAYING US FOR FOOLS, KUP.

THERE'S MORE.

DOOT

WE'VE BEEN REMOTELY MONITORING THE TALISMAN EVER SINCE IT APPEARED. WHEN WE *FIRST* SCANNED IT, IT WAS EMBEDDED ABOUT SIX METERS DEEP IN A STRATUM OF IGNEOUS ROCK.

TODAY? IT'S *ELEVEN* METERS DOWN.

SO IT'S SINKING?

NO. IT'S *TUNNELING.*

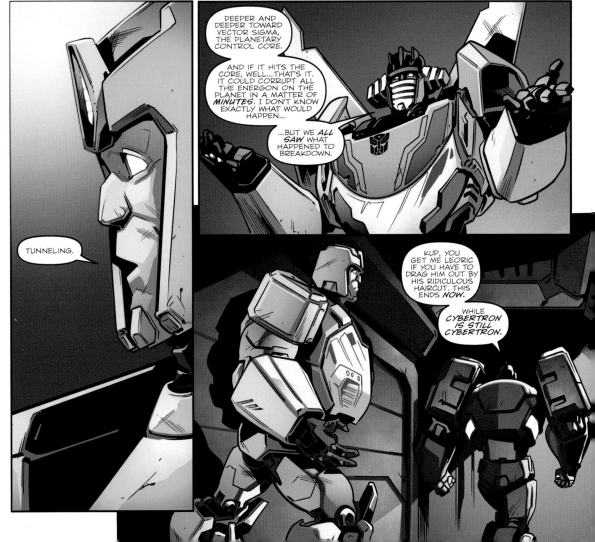

DEEPER AND DEEPER TOWARD VECTOR SIGMA, THE PLANETARY CONTROL CORE.

AND IF IT HITS THE CORE, WELL...THAT'S IT. IT COULD CORRUPT ALL THE ENERGON ON THE PLANET IN A MATTER OF *MINUTES.* I DON'T KNOW EXACTLY WHAT WOULD HAPPEN...

...BUT WE *ALL SAW* WHAT HAPPENED TO BREAKDOWN.

TUNNELING.

KUP, YOU GET ME LEORIC IF YOU HAVE TO DRAG HIM OUT BY HIS RIDICULOUS HAIRCUT. THIS ENDS *NOW.*

WHILE *CYBERTRON* IS STILL *CYBERTRON.*

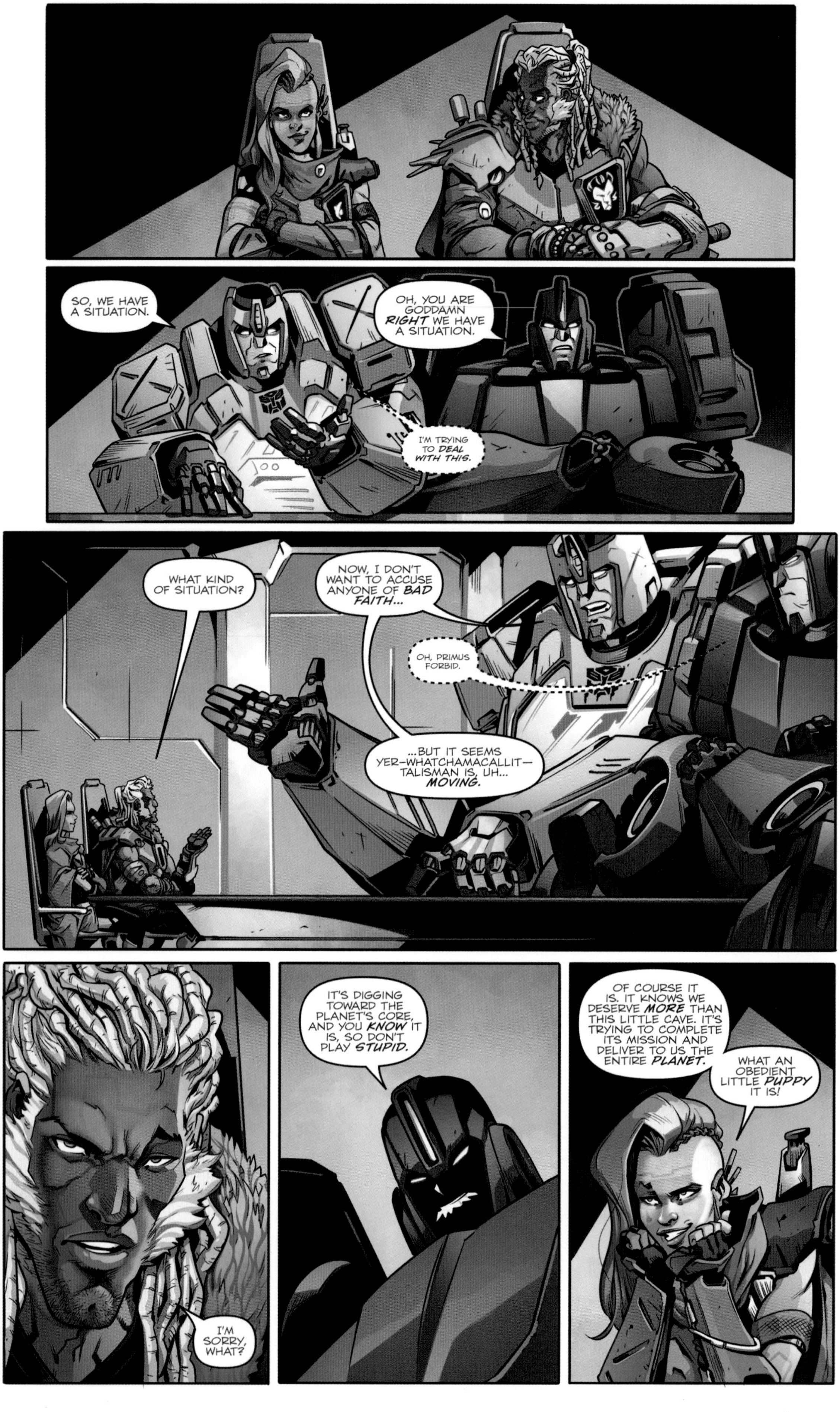
SO, WE HAVE A SITUATION.
OH, YOU ARE GODDAMN *RIGHT* WE HAVE A SITUATION.
I'M TRYING TO *DEAL WITH THIS.*
WHAT KIND OF SITUATION?
NOW, I DON'T WANT TO ACCUSE ANYONE OF *BAD FAITH*...
OH, PRIMUS FORBID.
...BUT IT SEEMS YER—WHATCHAMACALLIT—TALISMAN IS, UH... *MOVING.*
I'M SORRY, WHAT?
IT'S DIGGING TOWARD THE PLANET'S CORE, AND YOU *KNOW* IT IS, SO DON'T PLAY *STUPID.*
OF COURSE IT IS. IT KNOWS WE DESERVE *MORE* THAN THIS LITTLE CAVE. IT'S TRYING TO COMPLETE ITS MISSION AND DELIVER TO US THE ENTIRE *PLANET.*
WHAT AN OBEDIENT LITTLE *PUPPY* IT IS!

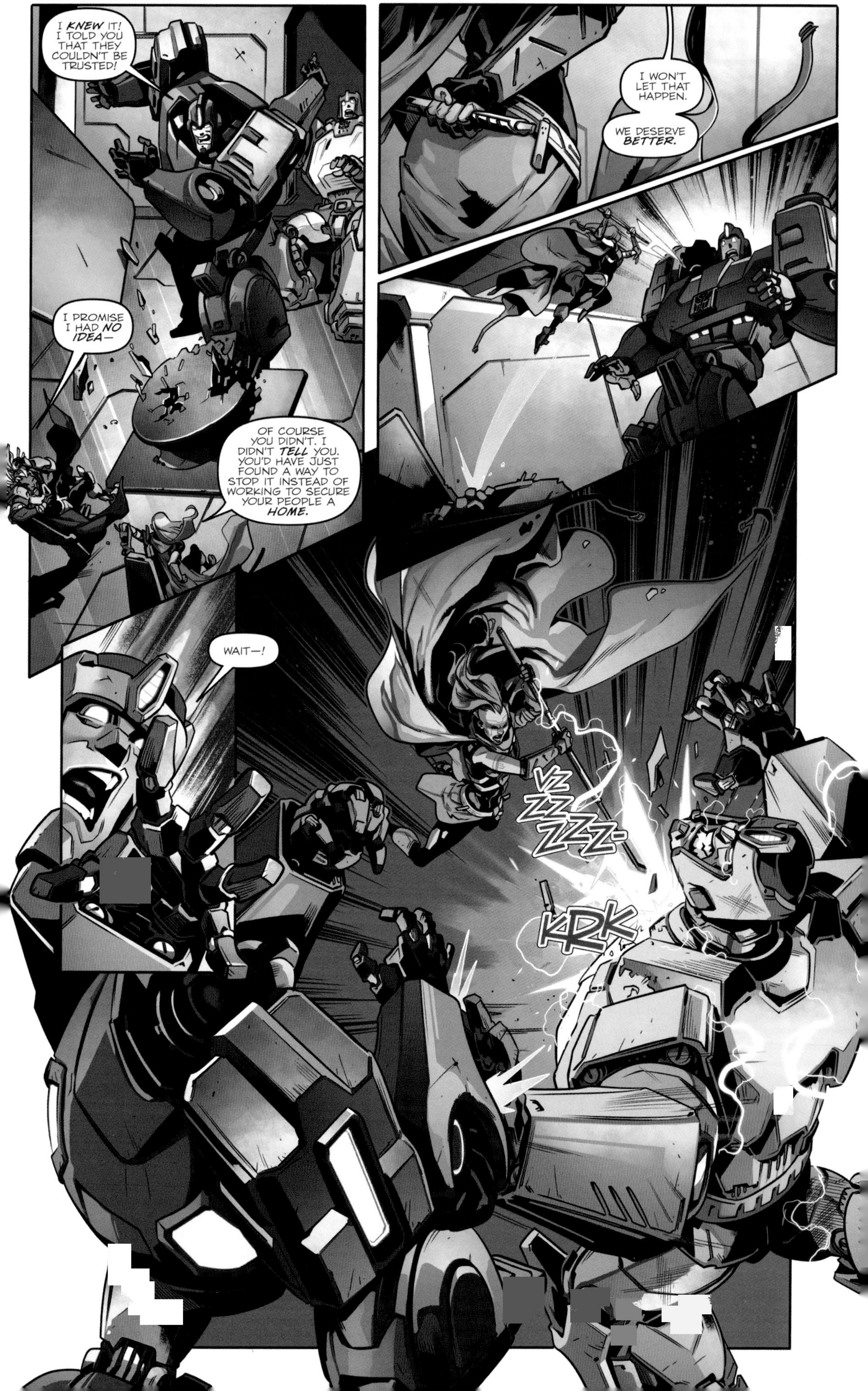
I KNEW IT! I TOLD YOU THAT THEY COULDN'T BE TRUSTED!
I PROMISE I HAD NO IDEA—
OF COURSE YOU DIDN'T. I DIDN'T TELL YOU. YOU'D HAVE JUST FOUND A WAY TO STOP IT INSTEAD OF WORKING TO SECURE YOUR PEOPLE A HOME.
I WON'T LET THAT HAPPEN.
WE DESERVE BETTER.
WAIT—!
VZZZZZZ-
KRK

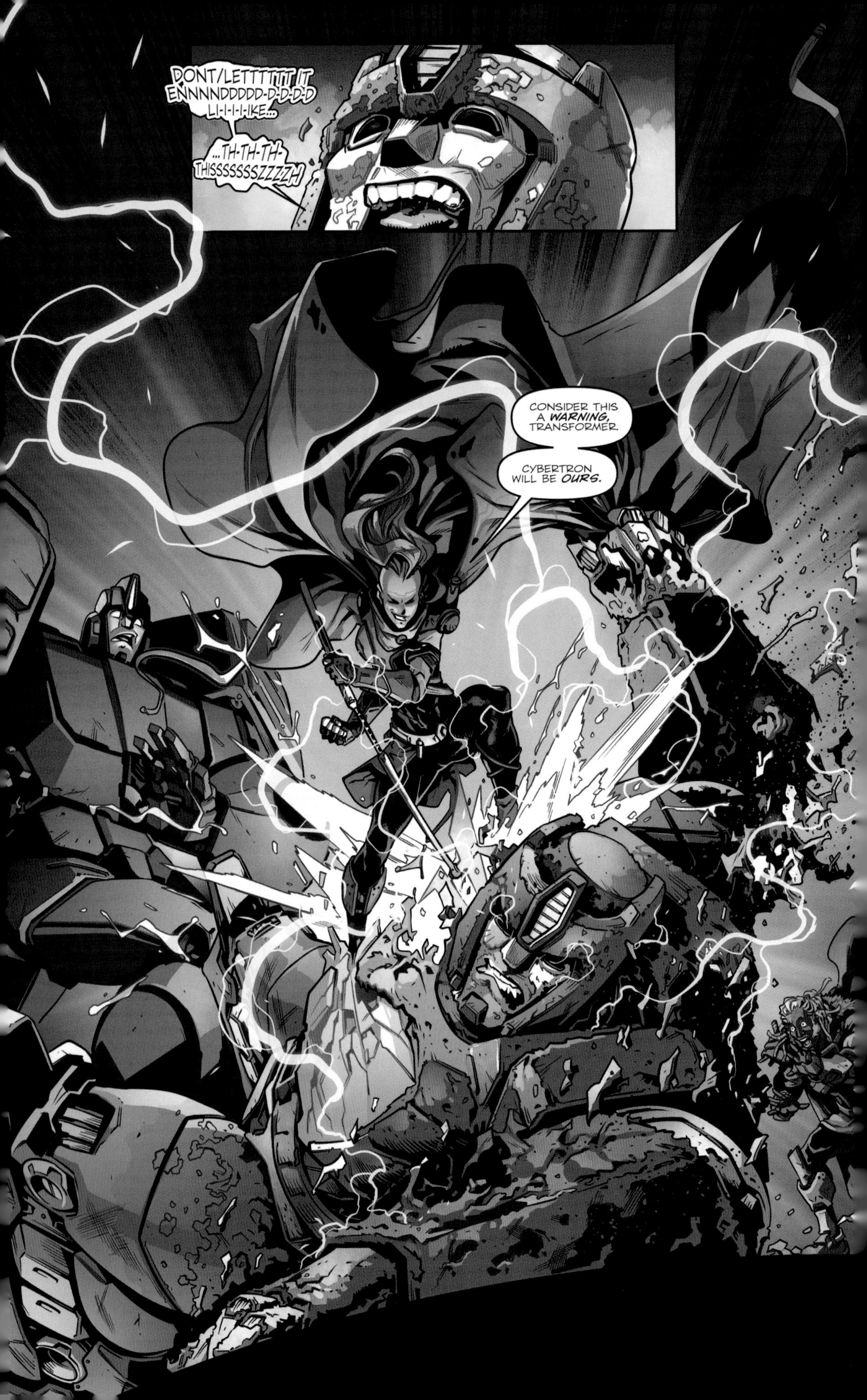
DONT/LETTTTTTT IT ENNNNDDDDD-D-D-D-D LI-I-I-I-IKE...
...TH-TH-TH-THISSSSSSSSZZZZH
CONSIDER THIS A *WARNING,* TRANSFORMER.
CYBERTRON WILL BE *OURS.*

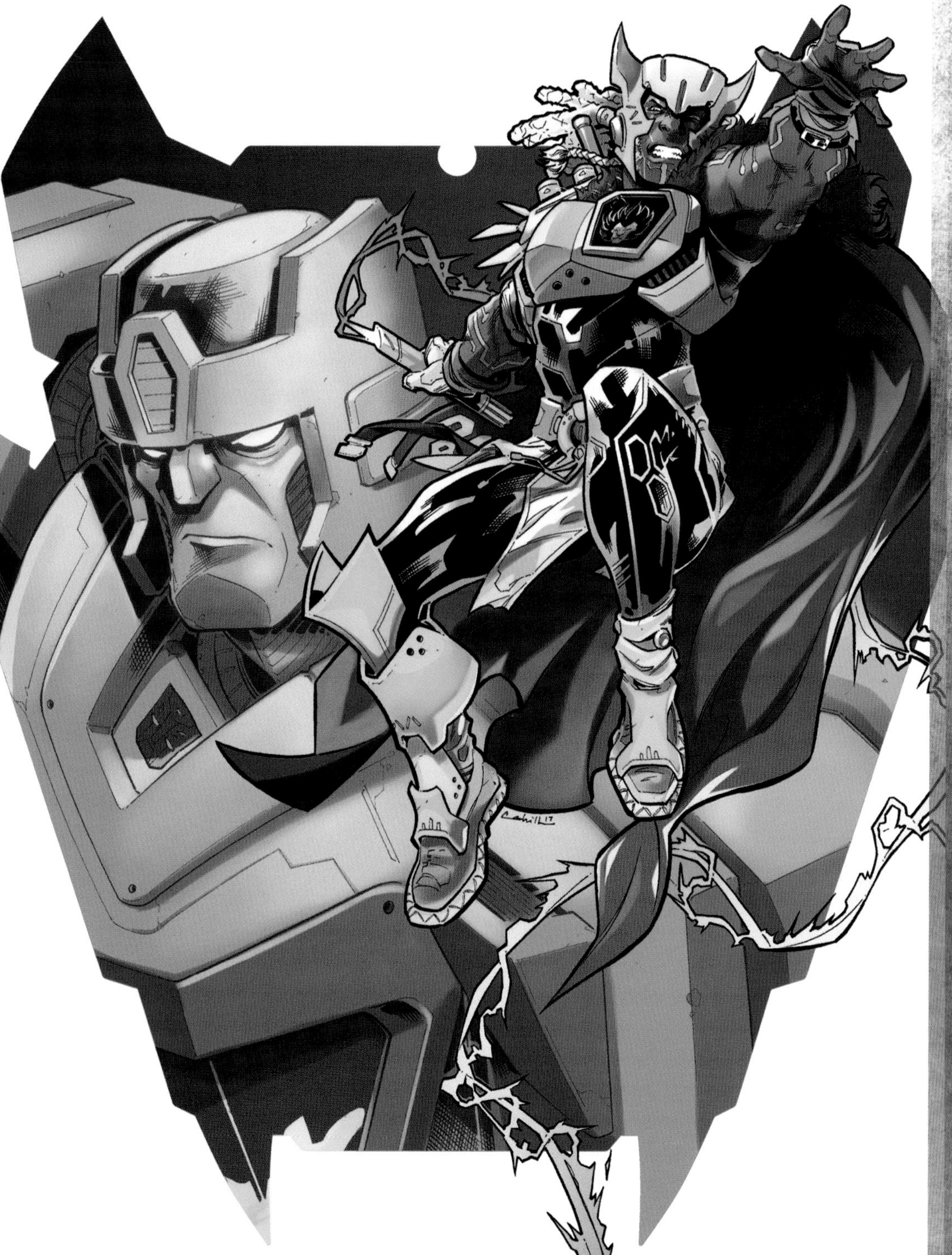
CAHILL 17

ART BY **BRENDAN CAHILL**
COLORS BY **LAUREN BENNETT**

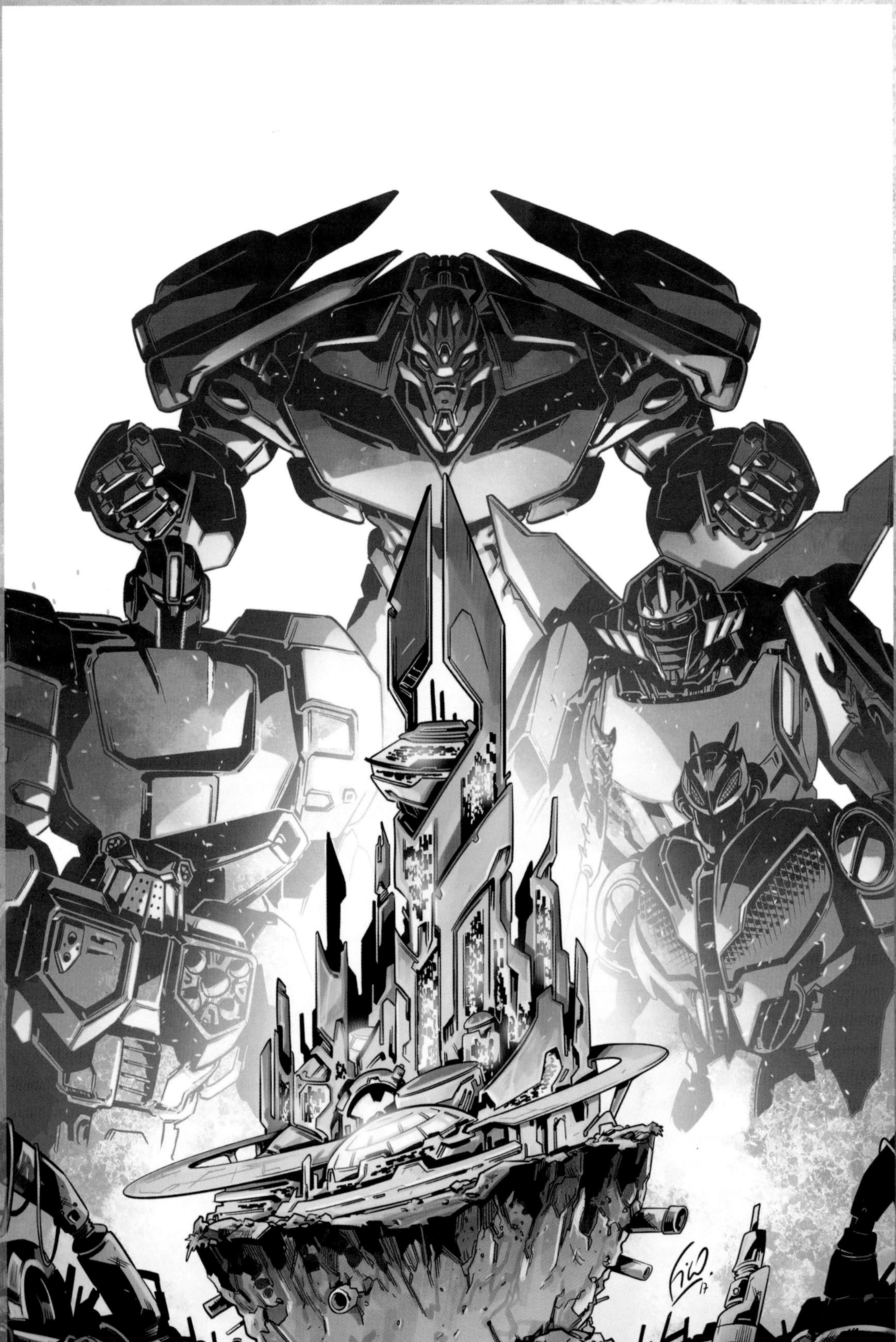

ART BY FICO OSSIO

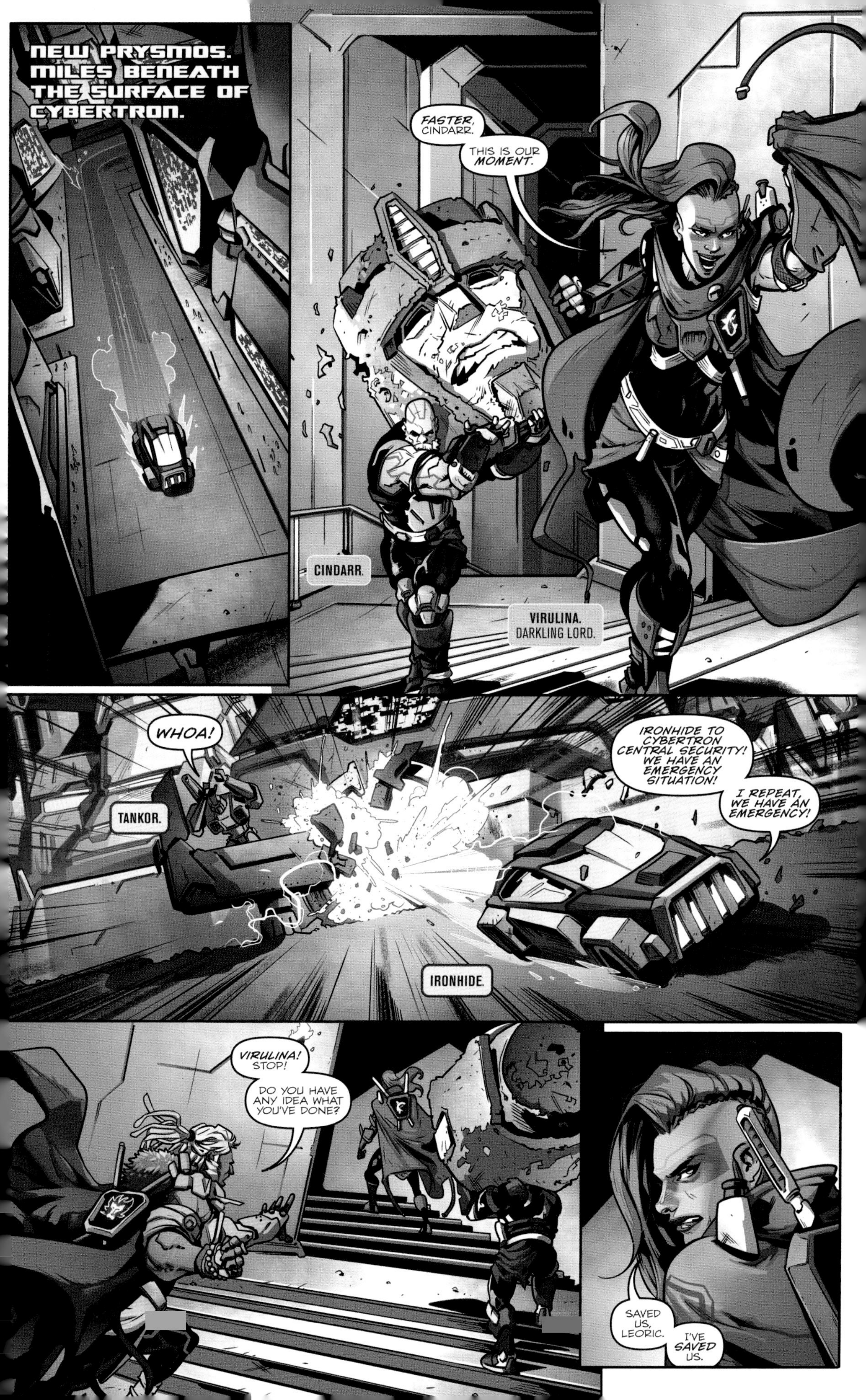
NEW PRYSMOS. MILES BENEATH THE SURFACE OF CYBERTRON.
FASTER, CINDARR.
THIS IS OUR MOMENT.
CINDARR.
VIRULINA. DARKLING LORD.
WHOA!
TANKOR.
IRONHIDE TO CYBERTRON CENTRAL SECURITY! WE HAVE AN EMERGENCY SITUATION!
I REPEAT, WE HAVE AN EMERGENCY!
IRONHIDE.
VIRULINA! STOP!
DO YOU HAVE ANY IDEA WHAT YOU'VE DONE?
SAVED US, LEORIC.
I'VE SAVED US.

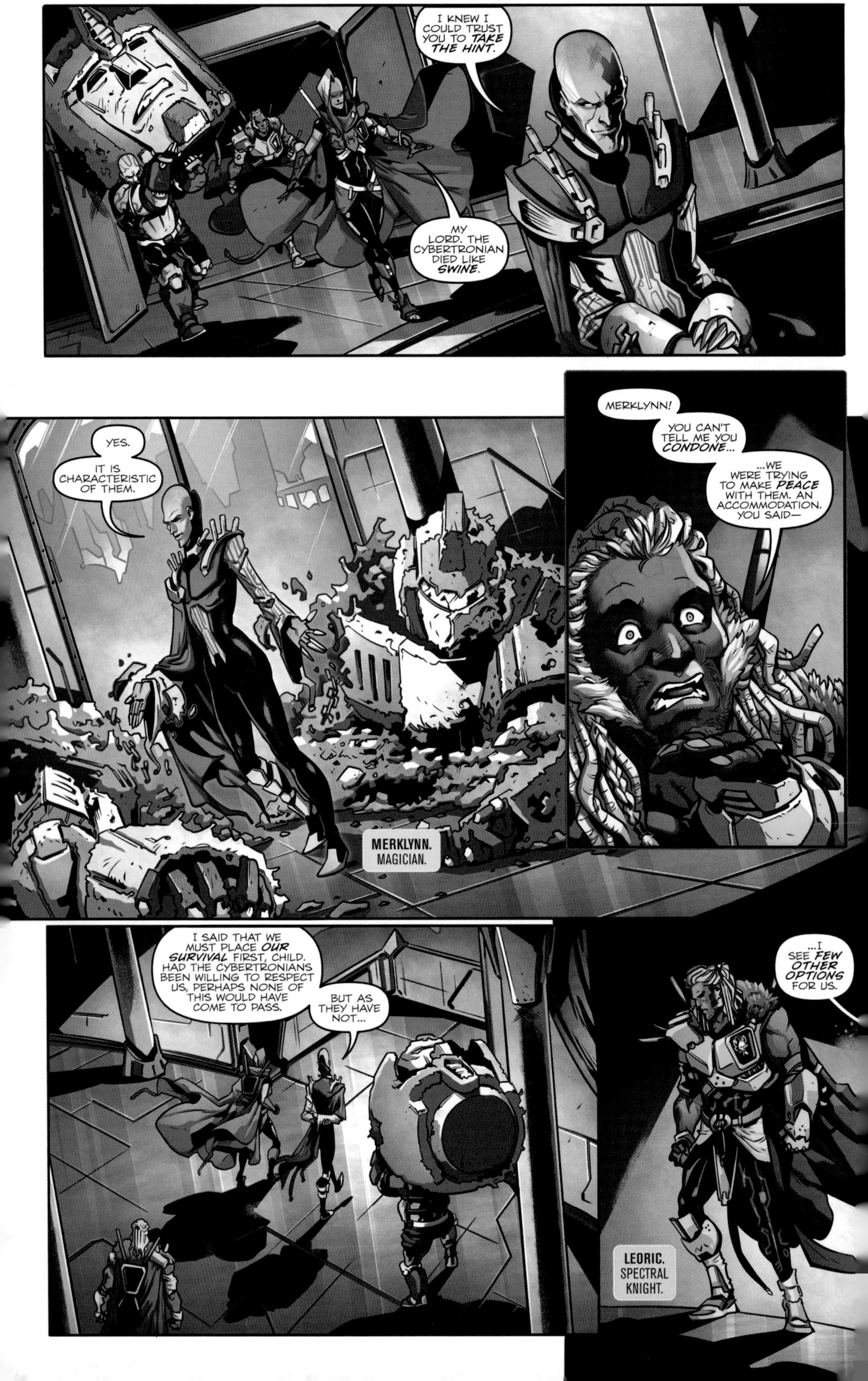
I KNEW I COULD TRUST YOU TO TAKE THE HINT.
MY LORD. THE CYBERTRONIAN DIED LIKE SWINE.
YES.
IT IS CHARACTERISTIC OF THEM.
MERKLYNN. MAGICIAN.
MERKLYNN!
YOU CAN'T TELL ME YOU CONDONE...
...WE WERE TRYING TO MAKE PEACE WITH THEM. AN ACCOMMODATION. YOU SAID—
I SAID THAT WE MUST PLACE OUR SURVIVAL FIRST, CHILD. HAD THE CYBERTRONIANS BEEN WILLING TO RESPECT US, PERHAPS NONE OF THIS WOULD HAVE COME TO PASS.
BUT AS THEY HAVE NOT...
...I SEE FEW OTHER OPTIONS FOR US.
LEORIC. SPECTRAL KNIGHT.

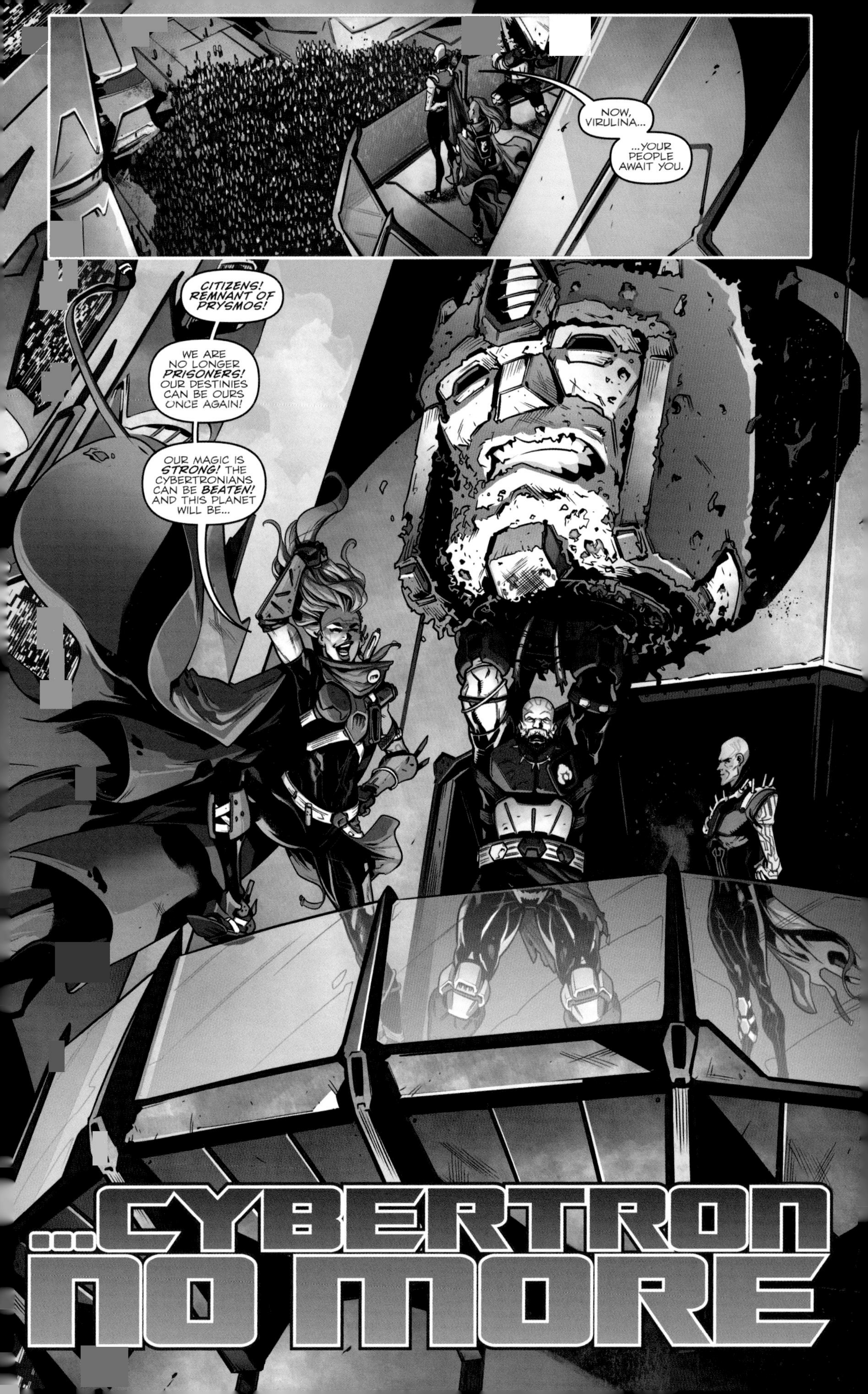
NOW, VIRULINA...
...YOUR PEOPLE AWAIT YOU.
CITIZENS! REMNANT OF PRYSMOS!
WE ARE NO LONGER PRISONERS! OUR DESTINIES CAN BE OURS ONCE AGAIN!
OUR MAGIC IS STRONG! THE CYBERTRONIANS CAN BE BEATEN! AND THIS PLANET WILL BE...
...CYBERTRON NO MORE

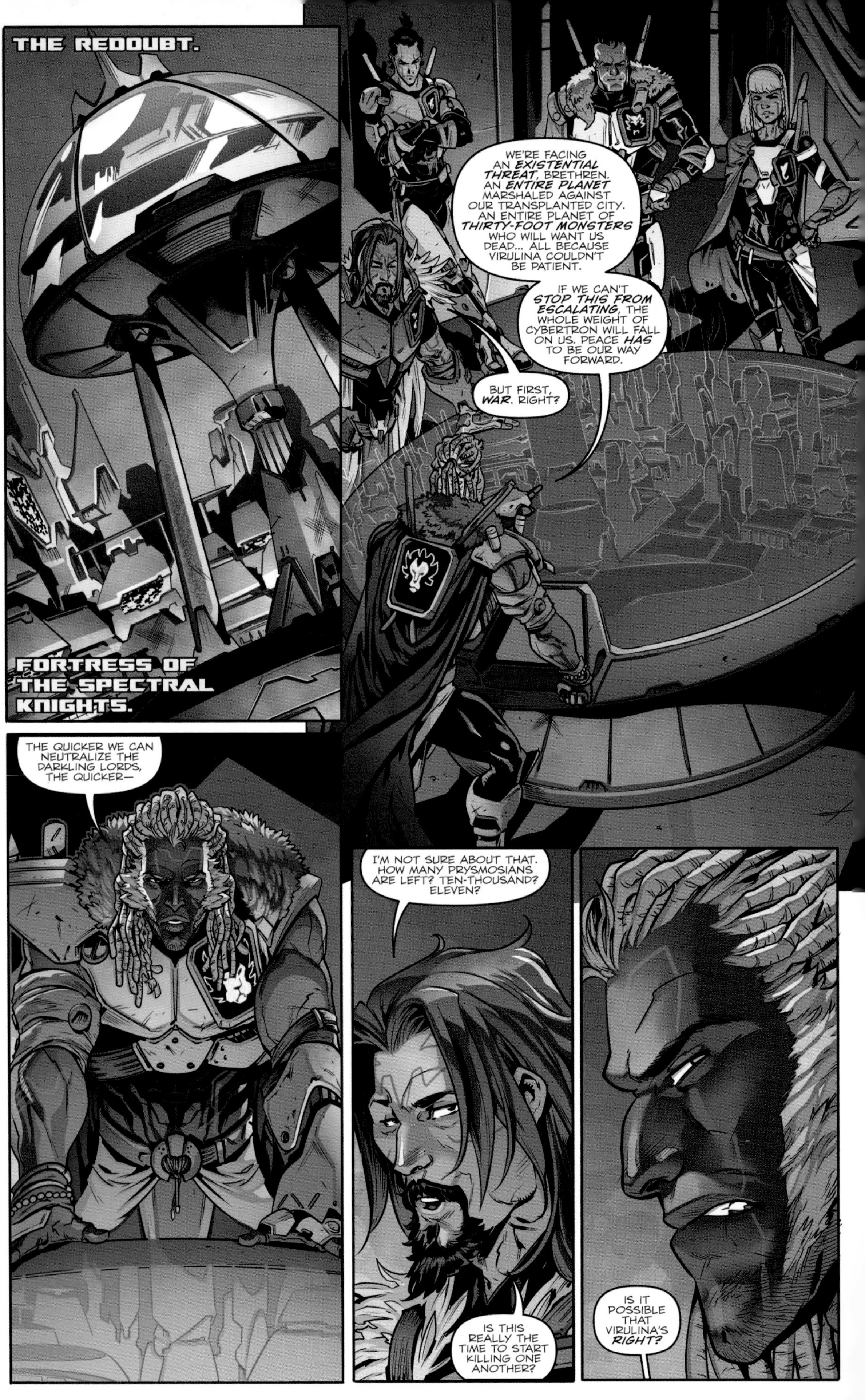
THE REDOUBT.
FORTRESS OF THE SPECTRAL KNIGHTS.
WE'RE FACING AN EXISTENTIAL THREAT, BRETHREN. AN ENTIRE PLANET MARSHALED AGAINST OUR TRANSPLANTED CITY. AN ENTIRE PLANET OF THIRTY-FOOT MONSTERS WHO WILL WANT US DEAD... ALL BECAUSE VIRULINA COULDN'T BE PATIENT.
IF WE CAN'T STOP THIS FROM ESCALATING, THE WHOLE WEIGHT OF CYBERTRON WILL FALL ON US. PEACE HAS TO BE OUR WAY FORWARD.
BUT FIRST, WAR. RIGHT?
THE QUICKER WE CAN NEUTRALIZE THE DARKLING LORDS, THE QUICKER—
I'M NOT SURE ABOUT THAT. HOW MANY PRYSMOSIANS ARE LEFT? TEN-THOUSAND? ELEVEN?
IS THIS REALLY THE TIME TO START KILLING ONE ANOTHER?
IS IT POSSIBLE THAT VIRULINA'S RIGHT?

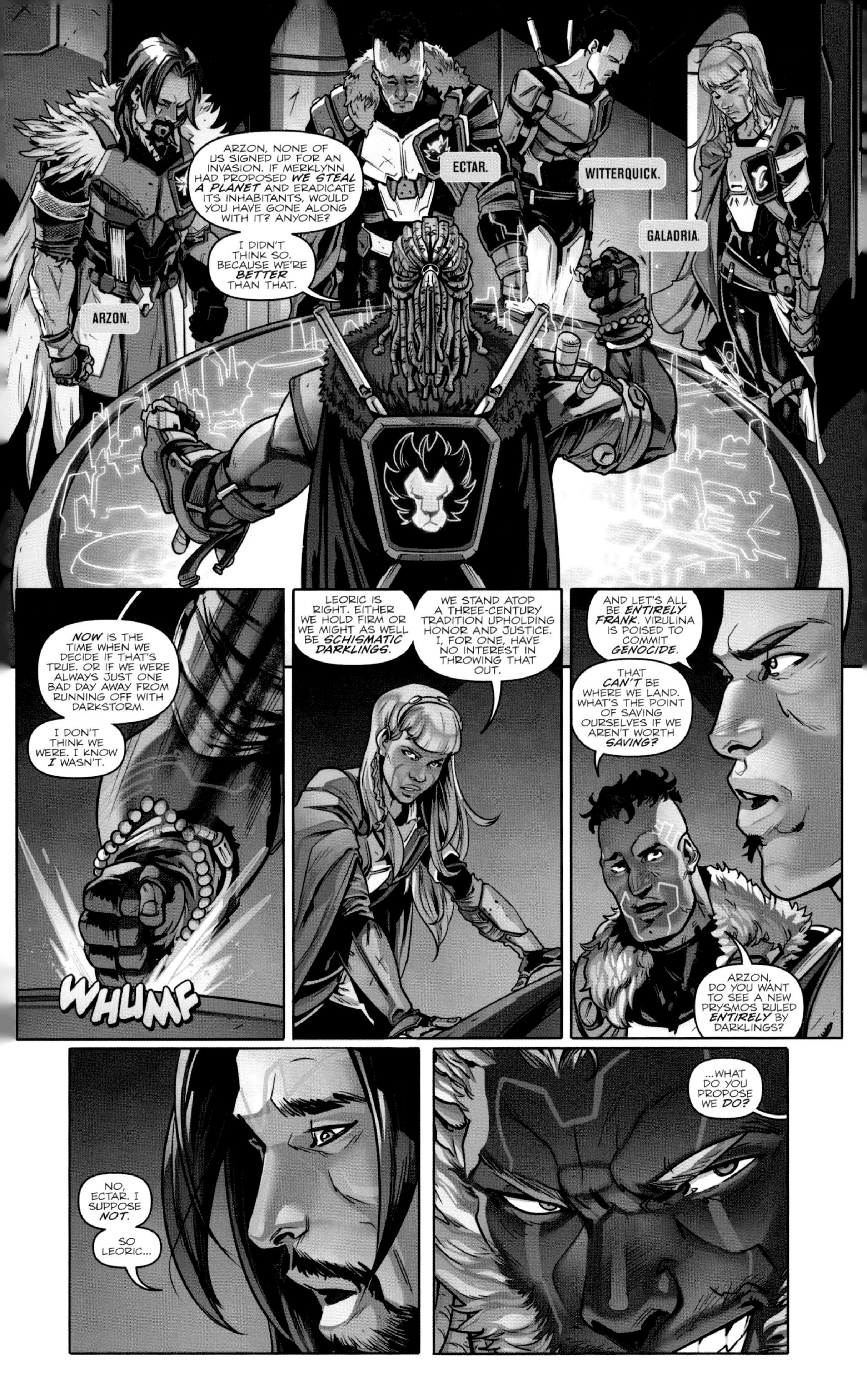
ARZON, NONE OF US SIGNED UP FOR AN INVASION. IF MERKLYNN HAD PROPOSED WE STEAL A PLANET AND ERADICATE ITS INHABITANTS, WOULD YOU HAVE GONE ALONG WITH IT? ANYONE?
I DIDN'T THINK SO. BECAUSE WE'RE BETTER THAN THAT.
ECTAR.
WITTERQUICK.
GALADRIA.
ARZON.
NOW IS THE TIME WHEN WE DECIDE IF THAT'S TRUE. OR IF WE WERE ALWAYS JUST ONE BAD DAY AWAY FROM RUNNING OFF WITH DARKSTORM.
I DON'T THINK WE WERE. I KNOW I WASN'T.
WHUMF
LEORIC IS RIGHT. EITHER WE HOLD FIRM OR WE MIGHT AS WELL BE SCHISMATIC DARKLINGS.
WE STAND ATOP A THREE-CENTURY TRADITION UPHOLDING HONOR AND JUSTICE. I, FOR ONE, HAVE NO INTEREST IN THROWING THAT OUT.
AND LET'S ALL BE ENTIRELY FRANK. VIRULINA IS POISED TO COMMIT GENOCIDE.
THAT CAN'T BE WHERE WE LAND. WHAT'S THE POINT OF SAVING OURSELVES IF WE AREN'T WORTH SAVING?
ARZON, DO YOU WANT TO SEE A NEW PRYSMOS RULED ENTIRELY BY DARKLINGS?
NO, ECTAR. I SUPPOSE NOT.
SO LEORIC...
...WHAT DO YOU PROPOSE WE DO?

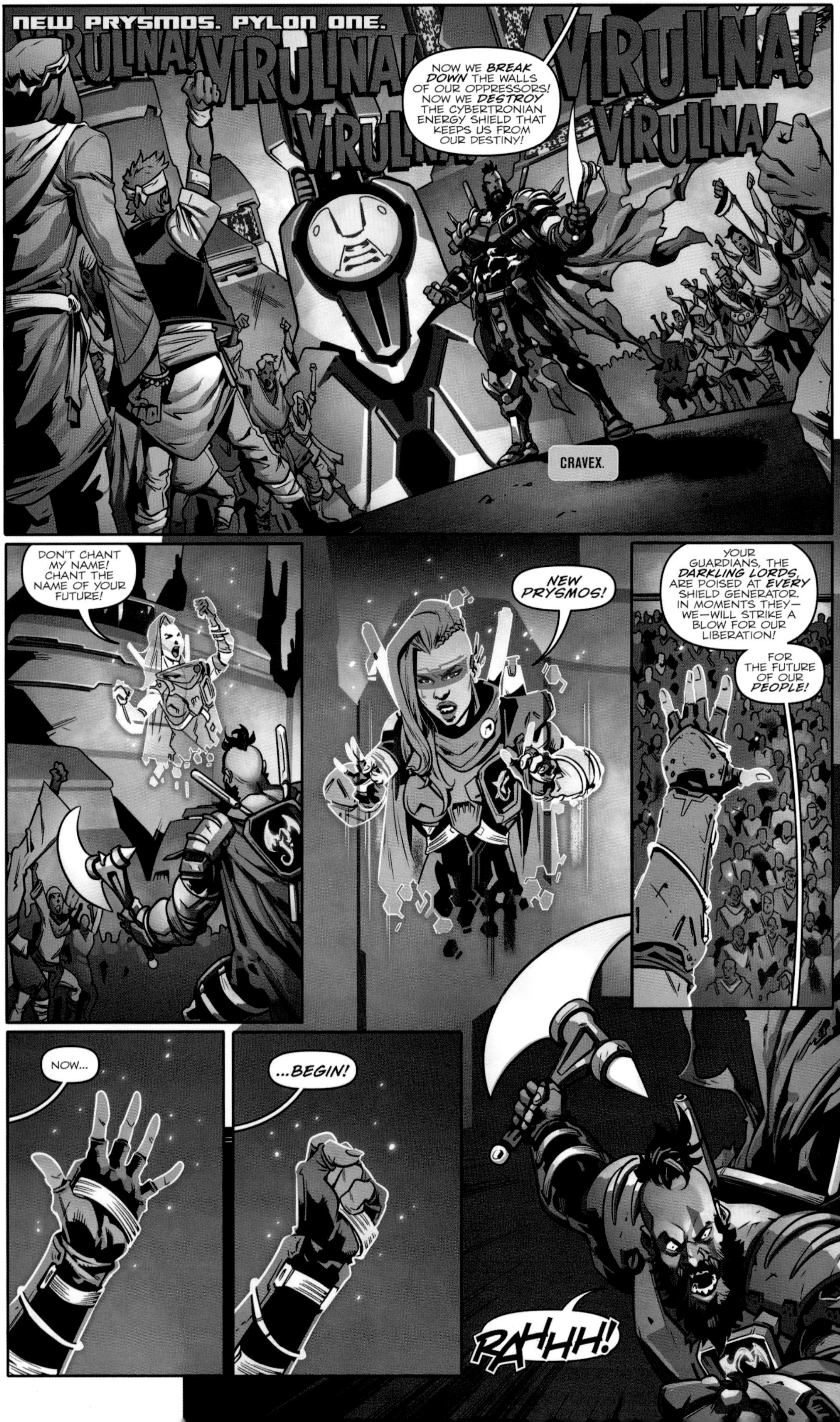
NEW PRYSMOS. PYLON ONE.
VIRULNA! VIRULNA! VIRULNA! VIRULNA! VIRULNA!
NOW WE BREAK DOWN THE WALLS OF OUR OPPRESSORS! NOW WE DESTROY THE CYBERTRONIAN ENERGY SHIELD THAT KEEPS US FROM OUR DESTINY!
CRAVEX.
DON'T CHANT MY NAME! CHANT THE NAME OF YOUR FUTURE!
NEW PRYSMOS!
YOUR GUARDIANS, THE DARKLING LORDS, ARE POISED AT EVERY SHIELD GENERATOR. IN MOMENTS THEY— WE—WILL STRIKE A BLOW FOR OUR LIBERATION!
FOR THE FUTURE OF OUR PEOPLE!
NOW...
...BEGIN!
RAHHH!

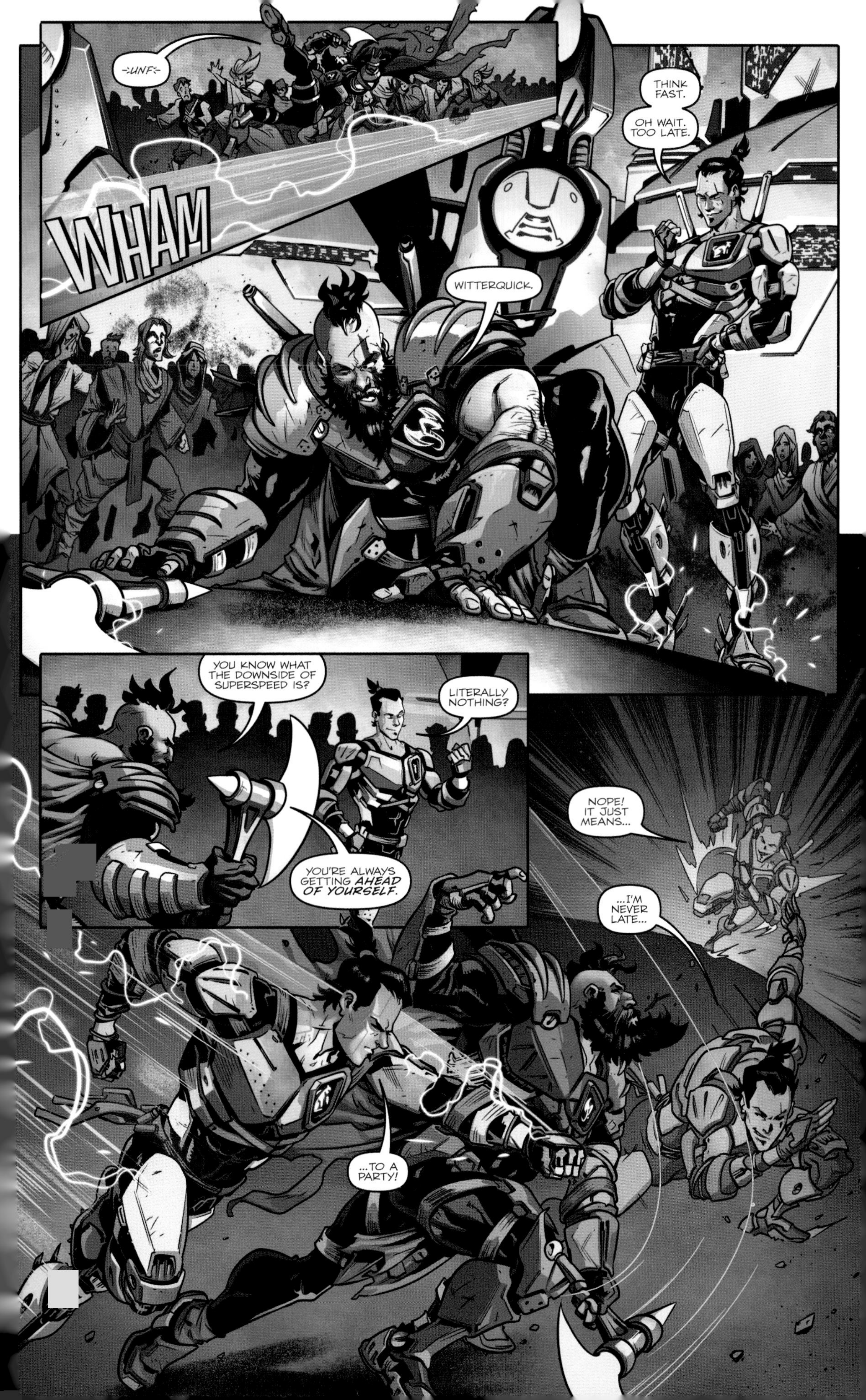
~UNF~
WHAM
THINK FAST.
OH WAIT. TOO LATE.
WITTERQUICK.
YOU KNOW WHAT THE DOWNSIDE OF SUPERSPEED IS?
LITERALLY NOTHING?
YOU'RE ALWAYS GETTING *AHEAD OF YOURSELF*.
NOPE! IT JUST MEANS...
...I'M NEVER LATE...
...TO A PARTY!

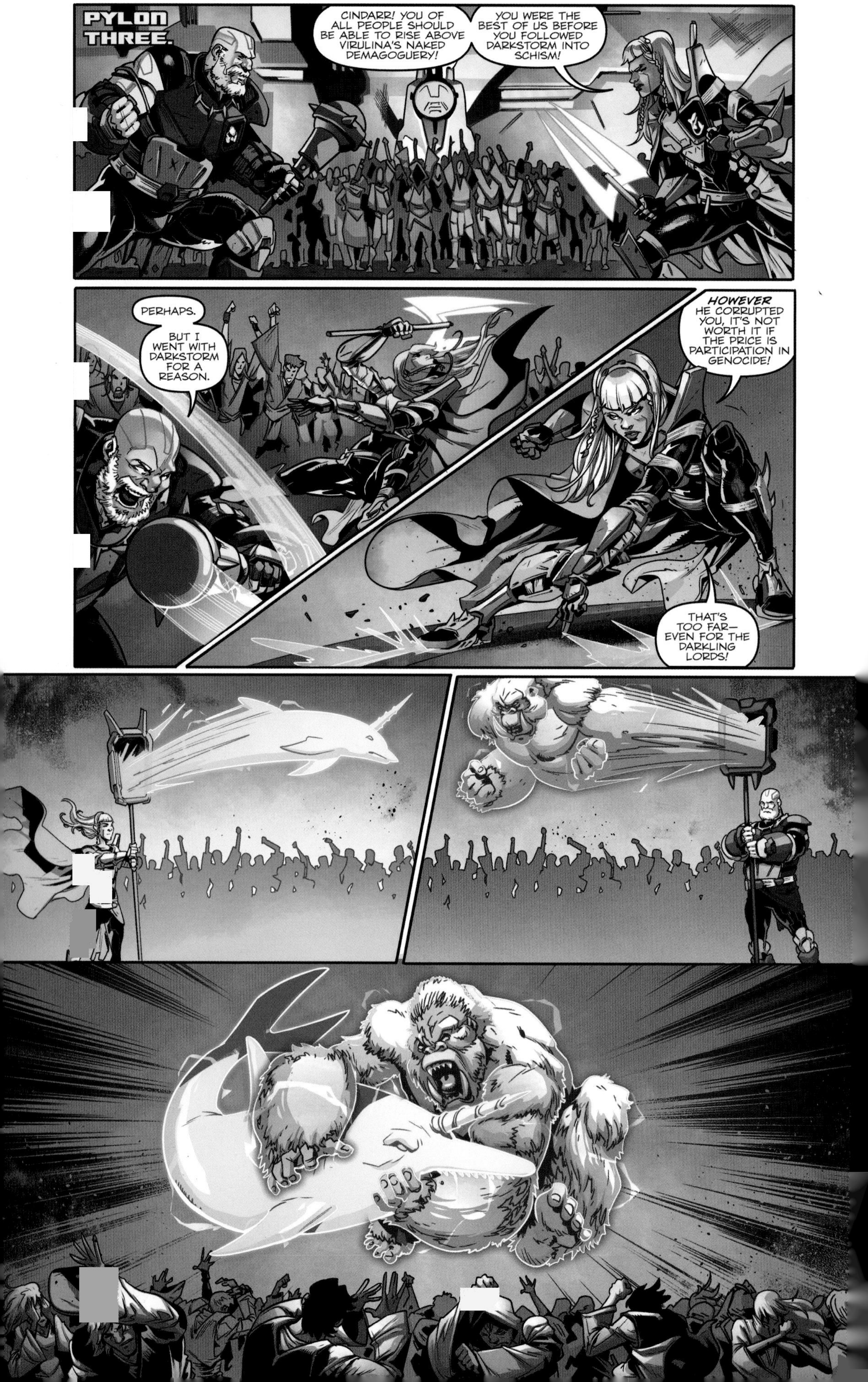
PYLON THREE.
CINDARR! YOU OF ALL PEOPLE SHOULD BE ABLE TO RISE ABOVE VIRULINA'S NAKED DEMAGOGUERY!
YOU WERE THE BEST OF US BEFORE YOU FOLLOWED DARKSTORM INTO SCHISM!
PERHAPS.
BUT I WENT WITH DARKSTORM FOR A REASON.
HOWEVER HE CORRUPTED YOU, IT'S NOT WORTH IT IF THE PRICE IS PARTICIPATION IN GENOCIDE!
THAT'S TOO FAR— EVEN FOR THE DARKLING LORDS!

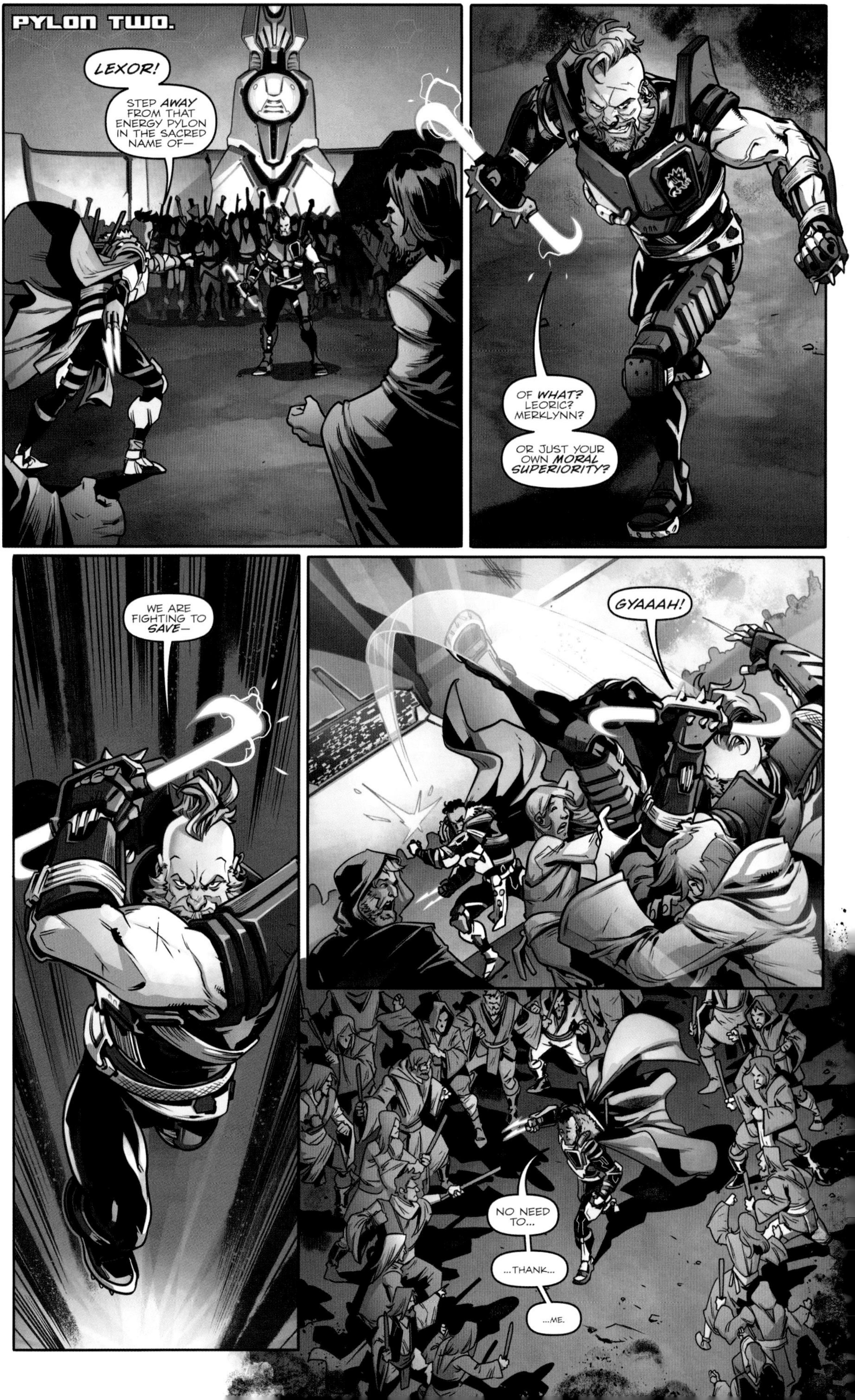
PYLON TWO.
LEXOR!
STEP AWAY FROM THAT ENERGY PYLON IN THE SACRED NAME OF—
OF WHAT? LEORIC? MERKLYNN?
OR JUST YOUR OWN MORAL SUPERIORITY?
WE ARE FIGHTING TO SAVE—
GYAAAH!
NO NEED TO...
...THANK...
...ME.

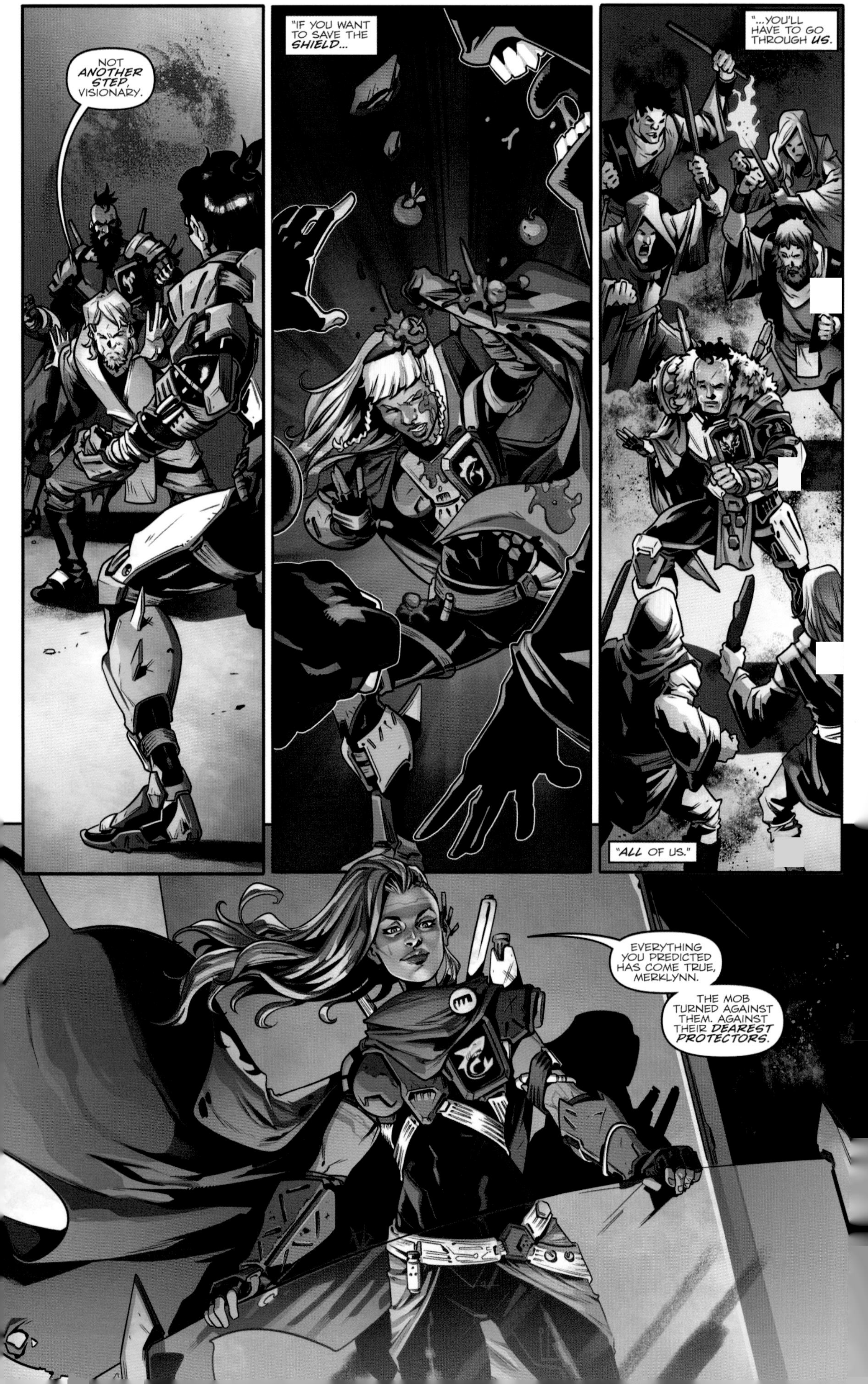
NOT ANOTHER STEP, VISIONARY.
"IF YOU WANT TO SAVE THE SHIELD...
"...YOU'LL HAVE TO GO THROUGH US.
"ALL OF US."
EVERYTHING YOU PREDICTED HAS COME TRUE, MERKLYNN.
THE MOB TURNED AGAINST THEM. AGAINST THEIR DEAREST PROTECTORS.

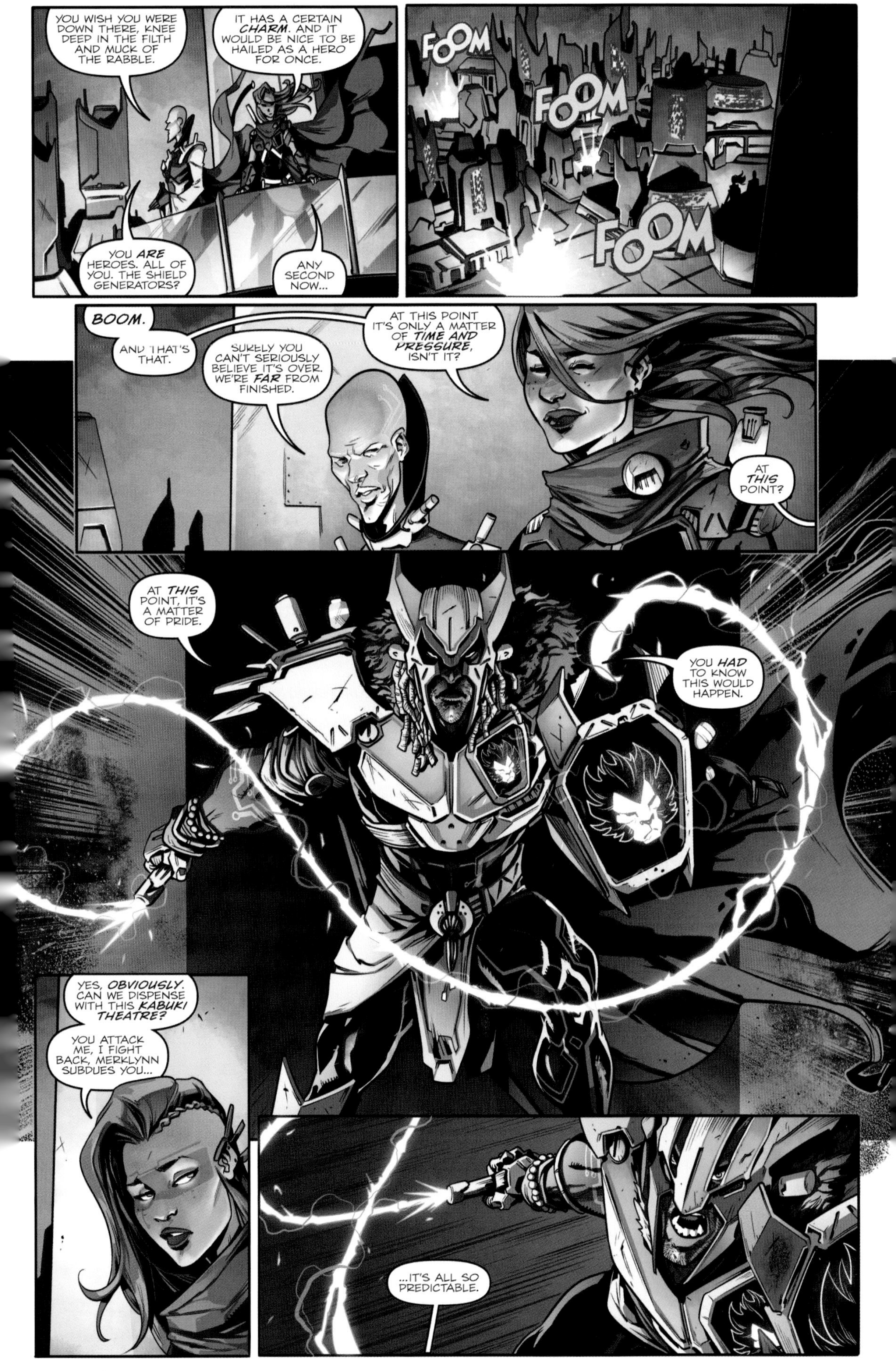

YOU WISH YOU WERE DOWN THERE, KNEE DEEP IN THE FILTH AND MUCK OF THE RABBLE.
IT HAS A CERTAIN CHARM. AND IT WOULD BE NICE TO BE HAILED AS A HERO FOR ONCE.
YOU ARE HEROES. ALL OF YOU. THE SHIELD GENERATORS?
ANY SECOND NOW...
FOOM
FOOM
FOOM
BOOM.
AND THAT'S THAT.
AT THIS POINT IT'S ONLY A MATTER OF TIME AND PRESSURE, ISN'T IT?
SURELY YOU CAN'T SERIOUSLY BELIEVE IT'S OVER. WE'RE FAR FROM FINISHED.
AT THIS POINT?
AT THIS POINT, IT'S A MATTER OF PRIDE.
YOU HAD TO KNOW THIS WOULD HAPPEN.
YES, OBVIOUSLY. CAN WE DISPENSE WITH THIS KABUKI THEATRE?
YOU ATTACK ME, I FIGHT BACK, MERKLYNN SUBDUES YOU...
...IT'S ALL SO PREDICTABLE.

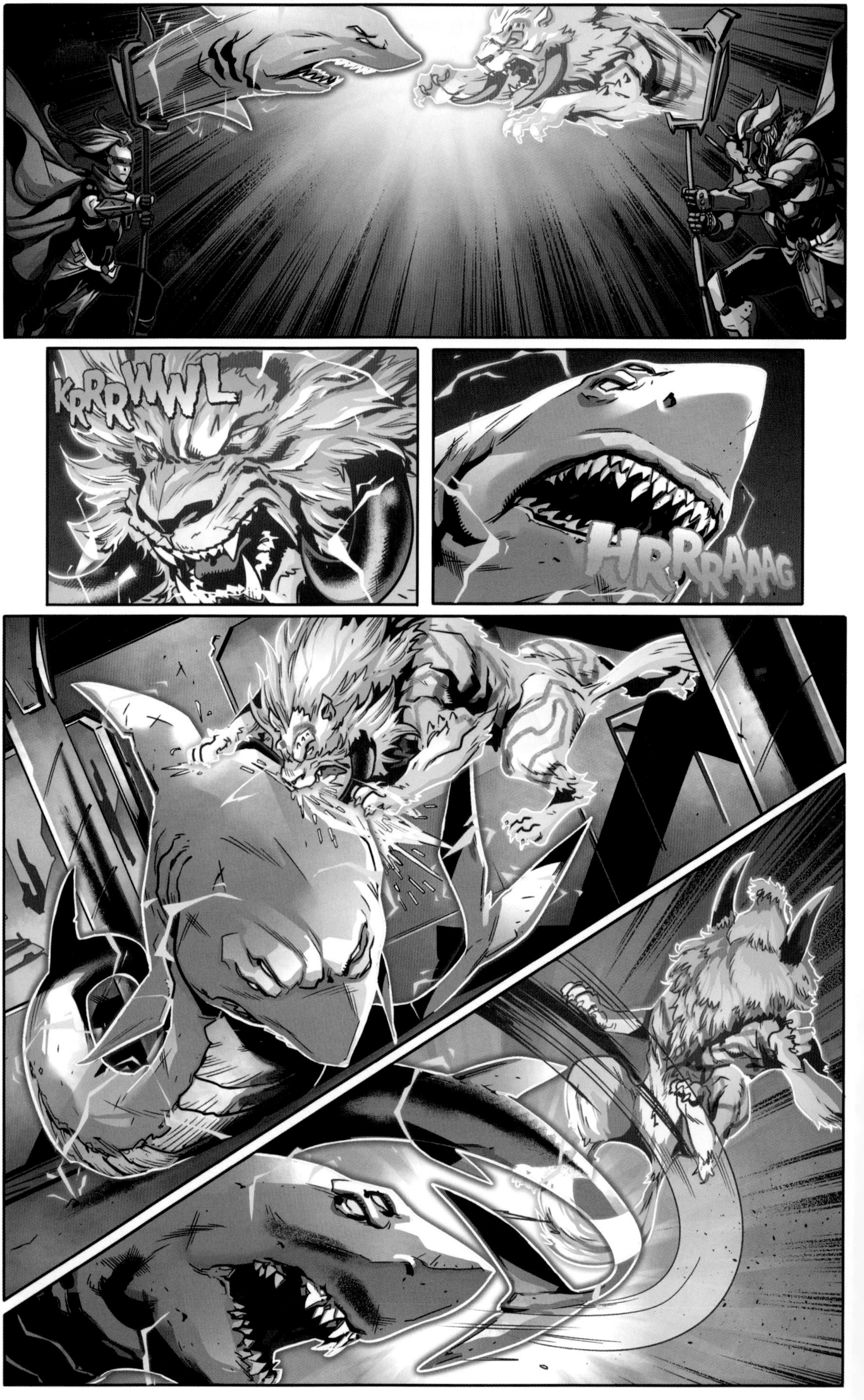
KRRRWWL
HRRRAAAG

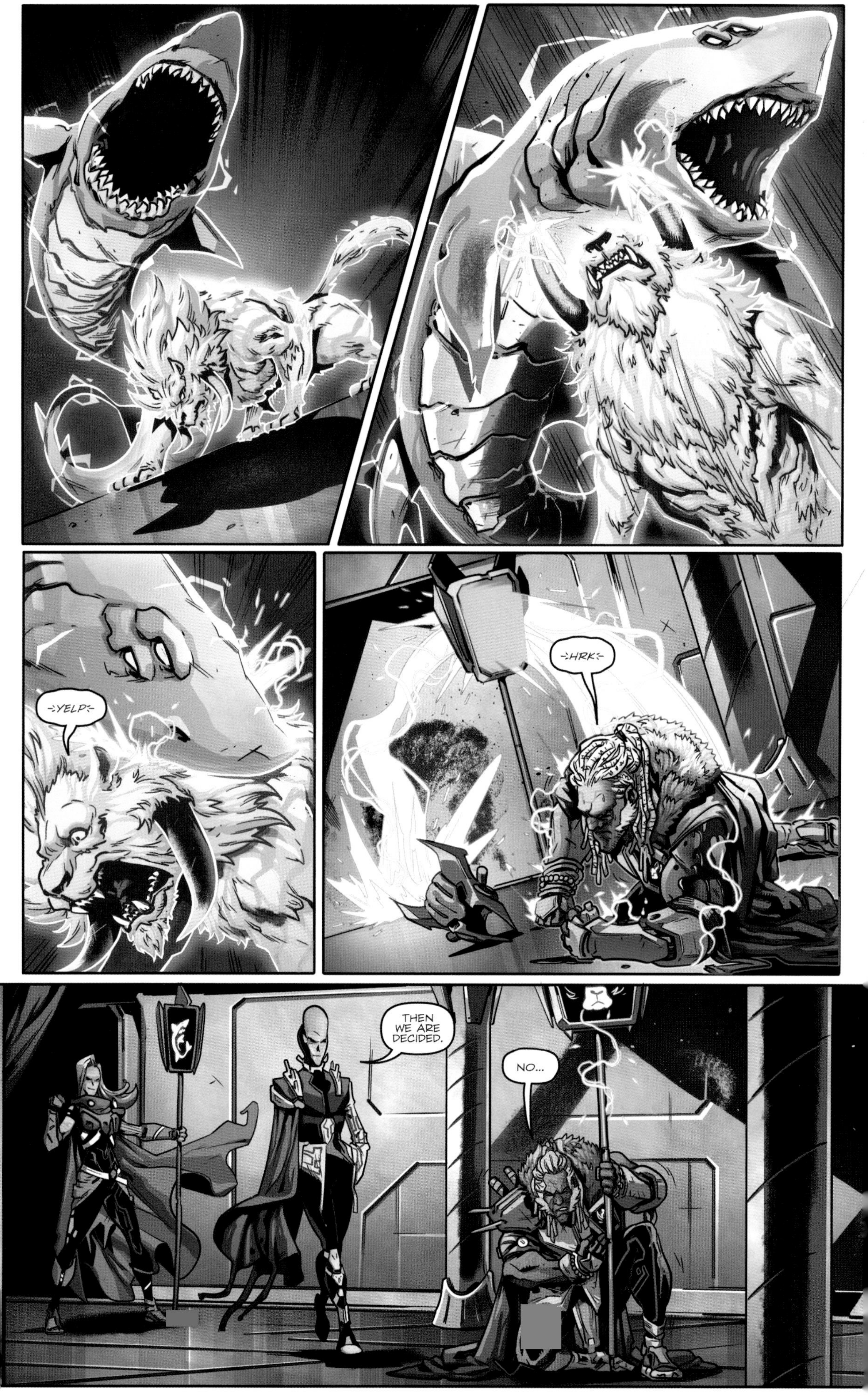
-YELP-
-HRK-
THEN WE ARE DECIDED.
NO...

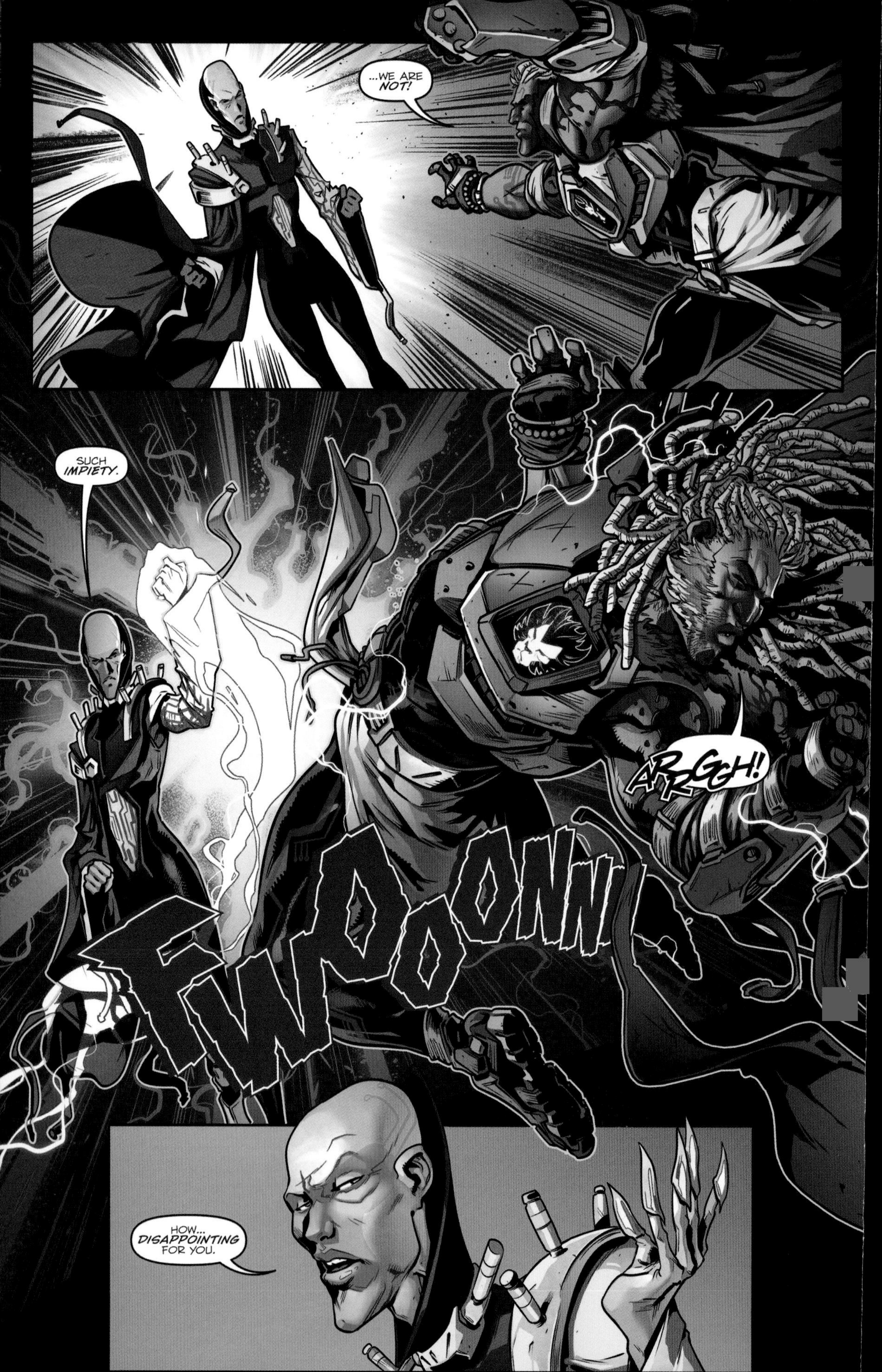
...WE ARE NOT!
SUCH IMPIETY.
ARRGGH!
FWOOONN
HOW... DISAPPOINTING FOR YOU.

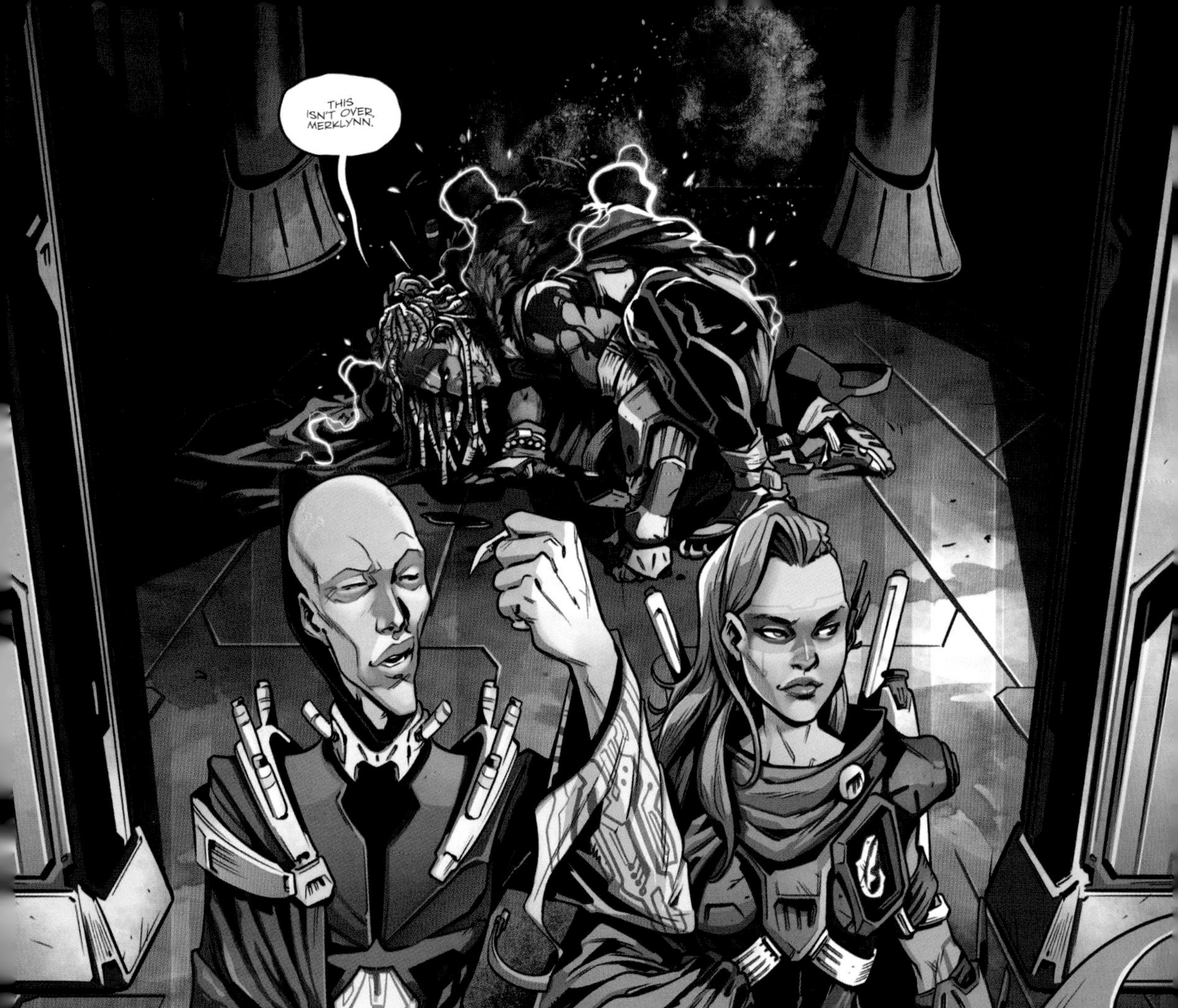
THIS ISN'T OVER, MERKLYNN.

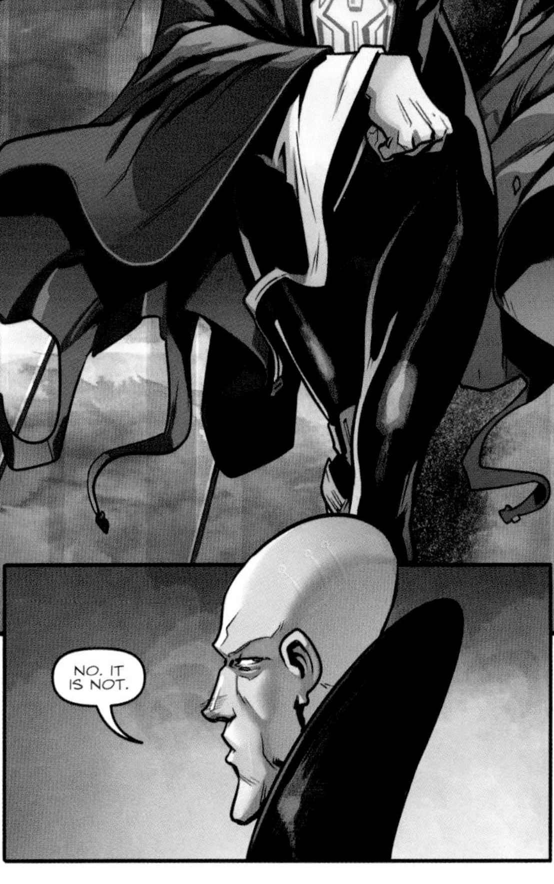
NO. IT IS NOT.

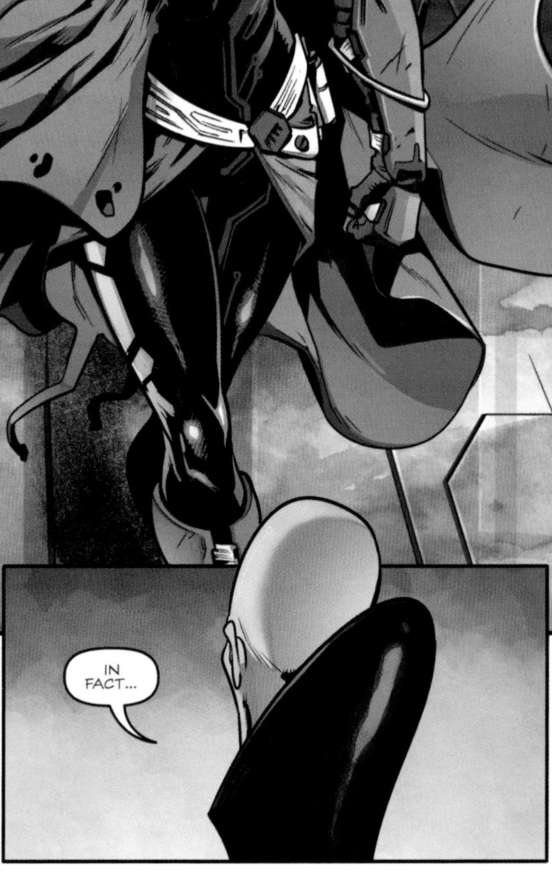
IN FACT...

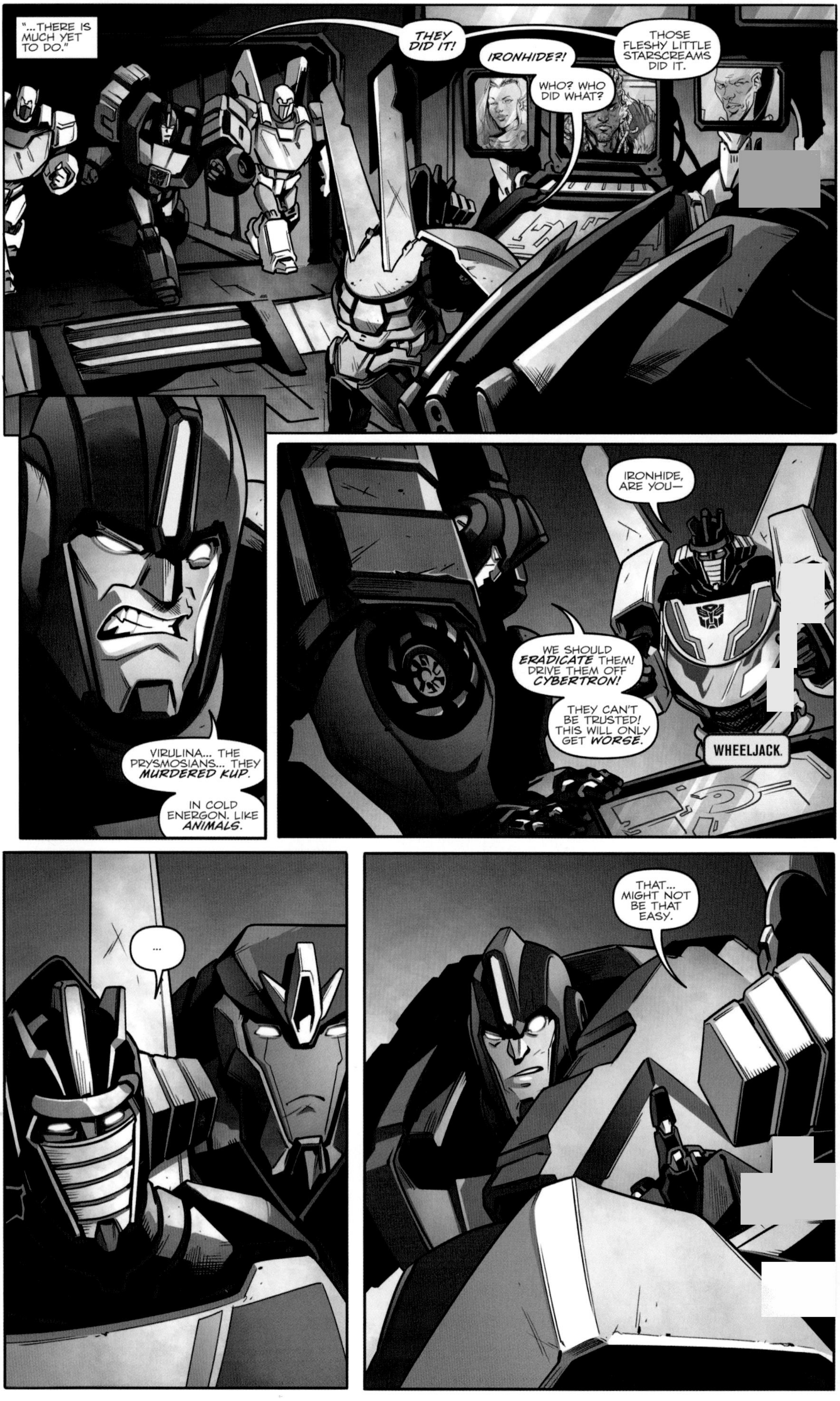
"...THERE IS MUCH YET TO DO."
THEY DID IT!
IRONHIDE?!
WHO? WHO DID WHAT?
THOSE FLESHY LITTLE STARSCREAMS DID IT.
VIRULINA... THE PRYSMOSIANS... THEY MURDERED KUP.
IN COLD ENERGON. LIKE ANIMALS.
IRONHIDE, ARE YOU—
WE SHOULD ERADICATE THEM! DRIVE THEM OFF CYBERTRON!
THEY CAN'T BE TRUSTED! THIS WILL ONLY GET WORSE.
WHEELJACK.
...
THAT... MIGHT NOT BE THAT EASY.

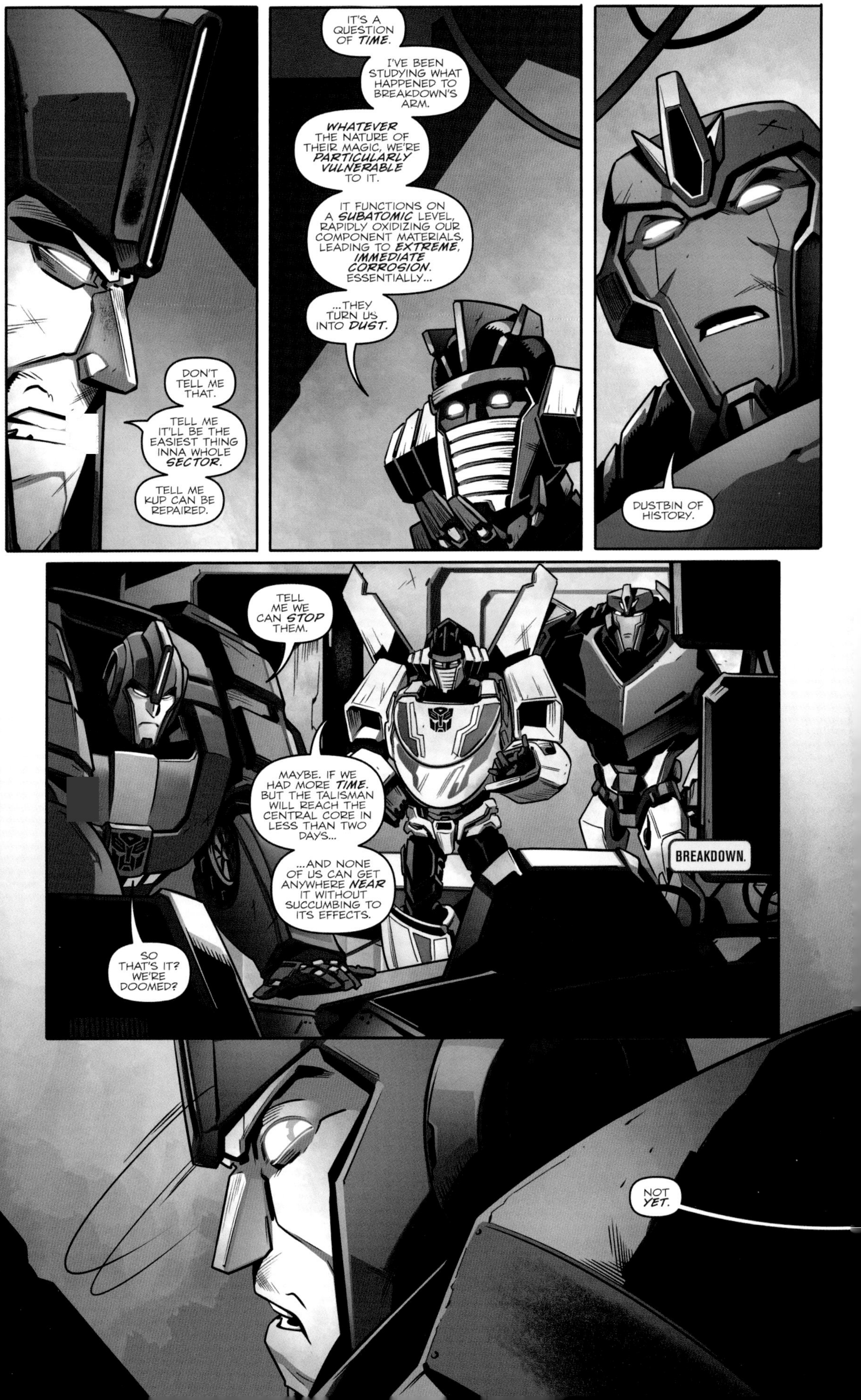
DON'T TELL ME THAT.
TELL ME IT'LL BE THE EASIEST THING INNA WHOLE SECTOR.
TELL ME KUP CAN BE REPAIRED.
IT'S A QUESTION OF TIME.
I'VE BEEN STUDYING WHAT HAPPENED TO BREAKDOWN'S ARM.
WHATEVER THE NATURE OF THEIR MAGIC, WE'RE PARTICULARLY VULNERABLE TO IT.
IT FUNCTIONS ON A SUBATOMIC LEVEL, RAPIDLY OXIDIZING OUR COMPONENT MATERIALS, LEADING TO EXTREME, IMMEDIATE CORROSION. ESSENTIALLY...
...THEY TURN US INTO DUST.
DUSTBIN OF HISTORY.
TELL ME WE CAN STOP THEM.
MAYBE. IF WE HAD MORE TIME. BUT THE TALISMAN WILL REACH THE CENTRAL CORE IN LESS THAN TWO DAYS...
...AND NONE OF US CAN GET ANYWHERE NEAR IT WITHOUT SUCCUMBING TO ITS EFFECTS.
SO THAT'S IT? WE'RE DOOMED?
BREAKDOWN.
NOT YET.

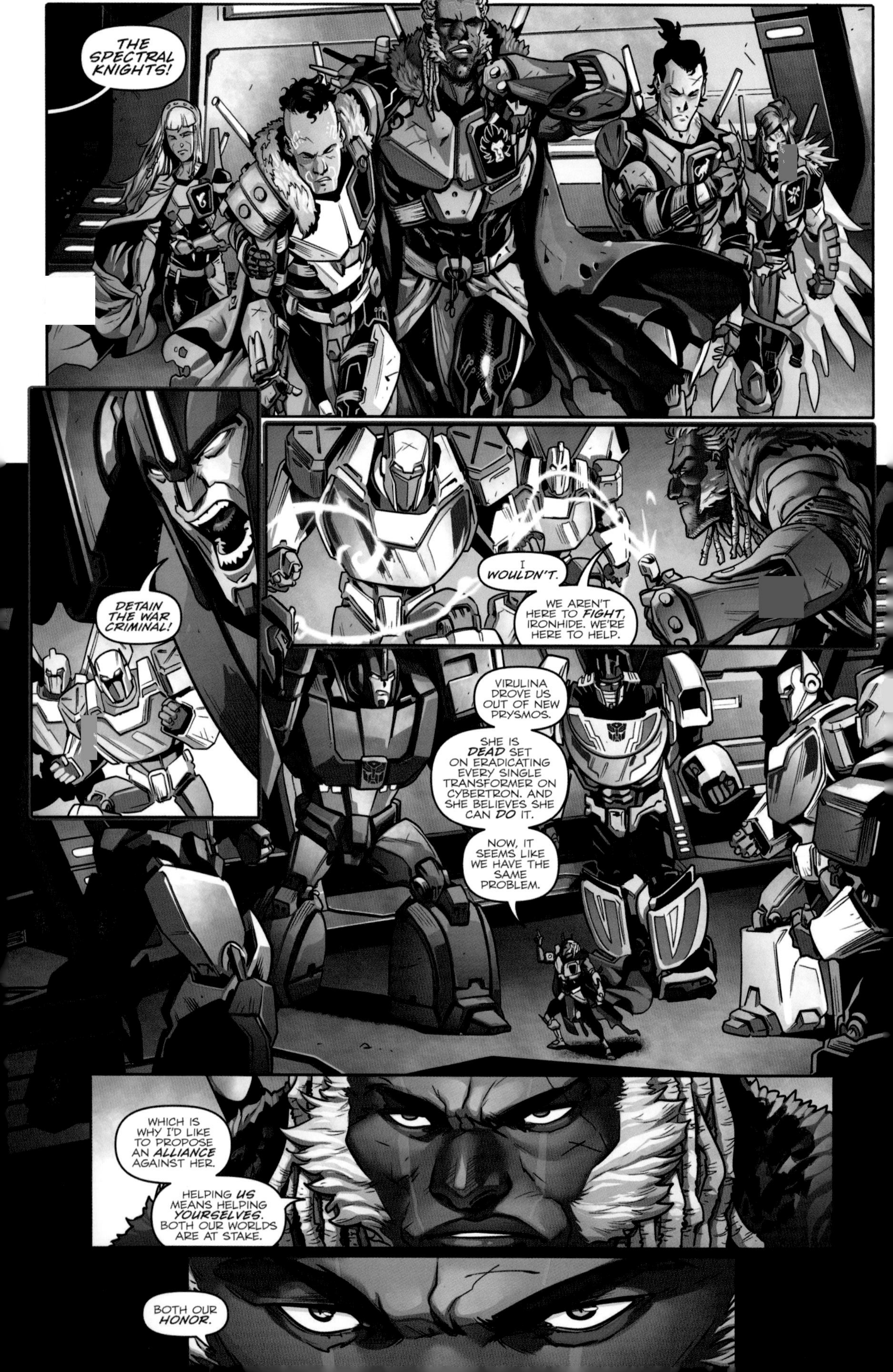
THE SPECTRAL KNIGHTS!
DETAIN THE WAR CRIMINAL!
I WOULDN'T.
WE AREN'T HERE TO FIGHT, IRONHIDE. WE'RE HERE TO HELP.
VIRULINA DROVE US OUT OF NEW PRYSMOS.
SHE IS DEAD SET ON ERADICATING EVERY SINGLE TRANSFORMER ON CYBERTRON. AND SHE BELIEVES SHE CAN DO IT.
NOW, IT SEEMS LIKE WE HAVE THE SAME PROBLEM.
WHICH IS WHY I'D LIKE TO PROPOSE AN ALLIANCE AGAINST HER.
HELPING US MEANS HELPING YOURSELVES. BOTH OUR WORLDS ARE AT STAKE.
BOTH OUR HONOR.

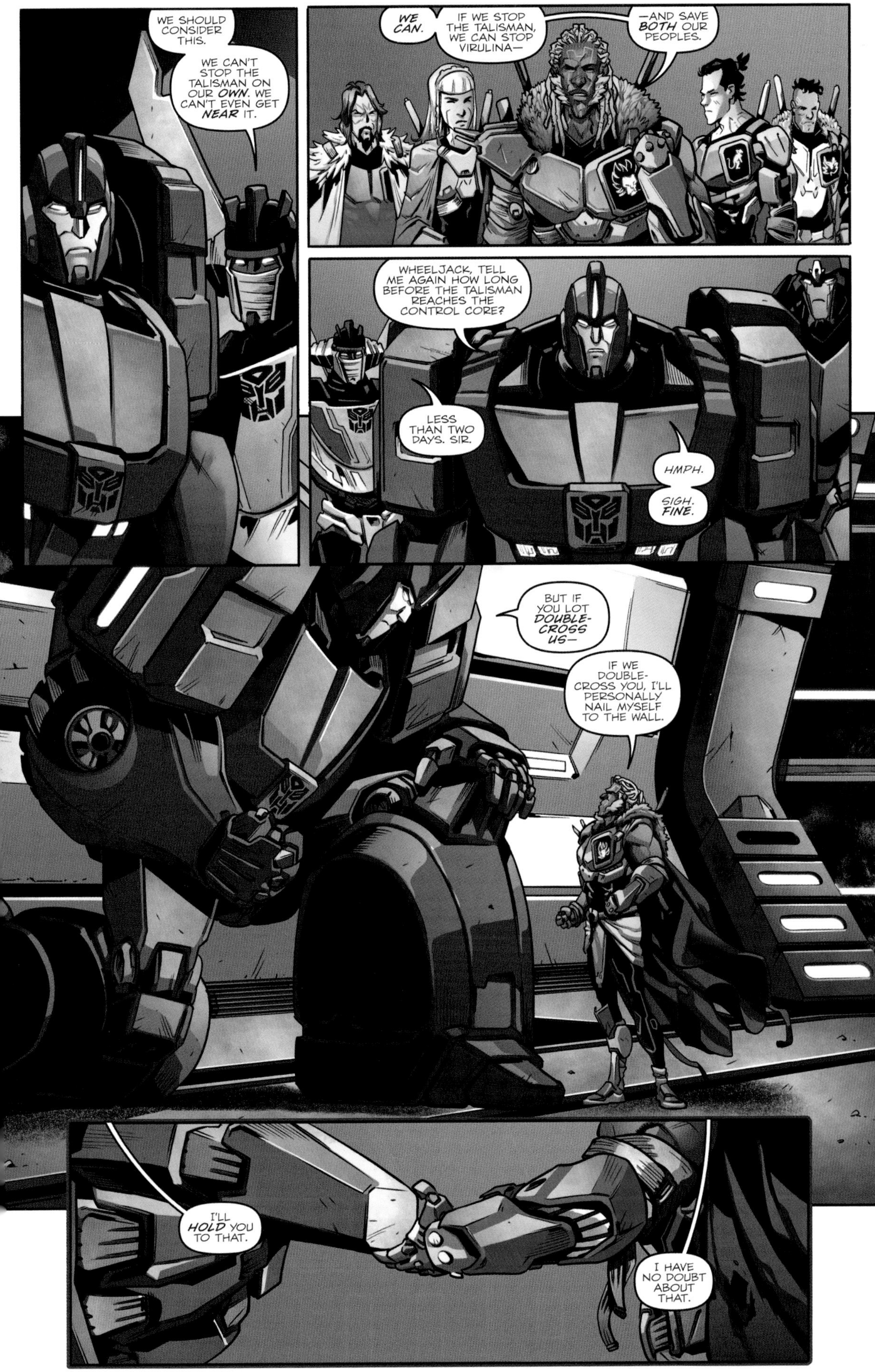
WE SHOULD CONSIDER THIS.
WE CAN'T STOP THE TALISMAN ON OUR OWN. WE CAN'T EVEN GET NEAR IT.
WE CAN.
IF WE STOP THE TALISMAN, WE CAN STOP VIRULINA—
—AND SAVE BOTH OUR PEOPLES.
WHEELJACK, TELL ME AGAIN HOW LONG BEFORE THE TALISMAN REACHES THE CONTROL CORE?
LESS THAN TWO DAYS. SIR.
HMPH.
SIGH. FINE.
BUT IF YOU LOT DOUBLE-CROSS US—
IF WE DOUBLE-CROSS YOU, I'LL PERSONALLY NAIL MYSELF TO THE WALL.
I'LL HOLD YOU TO THAT.
I HAVE NO DOUBT ABOUT THAT.

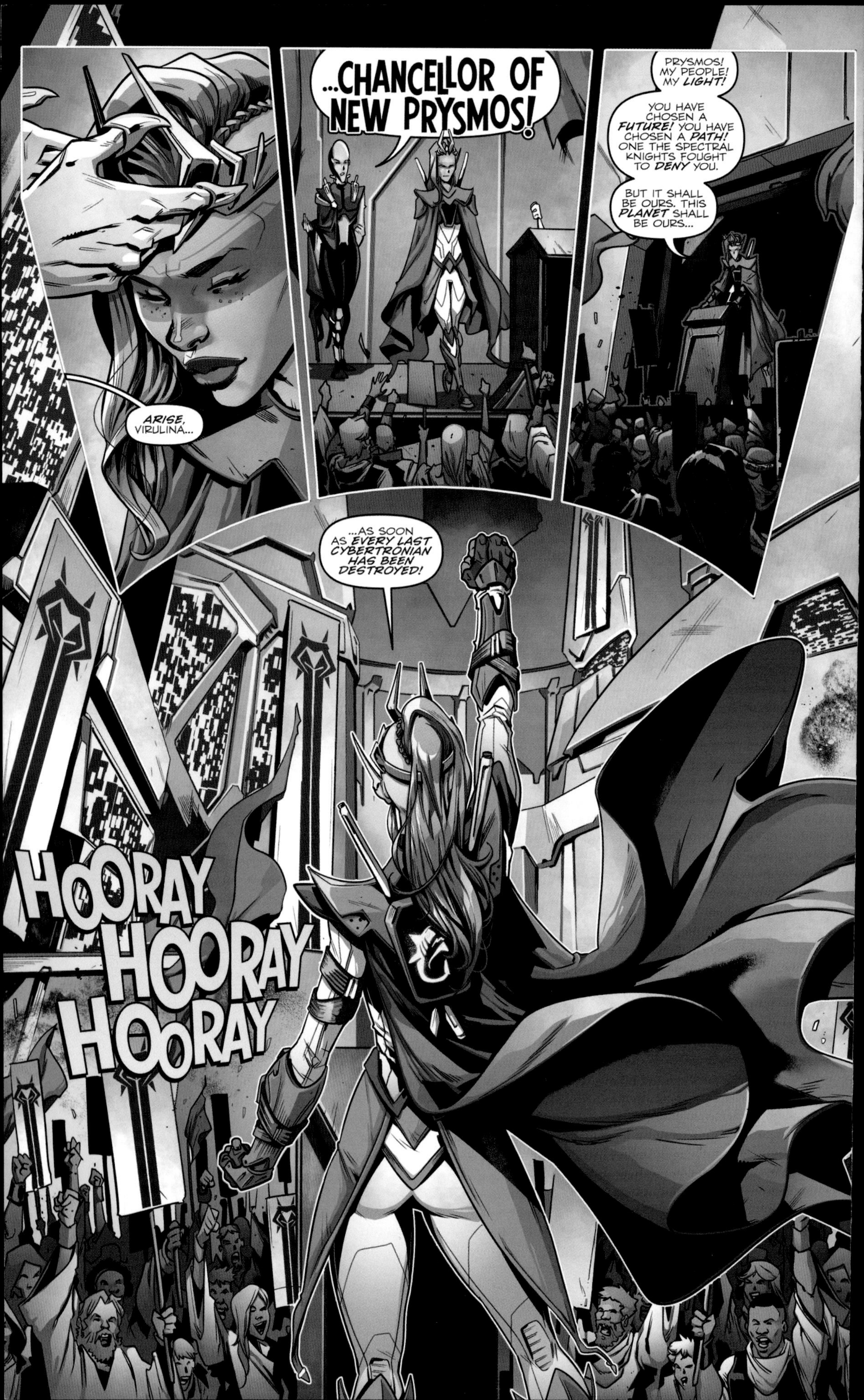
ARISE, VIRULINA...
...CHANCELLOR OF NEW PRYSMOS!
PRYSMOS! MY PEOPLE! MY LIGHT!
YOU HAVE CHOSEN A FUTURE! YOU HAVE CHOSEN A PATH! ONE THE SPECTRAL KNIGHTS FOUGHT TO DENY YOU.
BUT IT SHALL BE OURS. THIS PLANET SHALL BE OURS...
...AS SOON AS EVERY LAST CYBERTRONIAN HAS BEEN DESTROYED!
HOORAY HOORAY HOORAY

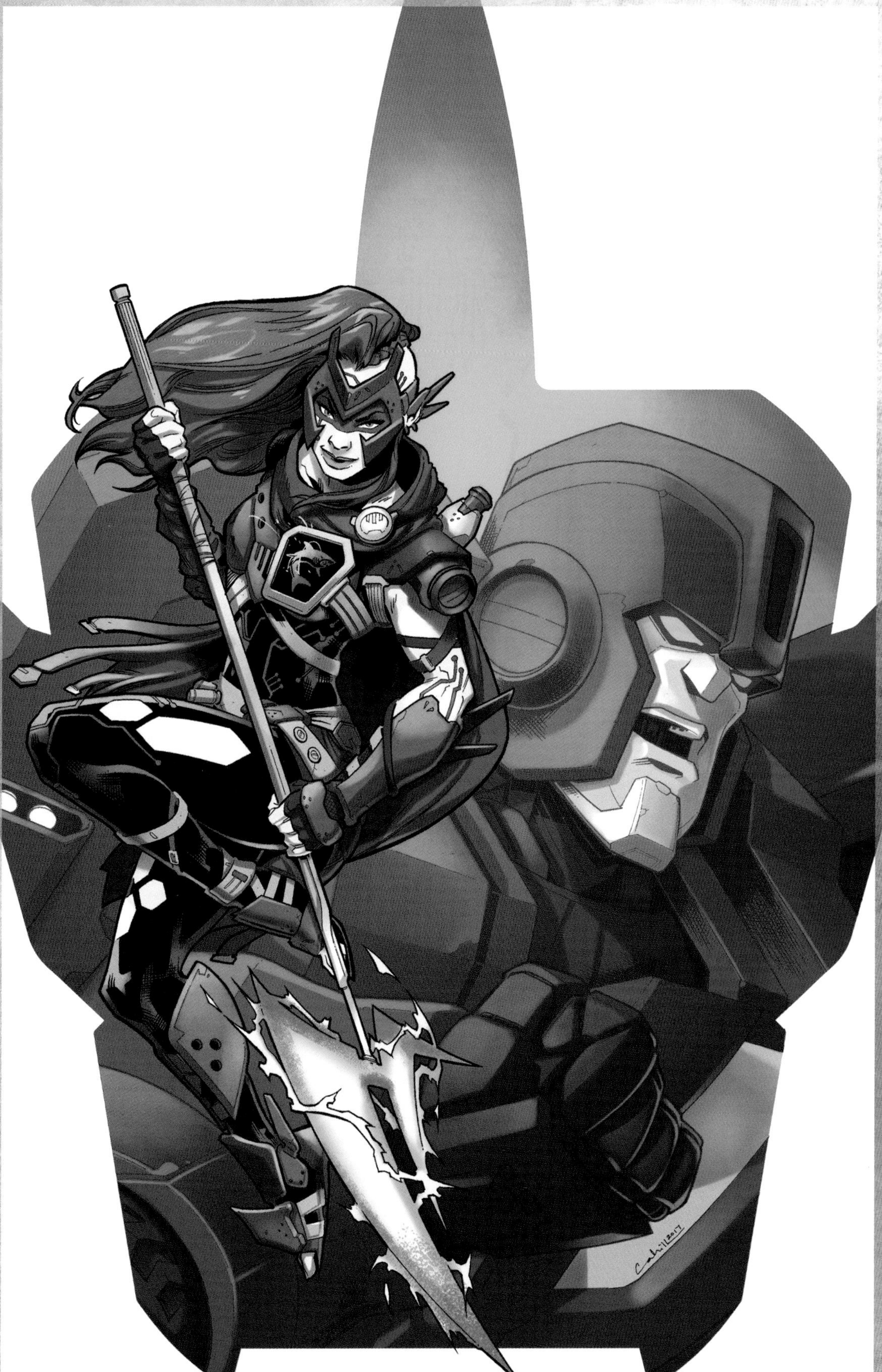

ART BY **BRENDAN CAHILL**
COLORS BY **LAUREN BENNETT**

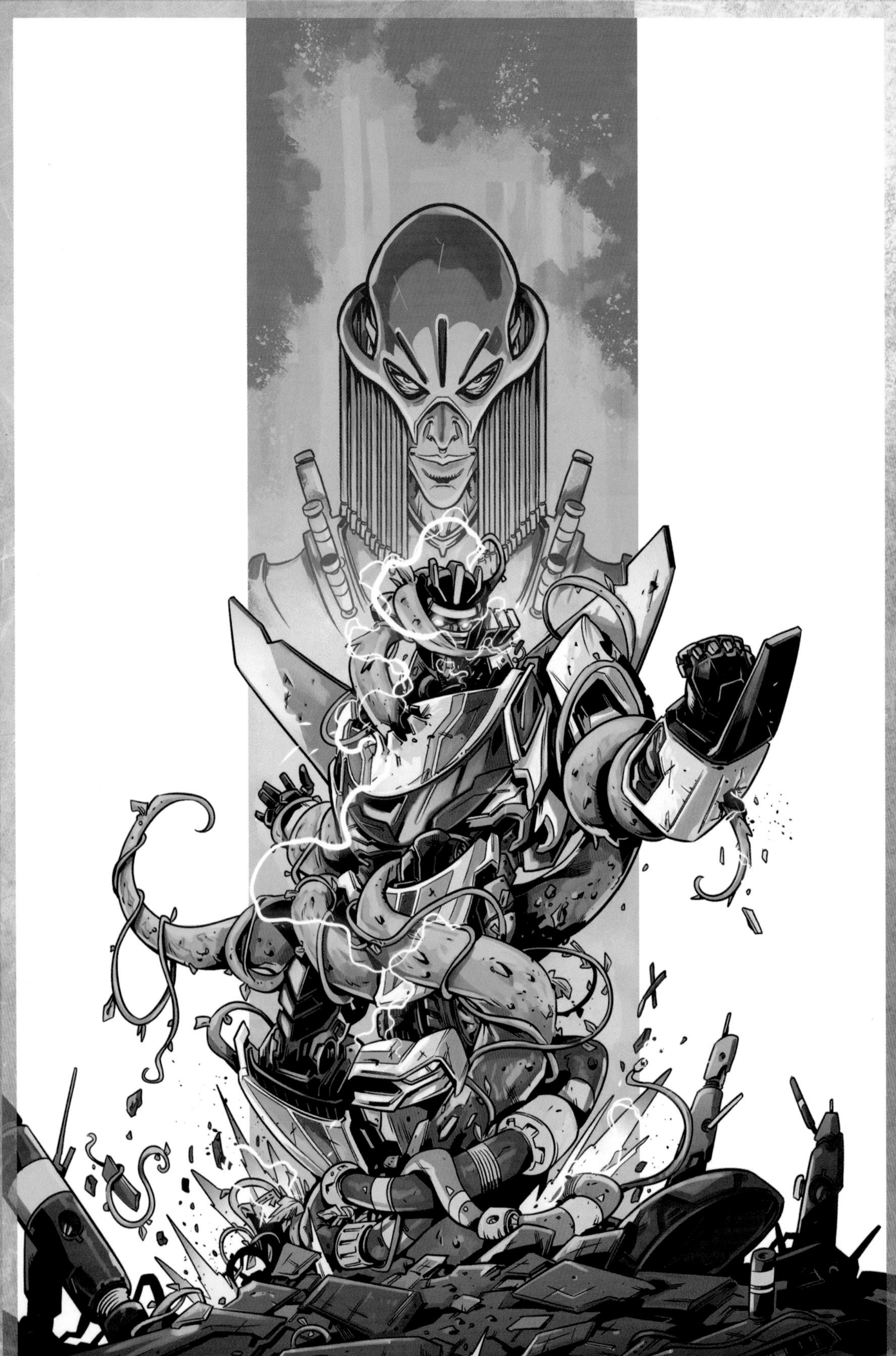

ART BY FICO OSSIO

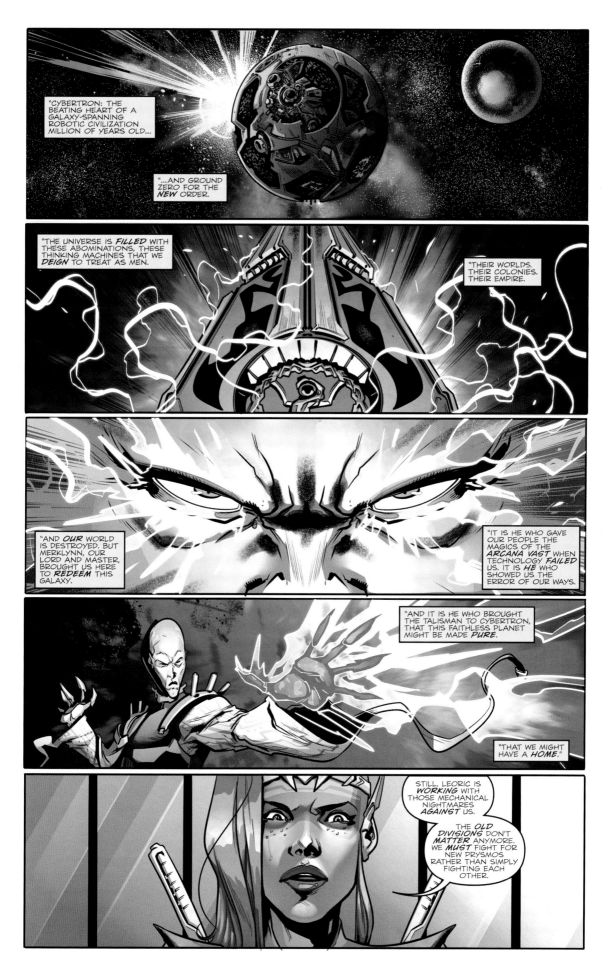

"CYBERTRON: THE BEATING HEART OF A GALAXY-SPANNING ROBOTIC CIVILIZATION MILLION OF YEARS OLD...

"...AND GROUND ZERO FOR THE *NEW* ORDER.

"THE UNIVERSE IS *FILLED* WITH THESE ABOMINATIONS, THESE THINKING MACHINES THAT WE *DEIGN* TO TREAT AS MEN.

"THEIR WORLDS. THEIR COLONIES. THEIR EMPIRE.

"AND *OUR* WORLD IS DESTROYED. BUT MERKLYNN, OUR LORD AND MASTER, BROUGHT US HERE TO *REDEEM* THIS GALAXY.

"IT IS HE WHO GAVE OUR PEOPLE THE MAGICS OF THE *ARCANA VAST* WHEN TECHNOLOGY *FAILED* US. IT IS *HE* WHO SHOWED US THE ERROR OF OUR WAYS.

"AND IT IS HE WHO BROUGHT THE TALISMAN TO CYBERTRON, THAT THIS FAITHLESS PLANET MIGHT BE MADE *PURE*.

"THAT WE MIGHT HAVE A *HOME*."

STILL, LEORIC IS *WORKING* WITH THOSE MECHANICAL NIGHTMARES *AGAINST* US.

THE *OLD DIVISIONS* DON'T *MATTER* ANYMORE. WE *MUST* FIGHT FOR NEW PRYSMOS RATHER THAN SIMPLY FIGHTING EACH OTHER.

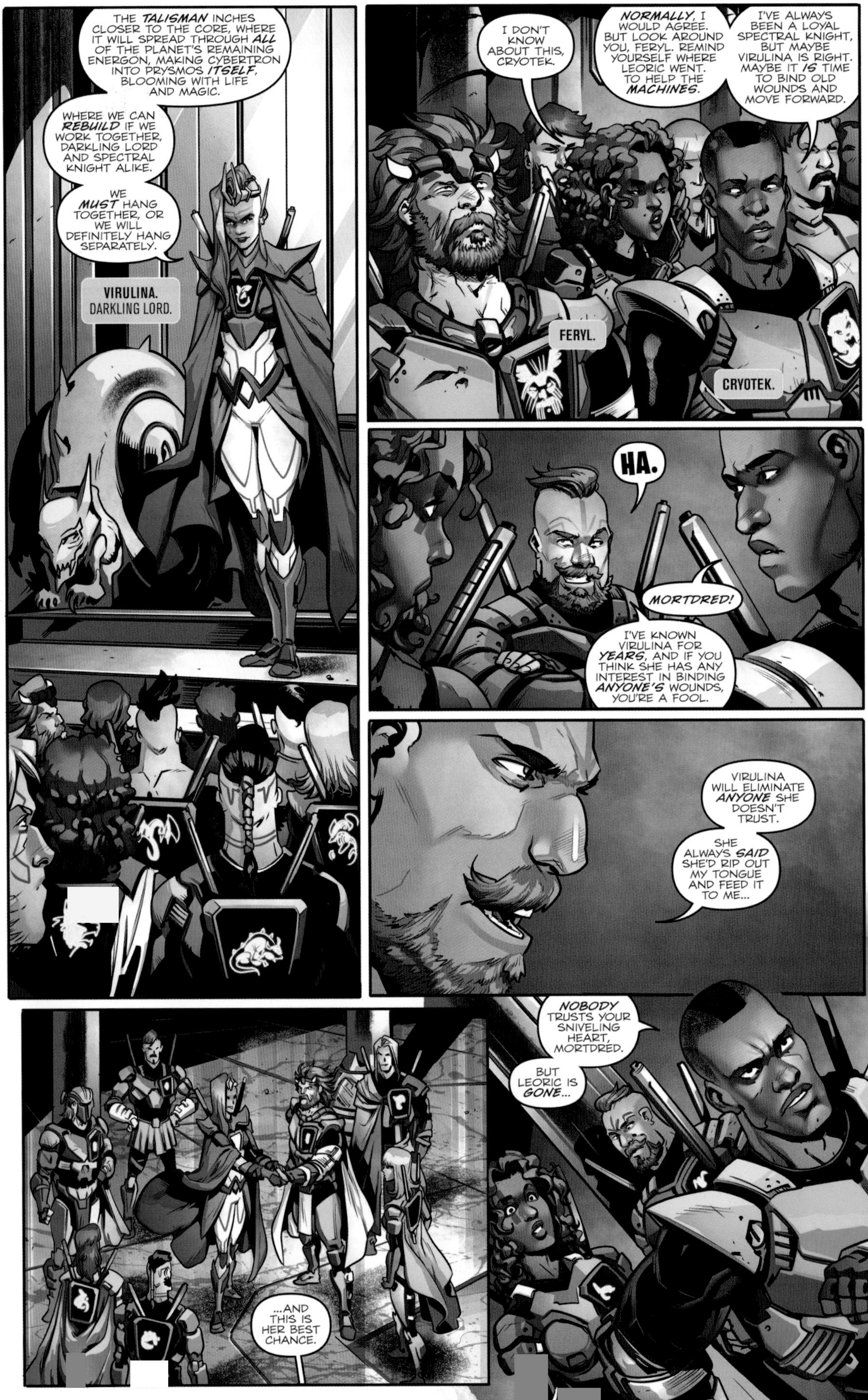
THE TALISMAN INCHES CLOSER TO THE CORE, WHERE IT WILL SPREAD THROUGH ALL OF THE PLANET'S REMAINING ENERGON, MAKING CYBERTRON INTO PRYSMOS ITSELF, BLOOMING WITH LIFE AND MAGIC.
WHERE WE CAN REBUILD IF WE WORK TOGETHER, DARKLING LORD AND SPECTRAL KNIGHT ALIKE.
WE MUST HANG TOGETHER, OR WE WILL DEFINITELY HANG SEPARATELY.
VIRULINA. DARKLING LORD.
I DON'T KNOW ABOUT THIS, CRYOTEK.
NORMALLY, I WOULD AGREE. BUT LOOK AROUND YOU, FERYL. REMIND YOURSELF WHERE LEORIC WENT. TO HELP THE MACHINES.
I'VE ALWAYS BEEN A LOYAL SPECTRAL KNIGHT, BUT MAYBE VIRULINA IS RIGHT. MAYBE IT IS TIME TO BIND OLD WOUNDS AND MOVE FORWARD.
FERYL.
CRYOTEK.
HA.
MORTDRED!
I'VE KNOWN VIRULINA FOR YEARS, AND IF YOU THINK SHE HAS ANY INTEREST IN BINDING ANYONE'S WOUNDS, YOU'RE A FOOL.
VIRULINA WILL ELIMINATE ANYONE SHE DOESN'T TRUST.
SHE ALWAYS SAID SHE'D RIP OUT MY TONGUE AND FEED IT TO ME...
...AND THIS IS HER BEST CHANCE.
NOBODY TRUSTS YOUR SNIVELING HEART, MORTDRED.
BUT LEORIC IS GONE...

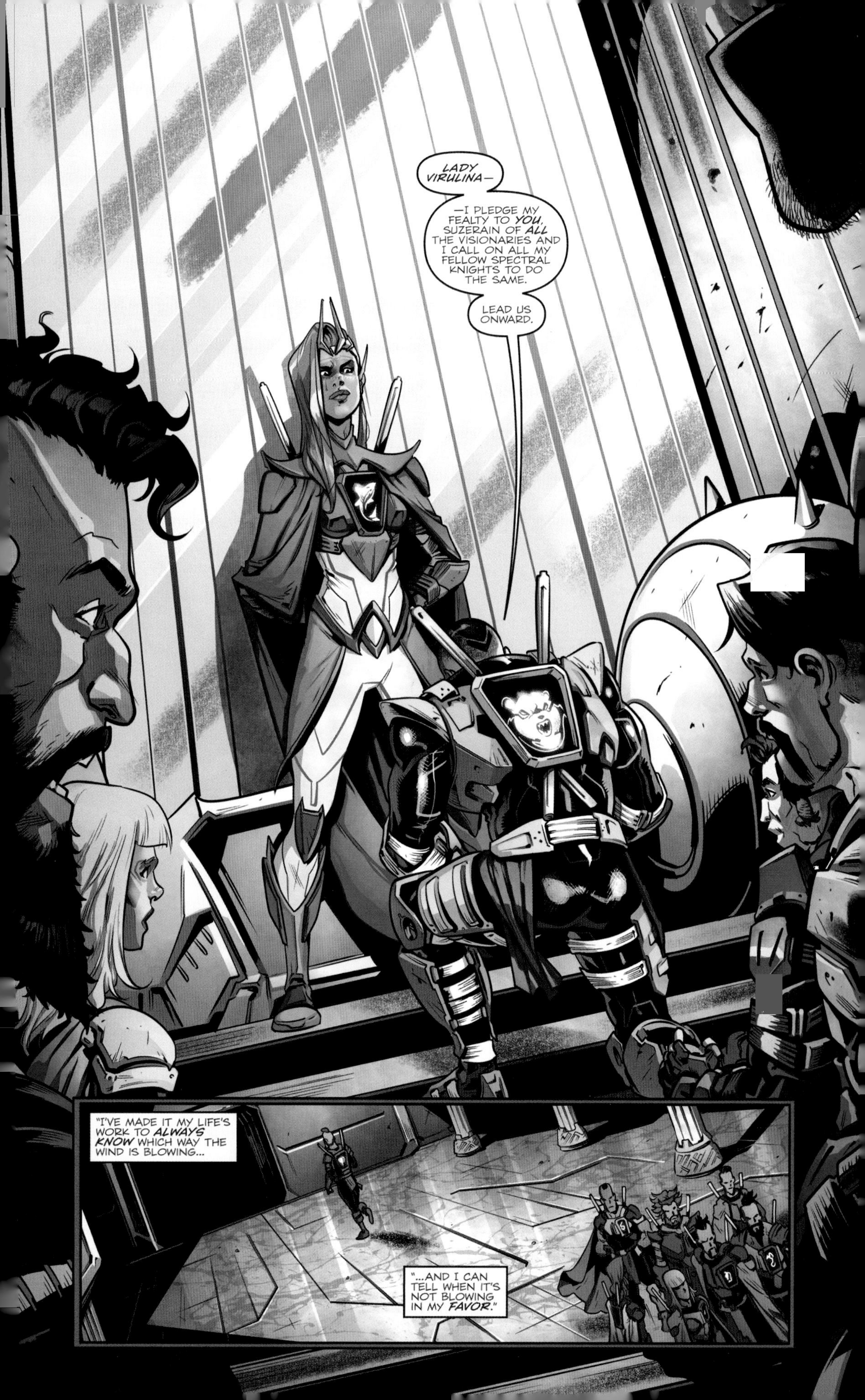
LADY VIRULINA—
—I PLEDGE MY FEALTY TO YOU, SUZERAIN OF ALL THE VISIONARIES AND I CALL ON ALL MY FELLOW SPECTRAL KNIGHTS TO DO THE SAME.
LEAD US ONWARD.
"I'VE MADE IT MY LIFE'S WORK TO ALWAYS KNOW WHICH WAY THE WIND IS BLOWING...
"...AND I CAN TELL WHEN IT'S NOT BLOWING IN MY FAVOR."

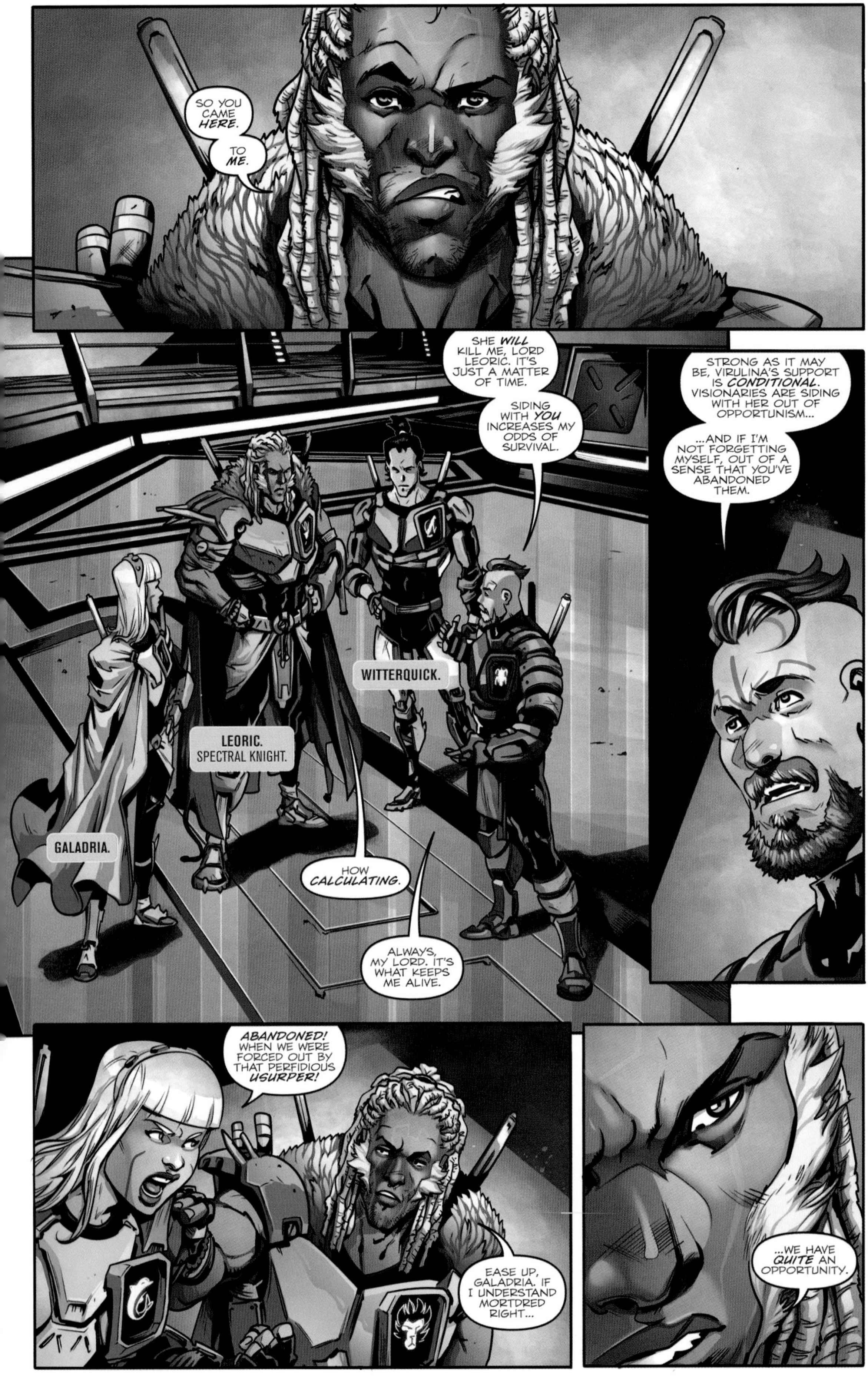
SO YOU CAME HERE.
TO ME.
SHE WILL KILL ME, LORD LEORIC. IT'S JUST A MATTER OF TIME.
SIDING WITH YOU INCREASES MY ODDS OF SURVIVAL.
WITTERQUICK.
LEORIC. SPECTRAL KNIGHT.
GALADRIA.
HOW CALCULATING.
ALWAYS, MY LORD. IT'S WHAT KEEPS ME ALIVE.
STRONG AS IT MAY BE, VIRULINA'S SUPPORT IS CONDITIONAL. VISIONARIES ARE SIDING WITH HER OUT OF OPPORTUNISM...
...AND IF I'M NOT FORGETTING MYSELF, OUT OF A SENSE THAT YOU'VE ABANDONED THEM.
ABANDONED! WHEN WE WERE FORCED OUT BY THAT PERFIDIOUS USURPER!
EASE UP, GALADRIA. IF I UNDERSTAND MORTDRED RIGHT...
...WE HAVE QUITE AN OPPORTUNITY.

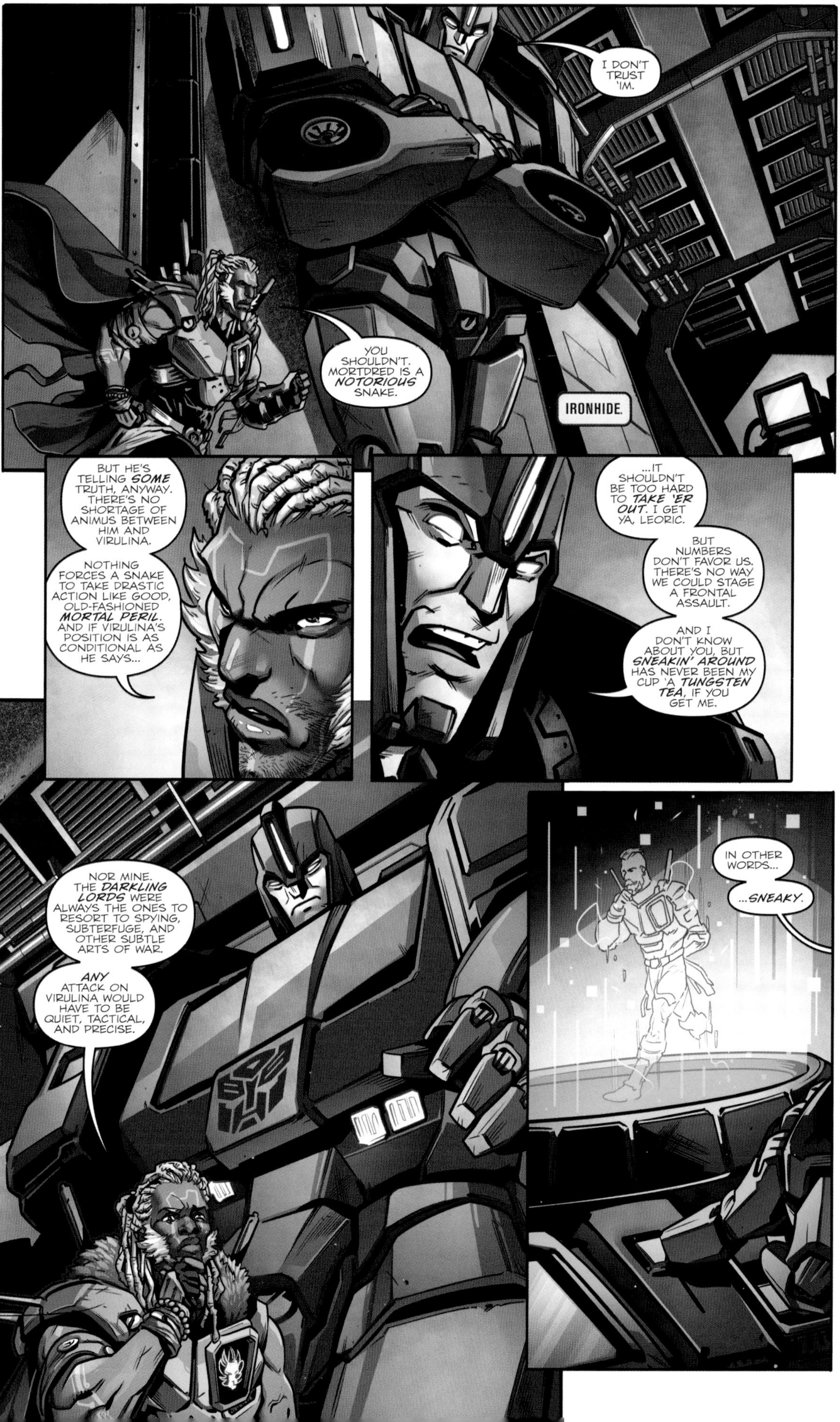
I DON'T TRUST 'IM.
YOU SHOULDN'T. MORTDRED IS A NOTORIOUS SNAKE.
IRONHIDE.
BUT HE'S TELLING SOME TRUTH, ANYWAY. THERE'S NO SHORTAGE OF ANIMUS BETWEEN HIM AND VIRULINA.
NOTHING FORCES A SNAKE TO TAKE DRASTIC ACTION LIKE GOOD, OLD-FASHIONED MORTAL PERIL. AND IF VIRULINA'S POSITION IS AS CONDITIONAL AS HE SAYS...
...IT SHOULDN'T BE TOO HARD TO TAKE 'ER OUT. I GET YA, LEORIC.
BUT NUMBERS DON'T FAVOR US. THERE'S NO WAY WE COULD STAGE A FRONTAL ASSAULT.
AND I DON'T KNOW ABOUT YOU, BUT SNEAKIN' AROUND HAS NEVER BEEN MY CUP 'A TUNGSTEN TEA, IF YOU GET ME.
NOR MINE. THE DARKLING LORDS WERE ALWAYS THE ONES TO RESORT TO SPYING, SUBTERFUGE, AND OTHER SUBTLE ARTS OF WAR.
ANY ATTACK ON VIRULINA WOULD HAVE TO BE QUIET, TACTICAL, AND PRECISE.
IN OTHER WORDS...
...SNEAKY.

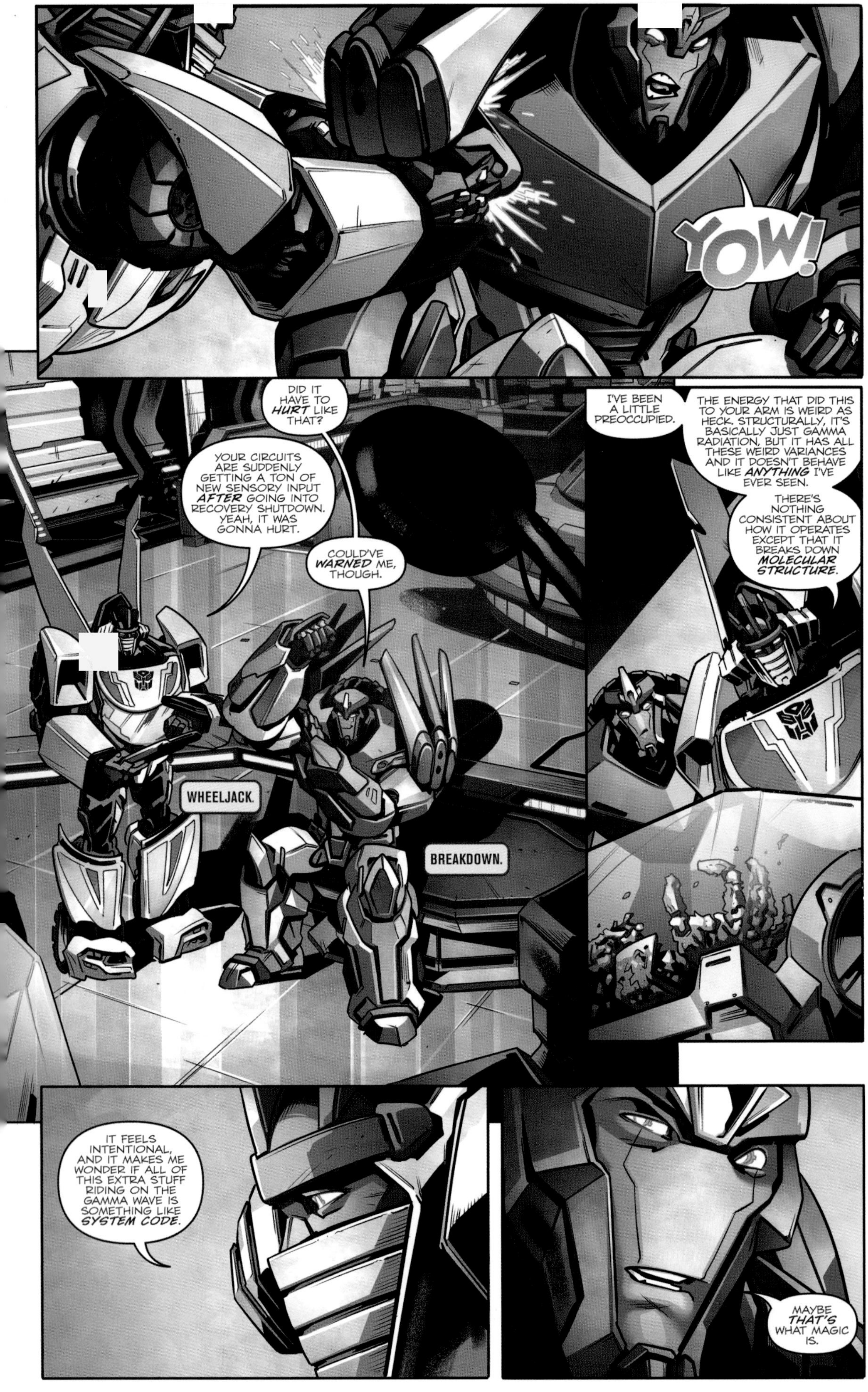
YOW!
DID IT HAVE TO *HURT* LIKE THAT?
YOUR CIRCUITS ARE SUDDENLY GETTING A TON OF NEW SENSORY INPUT *AFTER* GOING INTO RECOVERY SHUTDOWN. YEAH, IT WAS GONNA HURT.
COULD'VE *WARNED* ME, THOUGH.
WHEELJACK.
BREAKDOWN.
I'VE BEEN A LITTLE PREOCCUPIED.
THE ENERGY THAT DID THIS TO YOUR ARM IS WEIRD AS HECK. STRUCTURALLY, IT'S BASICALLY JUST GAMMA RADIATION, BUT IT HAS ALL THESE WEIRD VARIANCES AND IT DOESN'T BEHAVE LIKE *ANYTHING* I'VE EVER SEEN.
THERE'S NOTHING CONSISTENT ABOUT HOW IT OPERATES EXCEPT THAT IT BREAKS DOWN ***MOLECULAR STRUCTURE***.
IT FEELS INTENTIONAL, AND IT MAKES ME WONDER IF ALL OF THIS EXTRA STUFF RIDING ON THE GAMMA WAVE IS SOMETHING LIKE ***SYSTEM CODE***.
MAYBE *THAT'S* WHAT MAGIC IS.

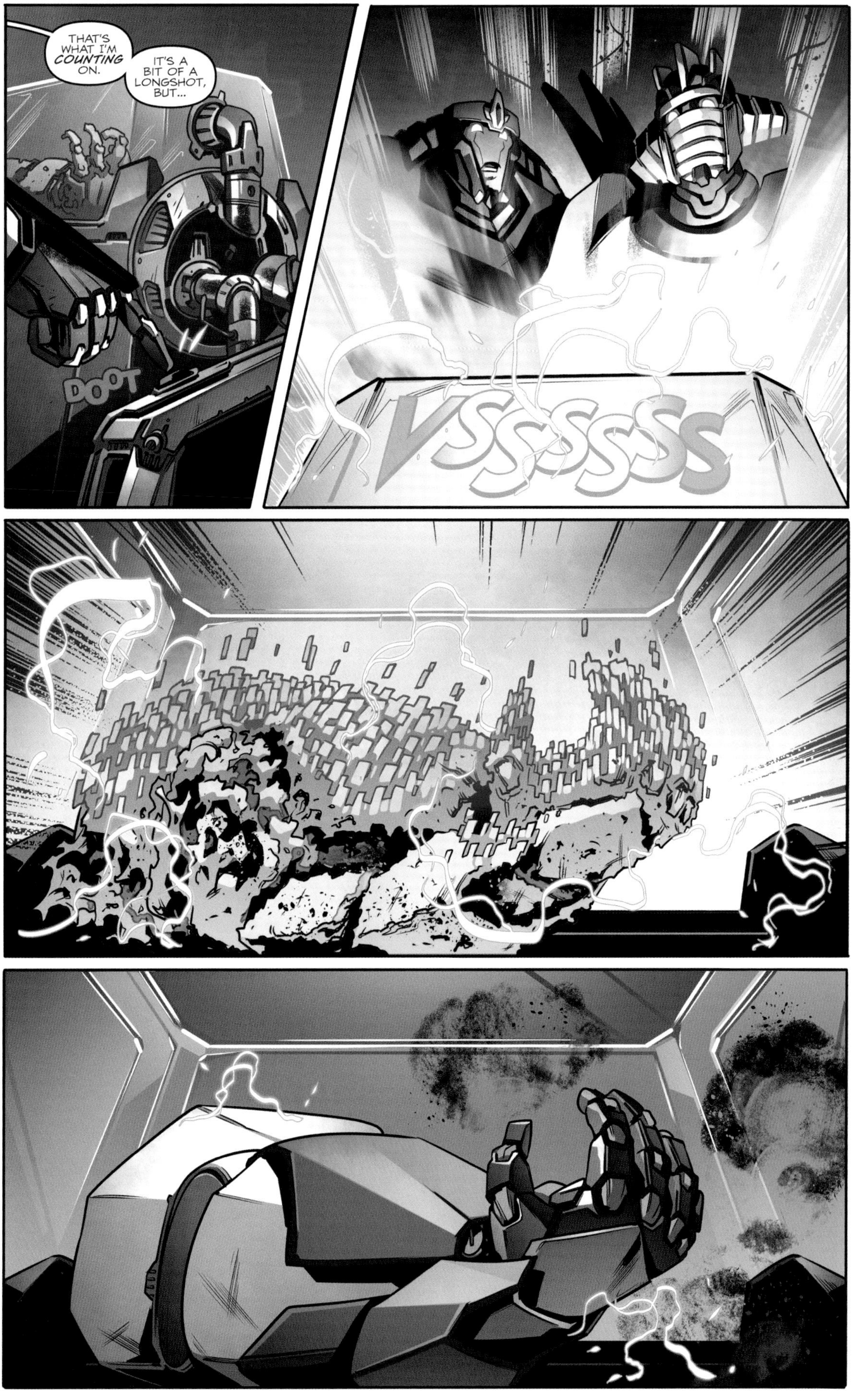
THAT'S WHAT I'M *COUNTING* ON.
IT'S A BIT OF A LONGSHOT, BUT...
DOOT
VSSSSSS

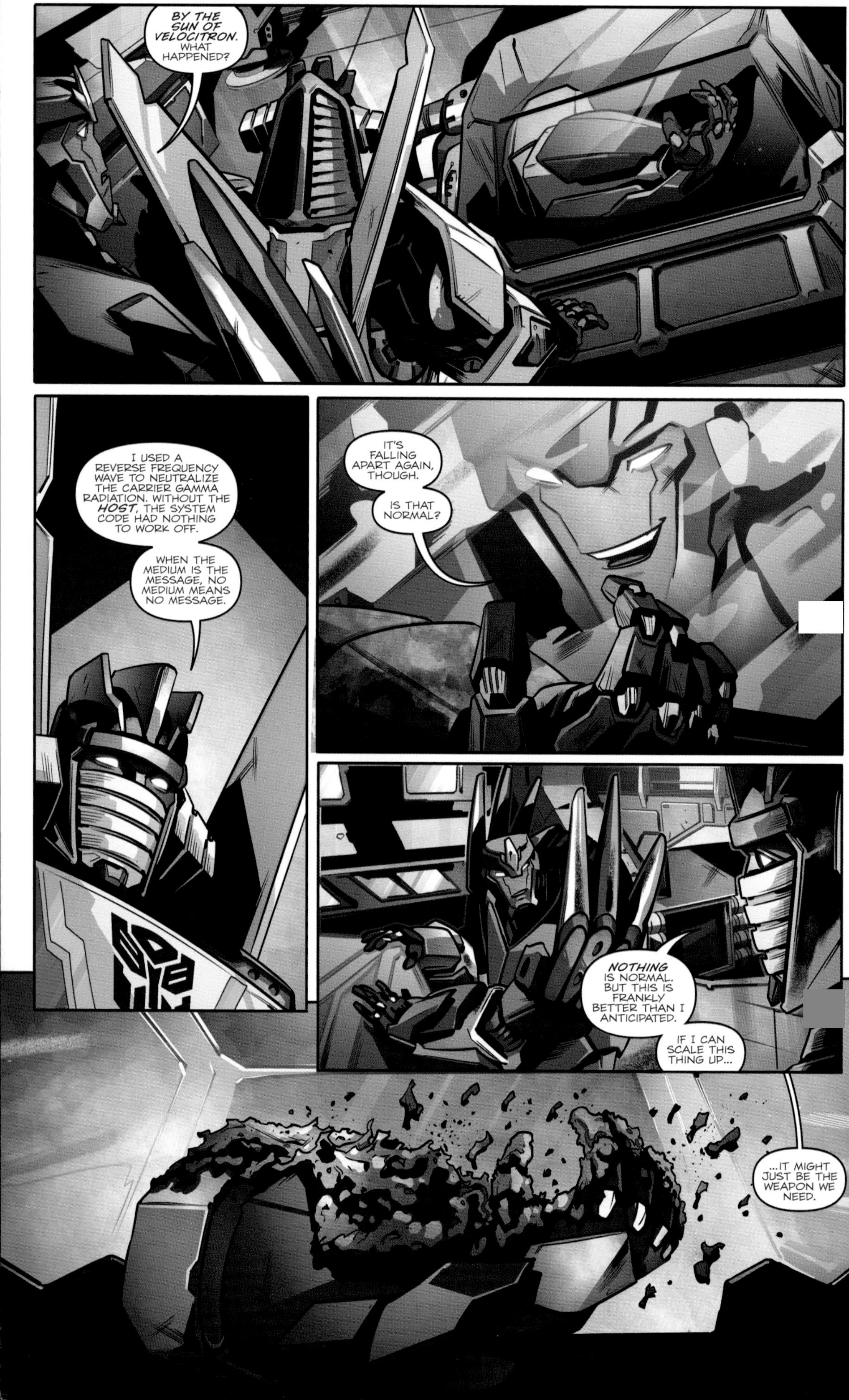
BY THE SUN OF VELOCITRON. WHAT HAPPENED?
I USED A REVERSE FREQUENCY WAVE TO NEUTRALIZE THE CARRIER GAMMA RADIATION. WITHOUT THE HOST, THE SYSTEM CODE HAD NOTHING TO WORK OFF.
WHEN THE MEDIUM IS THE MESSAGE, NO MEDIUM MEANS NO MESSAGE.
IT'S FALLING APART AGAIN, THOUGH.
IS THAT NORMAL?
NOTHING IS NORMAL. BUT THIS IS FRANKLY BETTER THAN I ANTICIPATED.
IF I CAN SCALE THIS THING UP...
...IT MIGHT JUST BE THE WEAPON WE NEED.

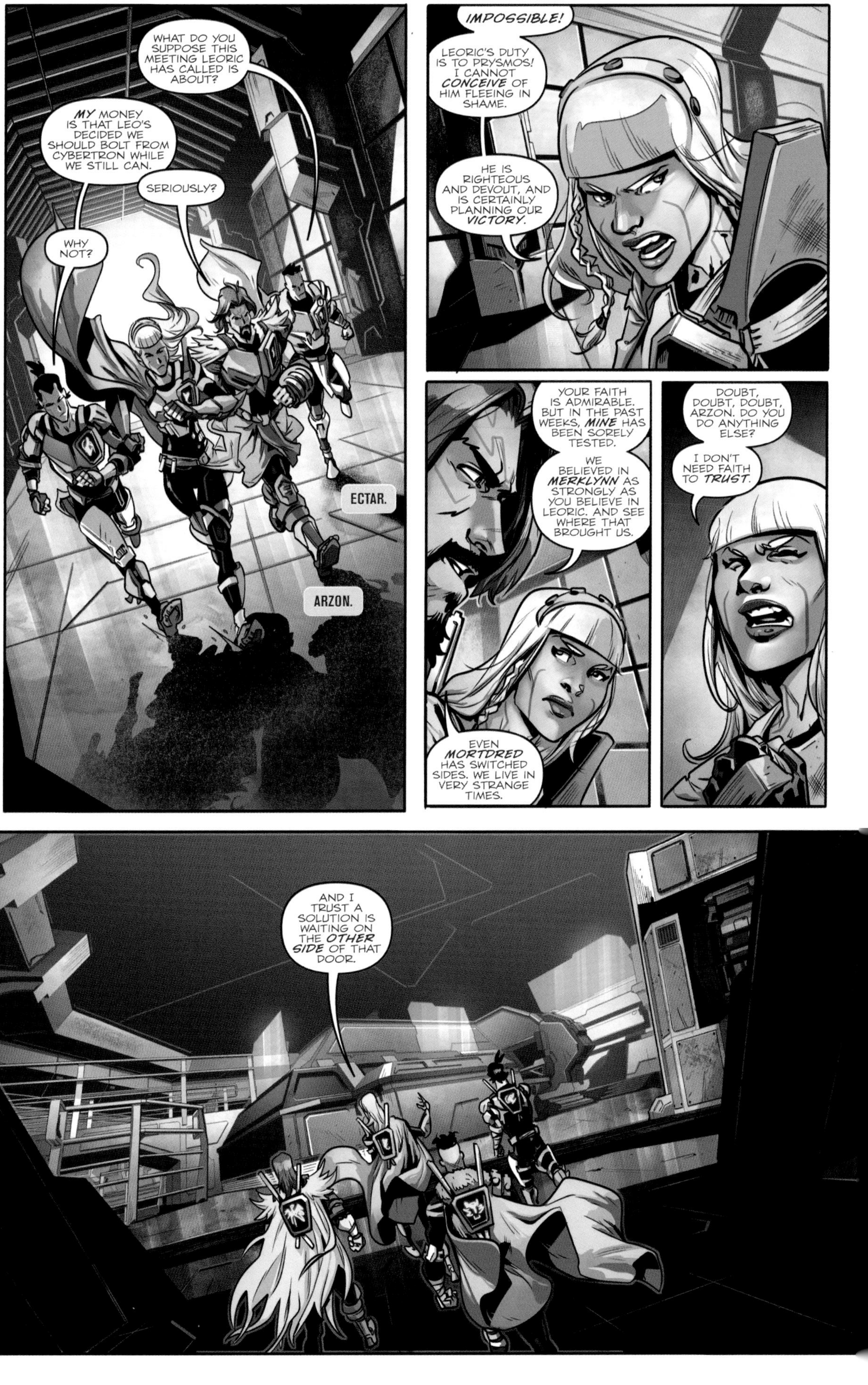
WHAT DO YOU SUPPOSE THIS MEETING LEORIC HAS CALLED IS ABOUT?
MY MONEY IS THAT LEO'S DECIDED WE SHOULD BOLT FROM CYBERTRON WHILE WE STILL CAN.
SERIOUSLY?
WHY NOT?
ECTAR.
ARZON.
IMPOSSIBLE!
LEORIC'S DUTY IS TO PRYSMOS! I CANNOT CONCEIVE OF HIM FLEEING IN SHAME.
HE IS RIGHTEOUS AND DEVOUT, AND IS CERTAINLY PLANNING OUR VICTORY.
YOUR FAITH IS ADMIRABLE. BUT IN THE PAST WEEKS, MINE HAS BEEN SORELY TESTED.
WE BELIEVED IN MERKLYNN AS STRONGLY AS YOU BELIEVE IN LEORIC. AND SEE WHERE THAT BROUGHT US.
EVEN MORTDRED HAS SWITCHED SIDES. WE LIVE IN VERY STRANGE TIMES.
DOUBT, DOUBT, DOUBT, ARZON. DO YOU DO ANYTHING ELSE?
I DON'T NEED FAITH TO TRUST.
AND I TRUST A SOLUTION IS WAITING ON THE OTHER SIDE OF THAT DOOR.

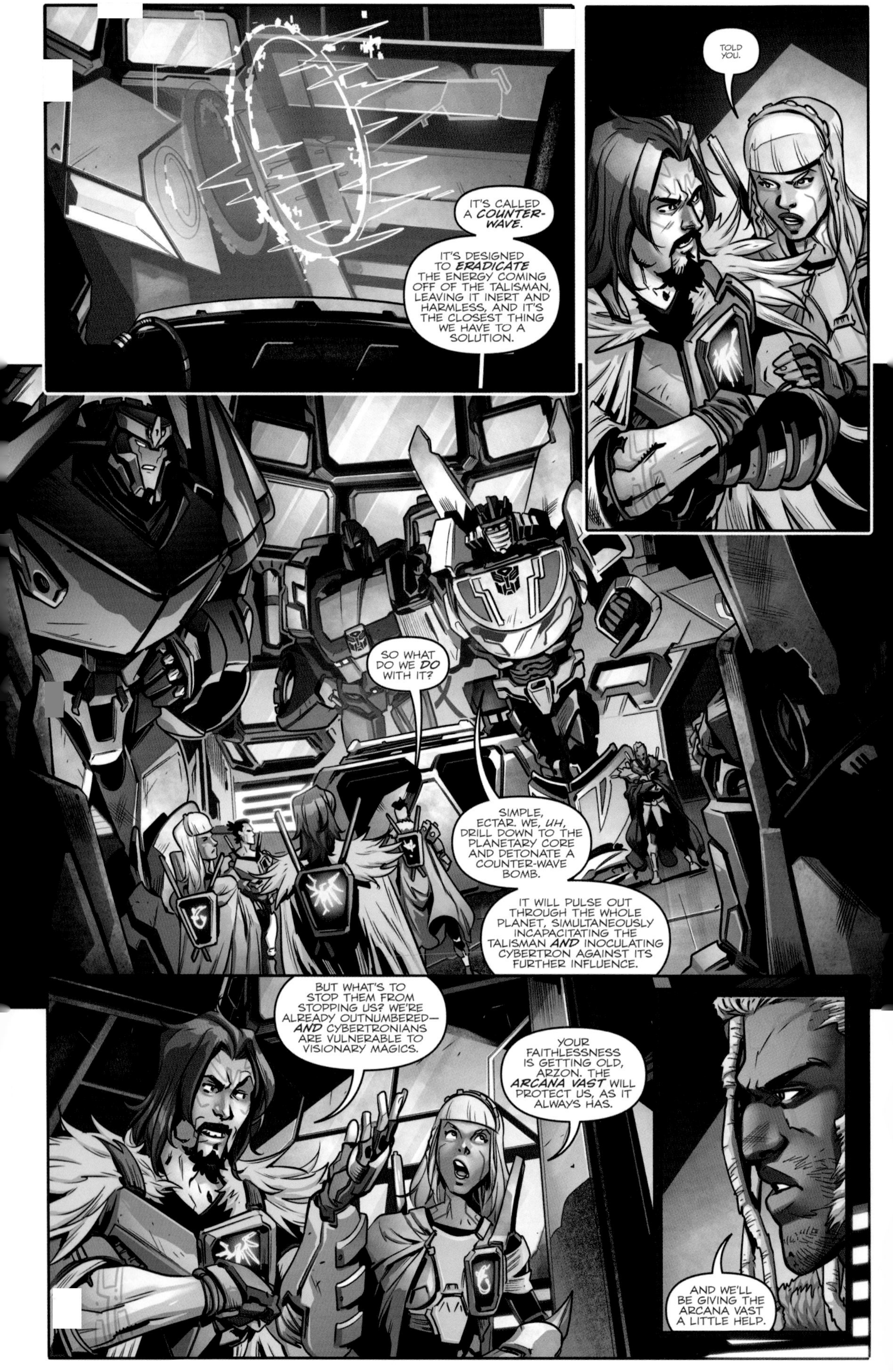
IT'S CALLED A COUNTER-WAVE.
IT'S DESIGNED TO ERADICATE THE ENERGY COMING OFF OF THE TALISMAN, LEAVING IT INERT AND HARMLESS, AND IT'S THE CLOSEST THING WE HAVE TO A SOLUTION.
TOLD YOU.
SO WHAT DO WE DO WITH IT?
SIMPLE, ECTAR. WE, UH, DRILL DOWN TO THE PLANETARY CORE AND DETONATE A COUNTER-WAVE BOMB.
IT WILL PULSE OUT THROUGH THE WHOLE PLANET, SIMULTANEOUSLY INCAPACITATING THE TALISMAN AND INOCULATING CYBERTRON AGAINST ITS FURTHER INFLUENCE.
BUT WHAT'S TO STOP THEM FROM STOPPING US? WE'RE ALREADY OUTNUMBERED— AND CYBERTRONIANS ARE VULNERABLE TO VISIONARY MAGICS.
YOUR FAITHLESSNESS IS GETTING OLD, ARZON. THE ARCANA VAST WILL PROTECT US, AS IT ALWAYS HAS.
AND WE'LL BE GIVING THE ARCANA VAST A LITTLE HELP.

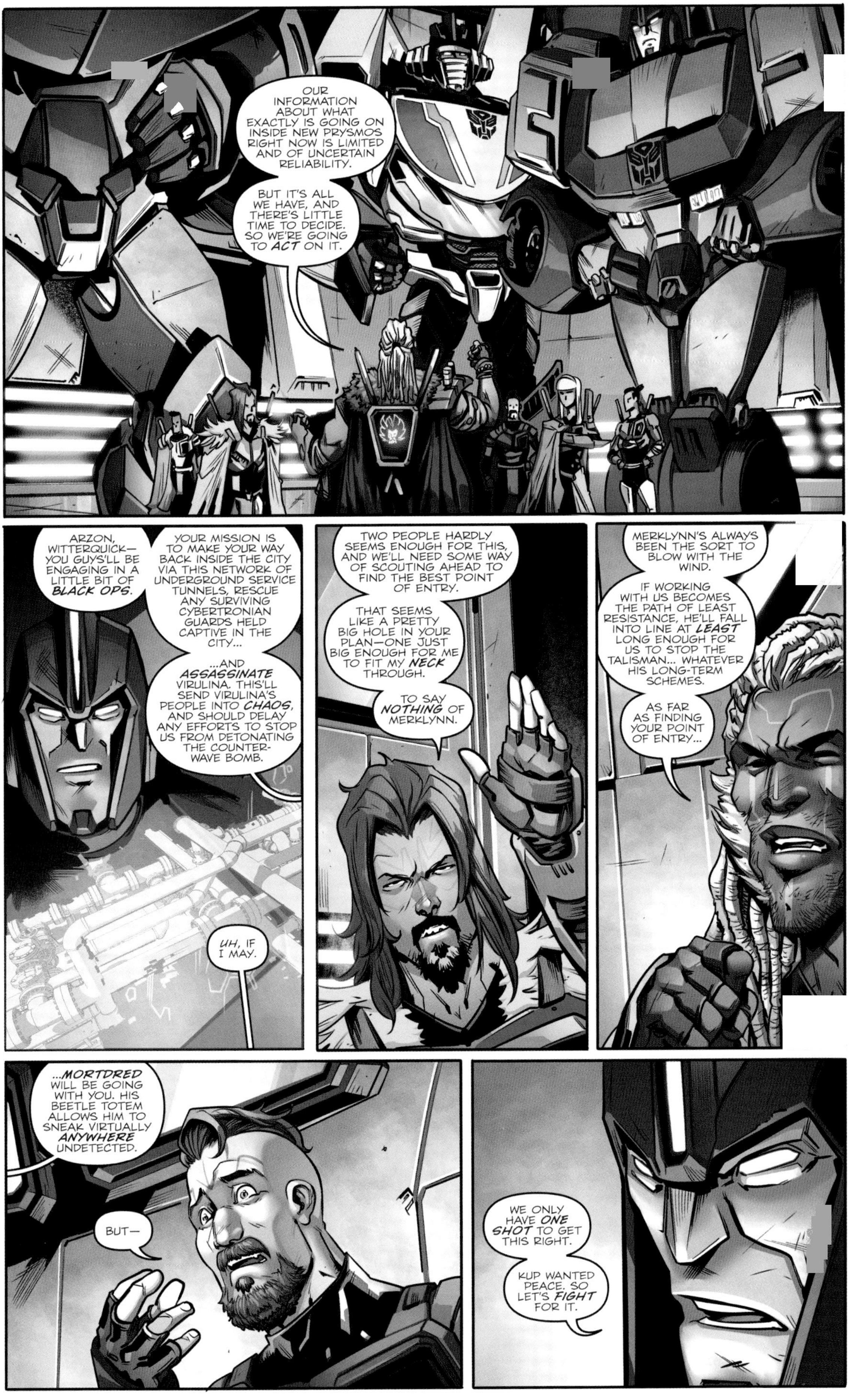

OUR INFORMATION ABOUT WHAT EXACTLY IS GOING ON INSIDE NEW PRYSMOS RIGHT NOW IS LIMITED AND OF UNCERTAIN RELIABILITY.
BUT IT'S ALL WE HAVE, AND THERE'S LITTLE TIME TO DECIDE. SO WE'RE GOING TO ACT ON IT.
ARZON, WITTERQUICK— YOU GUYS'LL BE ENGAGING IN A LITTLE BIT OF BLACK OPS.
YOUR MISSION IS TO MAKE YOUR WAY BACK INSIDE THE CITY VIA THIS NETWORK OF UNDERGROUND SERVICE TUNNELS, RESCUE ANY SURVIVING CYBERTRONIAN GUARDS HELD CAPTIVE IN THE CITY...
...AND ASSASSINATE VIRULINA. THIS'LL SEND VIRULINA'S PEOPLE INTO CHAOS, AND SHOULD DELAY ANY EFFORTS TO STOP US FROM DETONATING THE COUNTER-WAVE BOMB.
UH, IF I MAY.
TWO PEOPLE HARDLY SEEMS ENOUGH FOR THIS, AND WE'LL NEED SOME WAY OF SCOUTING AHEAD TO FIND THE BEST POINT OF ENTRY.
THAT SEEMS LIKE A PRETTY BIG HOLE IN YOUR PLAN—ONE JUST BIG ENOUGH FOR ME TO FIT MY NECK THROUGH.
TO SAY NOTHING OF MERKLYNN.
MERKLYNN'S ALWAYS BEEN THE SORT TO BLOW WITH THE WIND.
IF WORKING WITH US BECOMES THE PATH OF LEAST RESISTANCE, HE'LL FALL INTO LINE AT LEAST LONG ENOUGH FOR US TO STOP THE TALISMAN... WHATEVER HIS LONG-TERM SCHEMES.
AS FAR AS FINDING YOUR POINT OF ENTRY...
...MORTDRED WILL BE GOING WITH YOU. HIS BEETLE TOTEM ALLOWS HIM TO SNEAK VIRTUALLY ANYWHERE UNDETECTED.
BUT—
WE ONLY HAVE ONE SHOT TO GET THIS RIGHT.
KUP WANTED PEACE. SO LET'S FIGHT FOR IT.

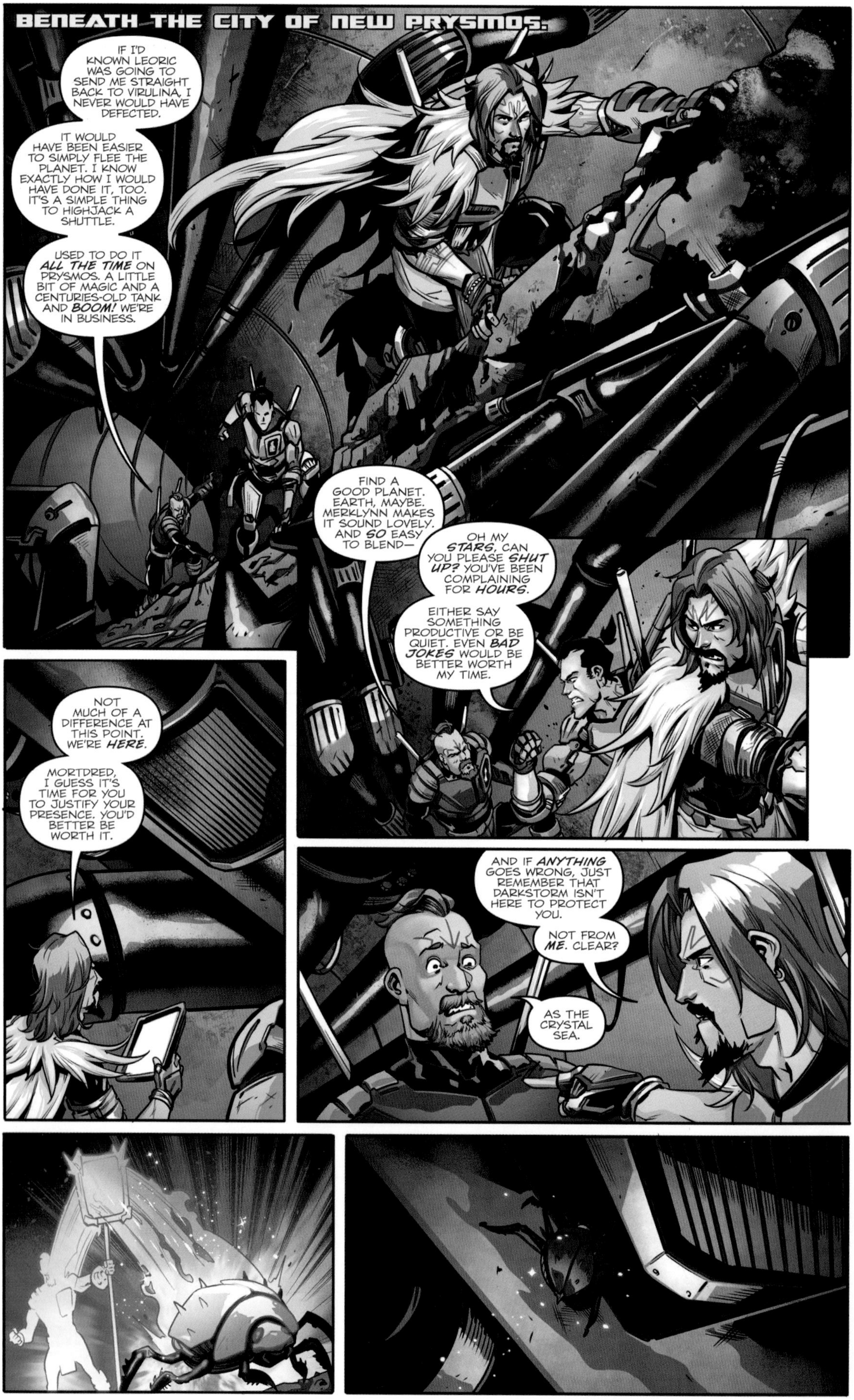
BENEATH THE CITY OF NEW PRYSMOS.
IF I'D KNOWN LEORIC WAS GOING TO SEND ME STRAIGHT BACK TO VIRULINA, I NEVER WOULD HAVE DEFECTED.
IT WOULD HAVE BEEN EASIER TO SIMPLY FLEE THE PLANET. I KNOW EXACTLY HOW I WOULD HAVE DONE IT, TOO. IT'S A SIMPLE THING TO HIGHJACK A SHUTTLE.
USED TO DO IT ALL THE TIME ON PRYSMOS. A LITTLE BIT OF MAGIC AND A CENTURIES-OLD TANK AND BOOM! WE'RE IN BUSINESS.
FIND A GOOD PLANET. EARTH, MAYBE. MERKLYNN MAKES IT SOUND LOVELY. AND SO EASY TO BLEND—
OH MY STARS, CAN YOU PLEASE SHUT UP? YOU'VE BEEN COMPLAINING FOR HOURS.
EITHER SAY SOMETHING PRODUCTIVE OR BE QUIET. EVEN BAD JOKES WOULD BE BETTER WORTH MY TIME.
NOT MUCH OF A DIFFERENCE AT THIS POINT. WE'RE HERE.
MORTDRED, I GUESS IT'S TIME FOR YOU TO JUSTIFY YOUR PRESENCE. YOU'D BETTER BE WORTH IT.
AND IF ANYTHING GOES WRONG, JUST REMEMBER THAT DARKSTORM ISN'T HERE TO PROTECT YOU.
NOT FROM ME. CLEAR?
AS THE CRYSTAL SEA.

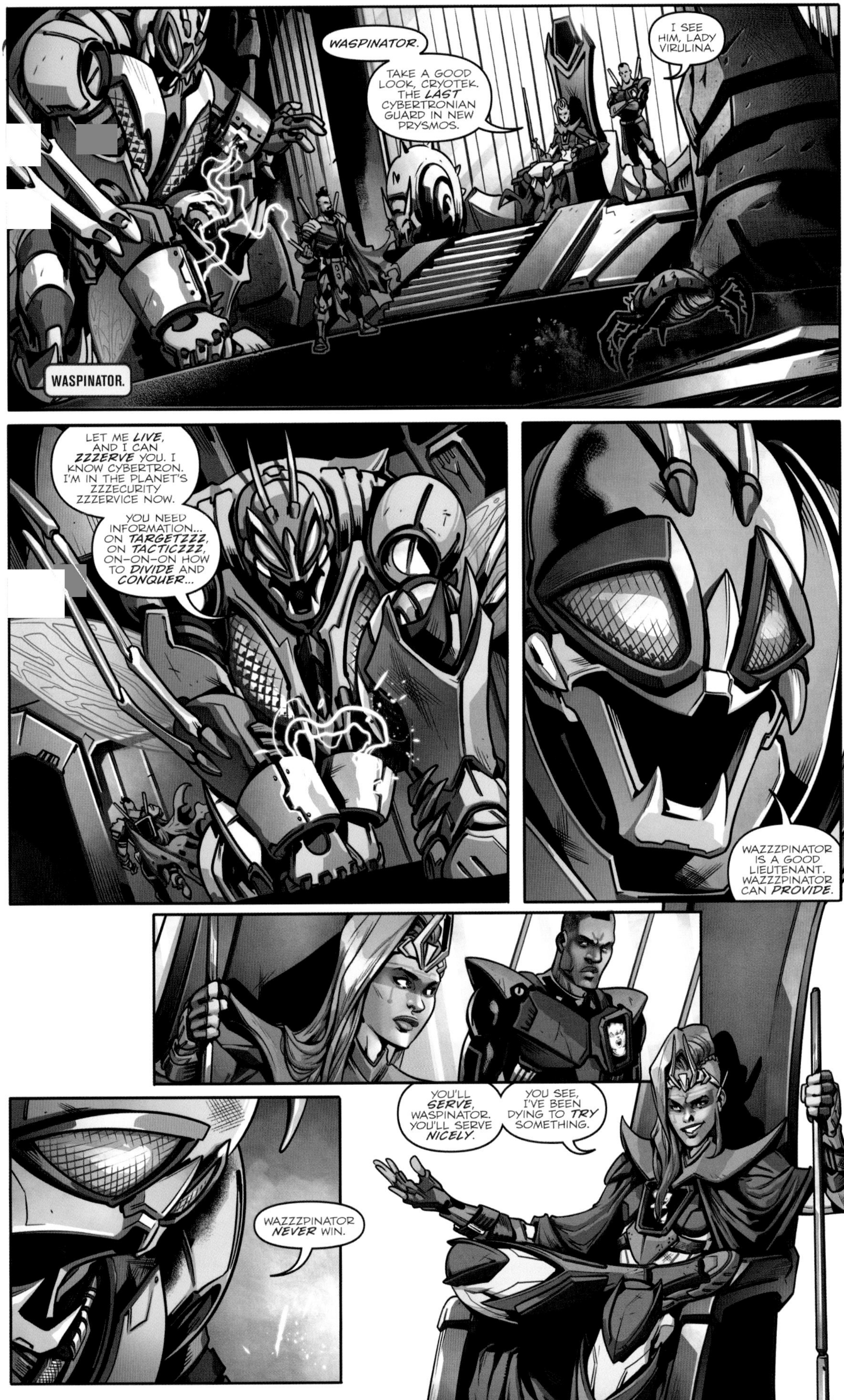
WASPINATOR.
TAKE A GOOD LOOK, CRYOTEK. THE LAST CYBERTRONIAN GUARD IN NEW PRYSMOS.
I SEE HIM, LADY VIRULINA.
WASPINATOR.
LET ME LIVE, AND I CAN ZZZERVE YOU. I KNOW CYBERTRON. I'M IN THE PLANET'S ZZZECURITY ZZZERVICE NOW.
YOU NEED INFORMATION... ON TARGETZZZ, ON TACTICZZZ, ON-ON-ON HOW TO DIVIDE AND CONQUER...
WAZZZPINATOR IS A GOOD LIEUTENANT. WAZZZPINATOR CAN PROVIDE.
WAZZZPINATOR NEVER WIN.
YOU'LL SERVE, WASPINATOR. YOU'LL SERVE NICELY.
YOU SEE, I'VE BEEN DYING TO TRY SOMETHING.

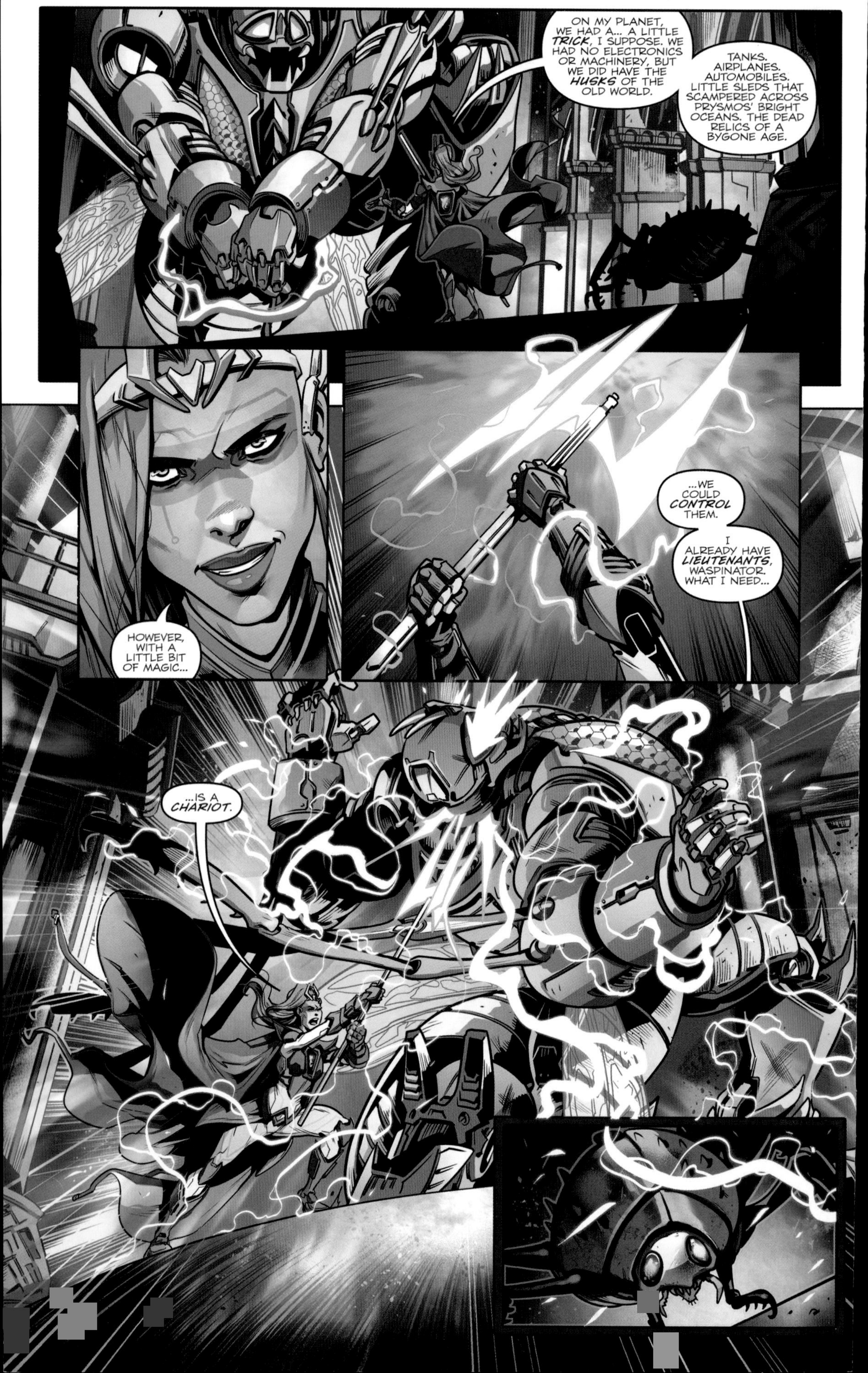
ON MY PLANET, WE HAD A... A LITTLE TRICK, I SUPPOSE. WE HAD NO ELECTRONICS OR MACHINERY, BUT WE DID HAVE THE HUSKS OF THE OLD WORLD.
TANKS. AIRPLANES. AUTOMOBILES. LITTLE SLEDS THAT SCAMPERED ACROSS PRYSMOS' BRIGHT OCEANS. THE DEAD RELICS OF A BYGONE AGE.
HOWEVER, WITH A LITTLE BIT OF MAGIC...
...WE COULD CONTROL THEM.
I ALREADY HAVE LIEUTENANTS, WASPINATOR. WHAT I NEED...
...IS A CHARIOT.

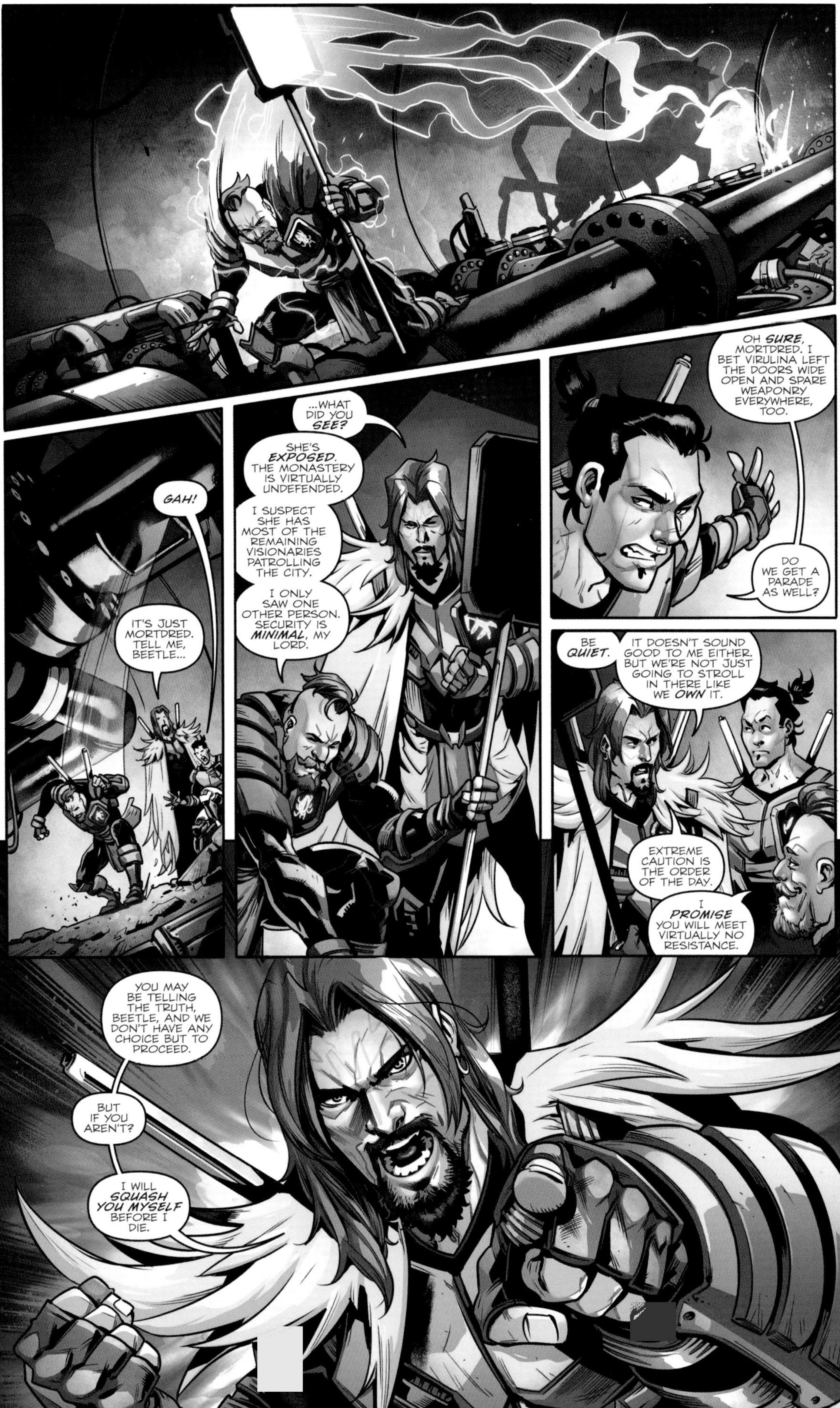

GAH!
IT'S JUST MORTDRED. TELL ME, BEETLE...
...WHAT DID YOU SEE?
SHE'S EXPOSED. THE MONASTERY IS VIRTUALLY UNDEFENDED.
I SUSPECT SHE HAS MOST OF THE REMAINING VISIONARIES PATROLLING THE CITY.
I ONLY SAW ONE OTHER PERSON. SECURITY IS MINIMAL, MY LORD.
OH SURE, MORTDRED. I BET VIRULINA LEFT THE DOORS WIDE OPEN AND SPARE WEAPONRY EVERYWHERE, TOO.
DO WE GET A PARADE AS WELL?
BE QUIET.
IT DOESN'T SOUND GOOD TO ME EITHER. BUT WE'RE NOT JUST GOING TO STROLL IN THERE LIKE WE OWN IT.
EXTREME CAUTION IS THE ORDER OF THE DAY.
I PROMISE YOU WILL MEET VIRTUALLY NO RESISTANCE.
YOU MAY BE TELLING THE TRUTH, BEETLE, AND WE DON'T HAVE ANY CHOICE BUT TO PROCEED.
BUT IF YOU AREN'T?
I WILL SQUASH YOU MYSELF BEFORE I DIE.

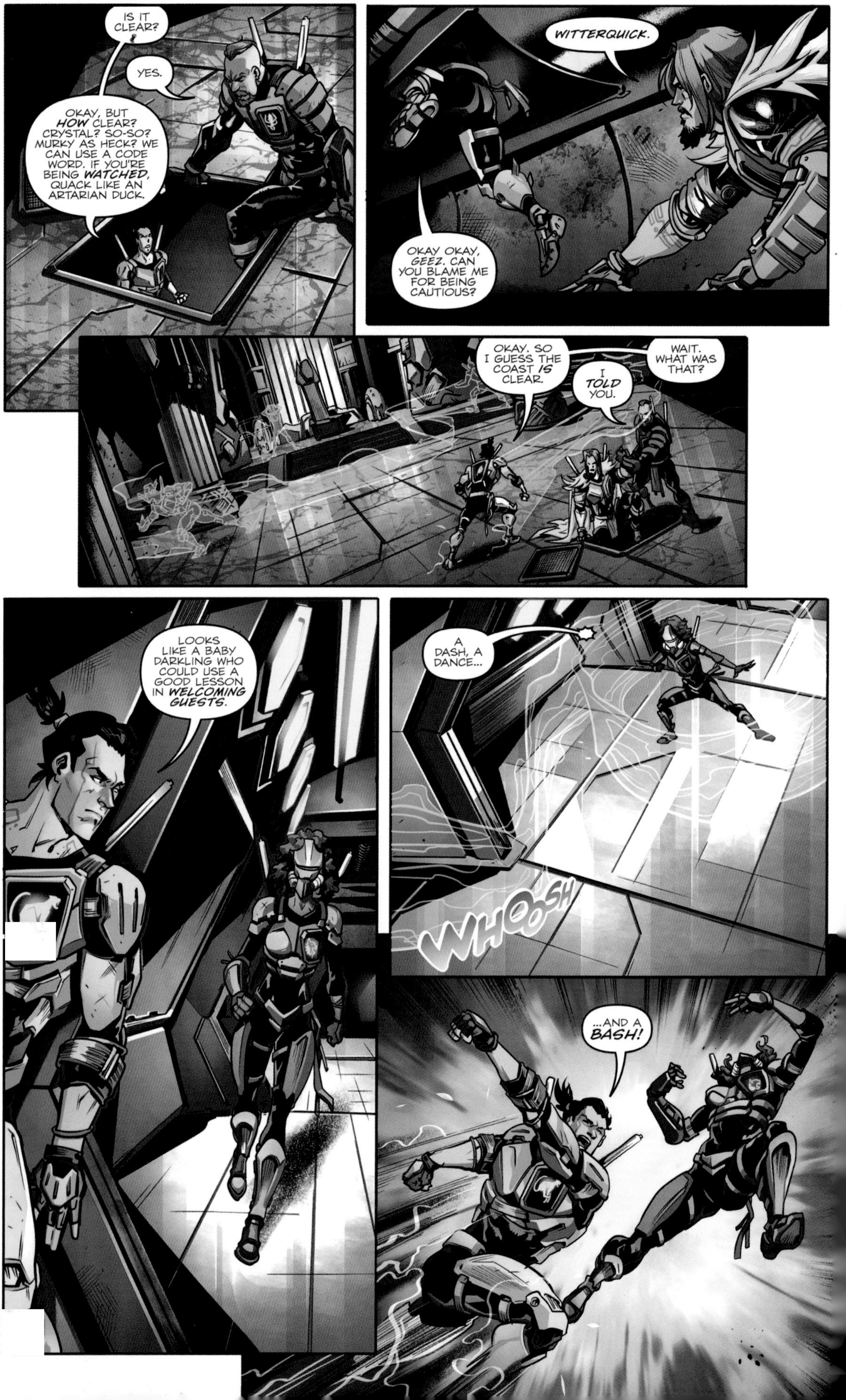

IS IT CLEAR?
YES.
OKAY, BUT HOW CLEAR? CRYSTAL? SO-SO? MURKY AS HECK? WE CAN USE A CODE WORD. IF YOU'RE BEING WATCHED, QUACK LIKE AN ARTARIAN DUCK.
WITTERQUICK.
OKAY OKAY, GEEZ. CAN YOU BLAME ME FOR BEING CAUTIOUS?
OKAY. SO I GUESS THE COAST IS CLEAR.
I TOLD YOU.
WAIT. WHAT WAS THAT?
LOOKS LIKE A BABY DARKLING WHO COULD USE A GOOD LESSON IN WELCOMING GUESTS.
A DASH, A DANCE...
WHOOOSH
...AND A BASH!

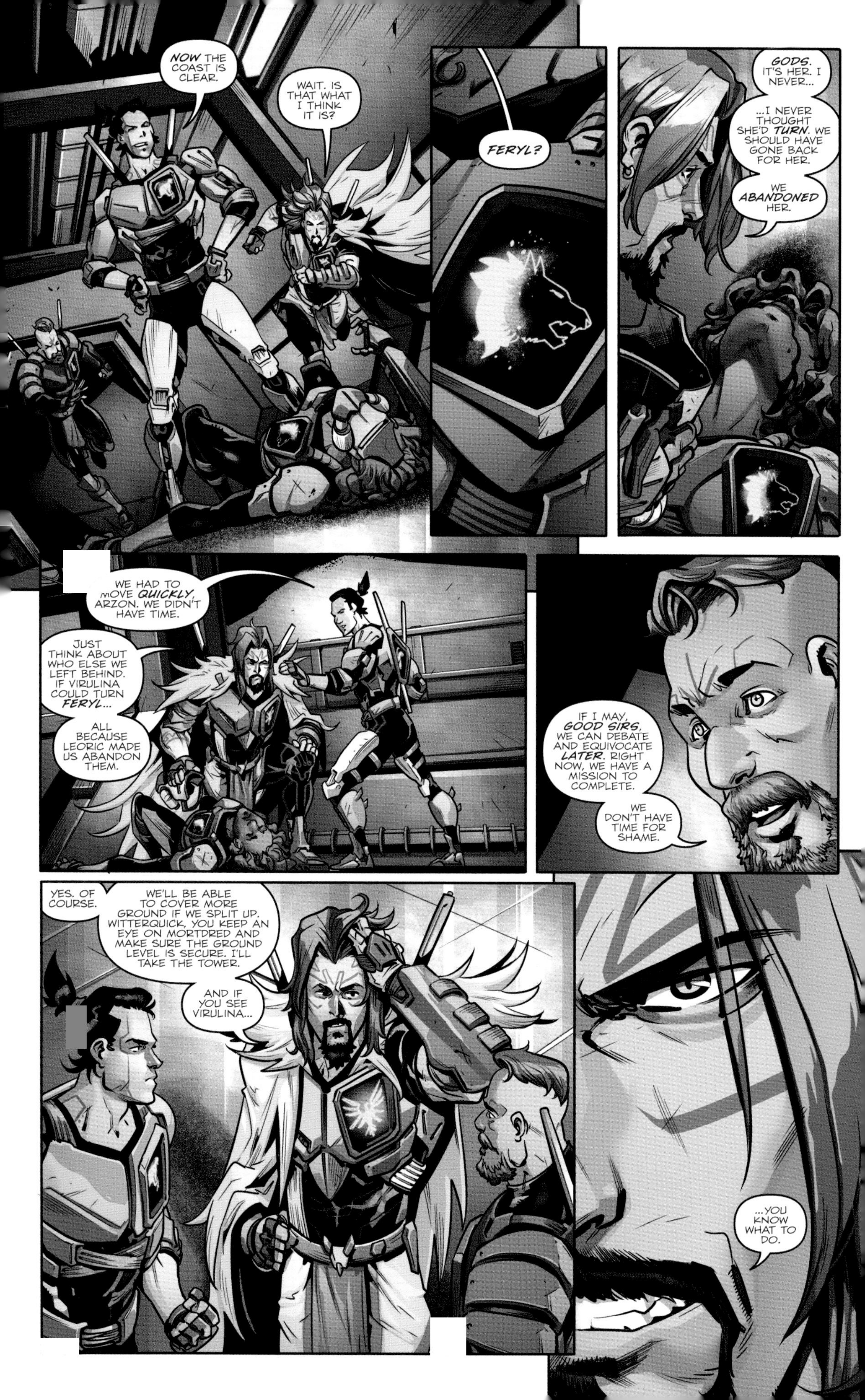
NOW THE COAST IS CLEAR.
WAIT. IS THAT WHAT I THINK IT IS?
FERYL?
GODS. IT'S HER. I NEVER...
...I NEVER THOUGHT SHE'D TURN. WE SHOULD HAVE GONE BACK FOR HER.
WE ABANDONED HER.
WE HAD TO MOVE QUICKLY, ARZON. WE DIDN'T HAVE TIME.
JUST THINK ABOUT WHO ELSE WE LEFT BEHIND. IF VIRULINA COULD TURN FERYL...
ALL BECAUSE LEORIC MADE US ABANDON THEM.
IF I MAY, GOOD SIRS, WE CAN DEBATE AND EQUIVOCATE LATER. RIGHT NOW, WE HAVE A MISSION TO COMPLETE.
WE DON'T HAVE TIME FOR SHAME.
YES. OF COURSE.
WE'LL BE ABLE TO COVER MORE GROUND IF WE SPLIT UP. WITTERQUICK, YOU KEEP AN EYE ON MORTDRED AND MAKE SURE THE GROUND LEVEL IS SECURE. I'LL TAKE THE TOWER.
AND IF YOU SEE VIRULINA...
...YOU KNOW WHAT TO DO.

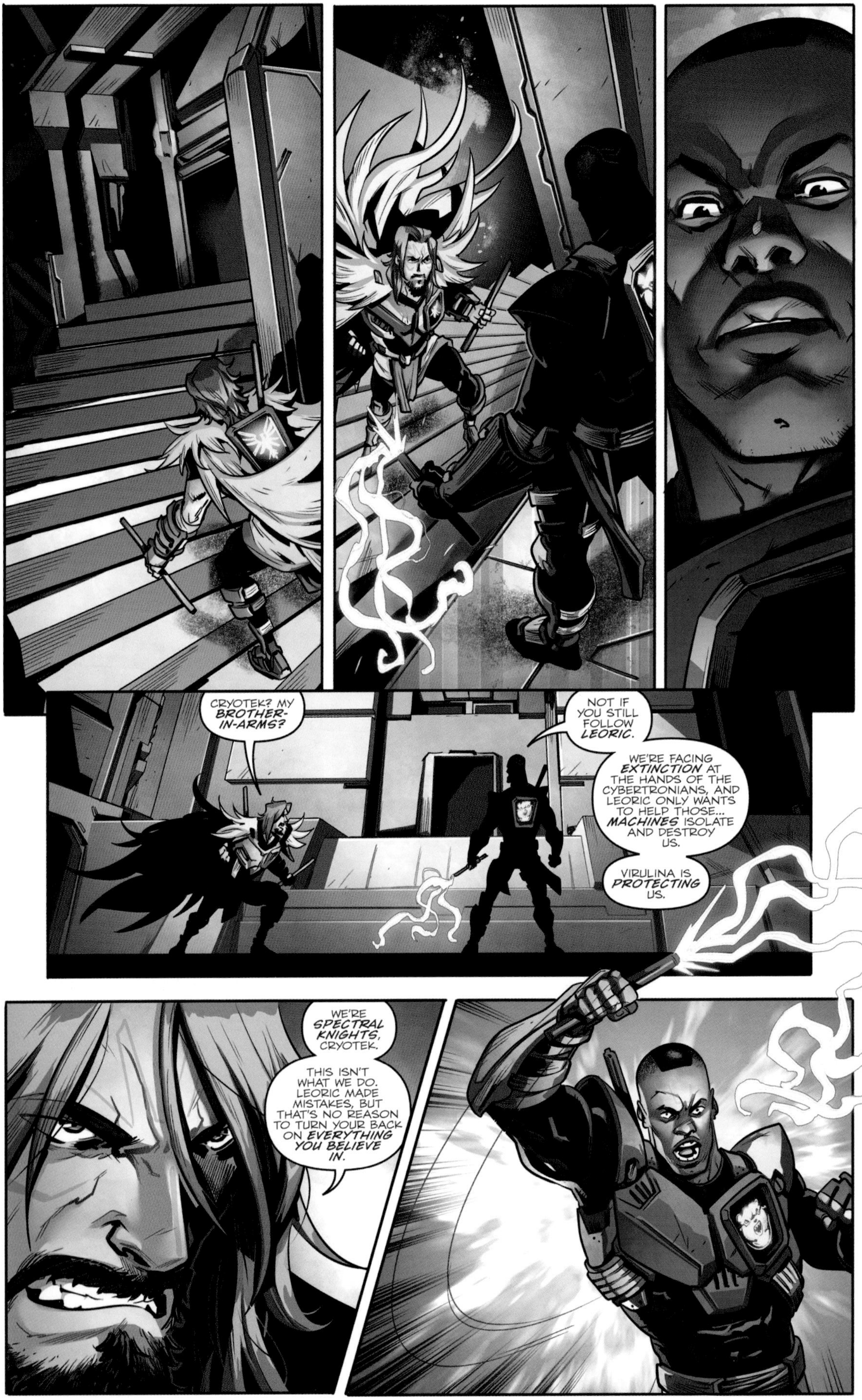
CRYOTEK? MY BROTHER-IN-ARMS?
NOT IF YOU STILL FOLLOW LEORIC.
WE'RE FACING EXTINCTION AT THE HANDS OF THE CYBERTRONIANS, AND LEORIC ONLY WANTS TO HELP THOSE... MACHINES ISOLATE AND DESTROY US.
VIRULINA IS PROTECTING US.
WE'RE SPECTRAL KNIGHTS, CRYOTEK.
THIS ISN'T WHAT WE DO. LEORIC MADE MISTAKES, BUT THAT'S NO REASON TO TURN YOUR BACK ON EVERYTHING YOU BELIEVE IN.

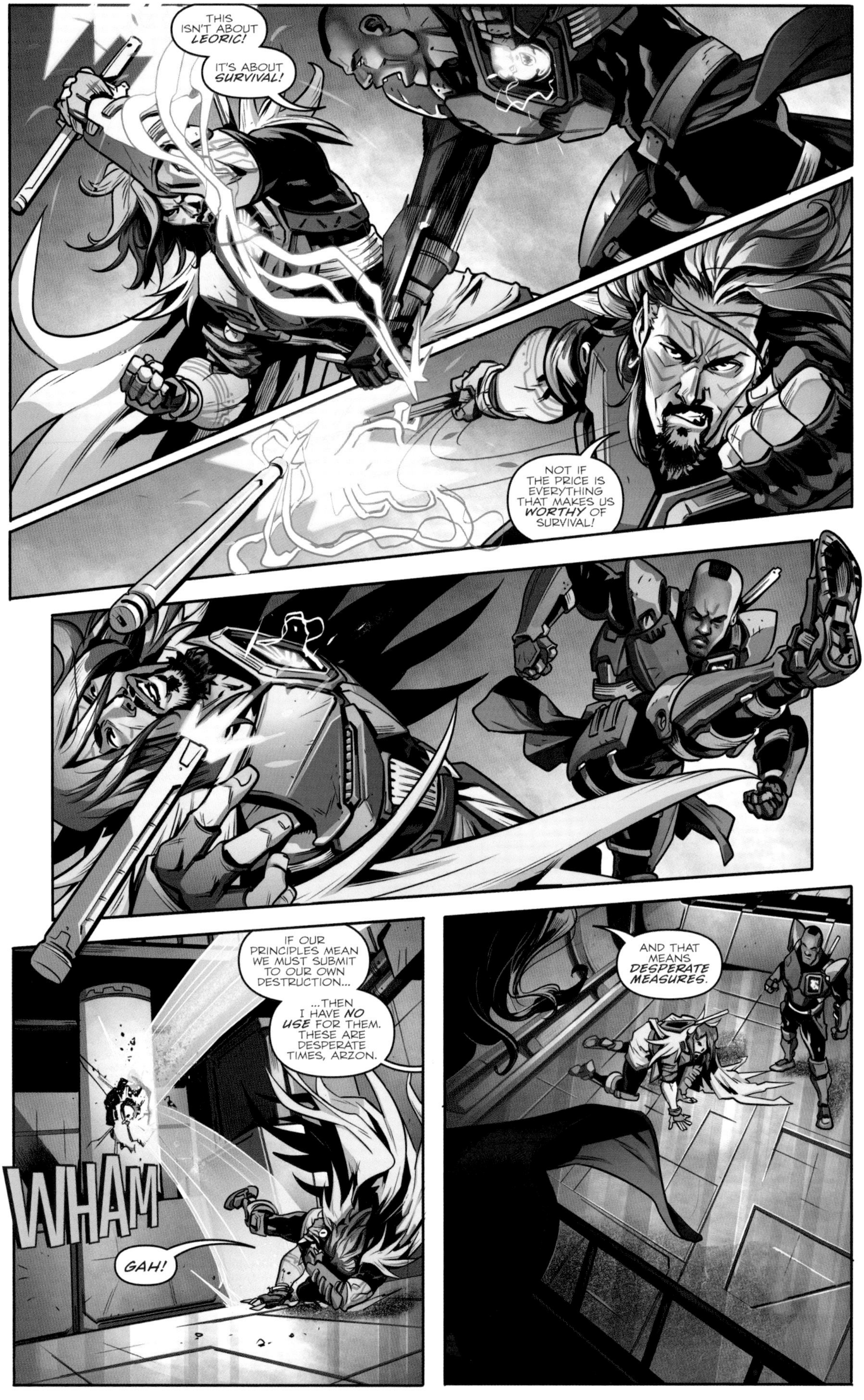
THIS ISN'T ABOUT *LEORIC!*
IT'S ABOUT *SURVIVAL!*
NOT IF THE PRICE IS EVERYTHING THAT MAKES US *WORTHY* OF SURVIVAL!
IF OUR PRINCIPLES MEAN WE MUST SUBMIT TO OUR OWN DESTRUCTION...
...THEN I HAVE *NO USE* FOR THEM. THESE ARE DESPERATE TIMES, ARZON.
WHAM
GAH!
AND THAT MEANS *DESPERATE MEASURES*.

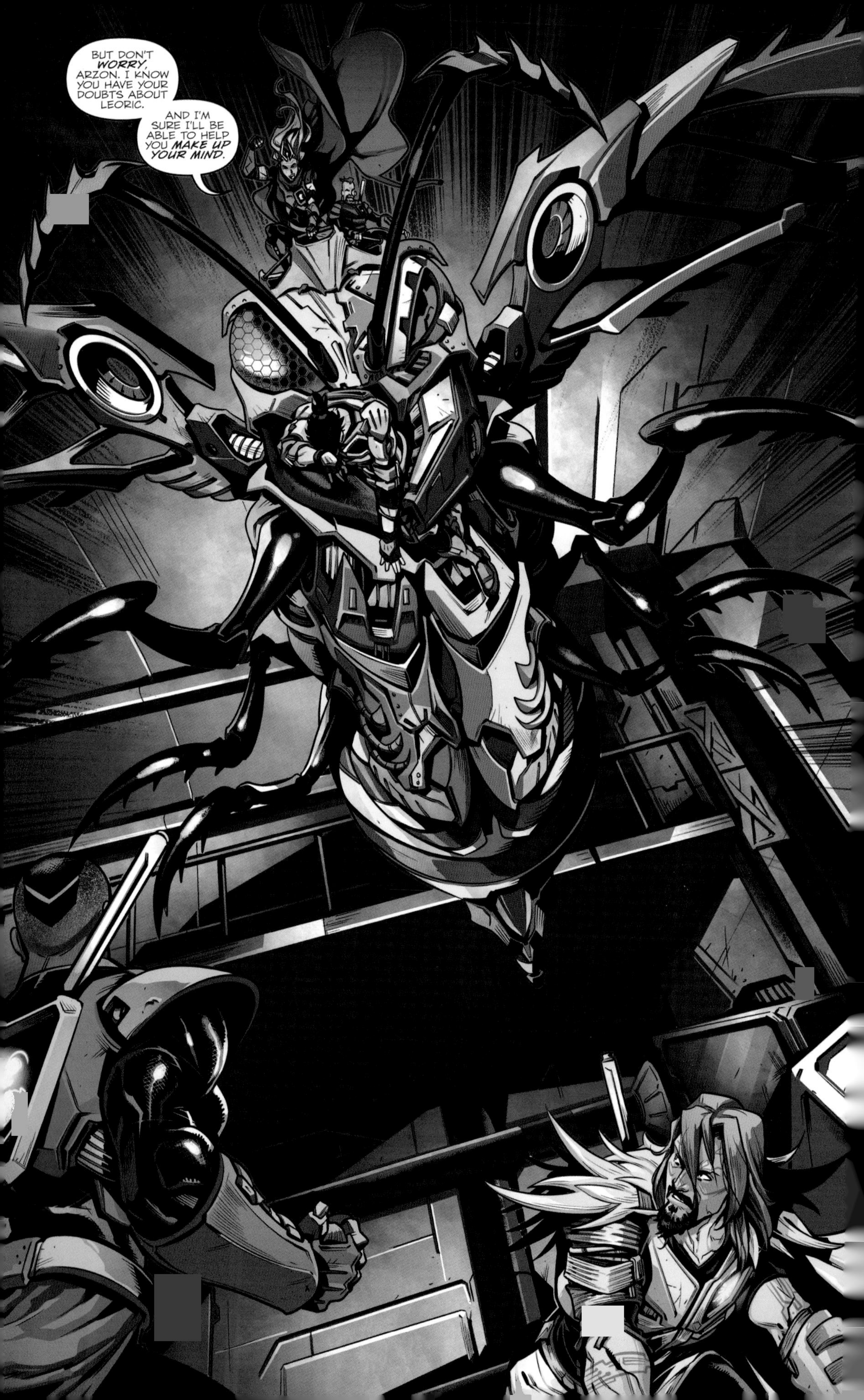
BUT DON'T **WORRY,** ARZON. I KNOW YOU HAVE YOUR DOUBTS ABOUT LEORIC.
AND I'M SURE I'LL BE ABLE TO HELP YOU **MAKE UP YOUR MIND.**

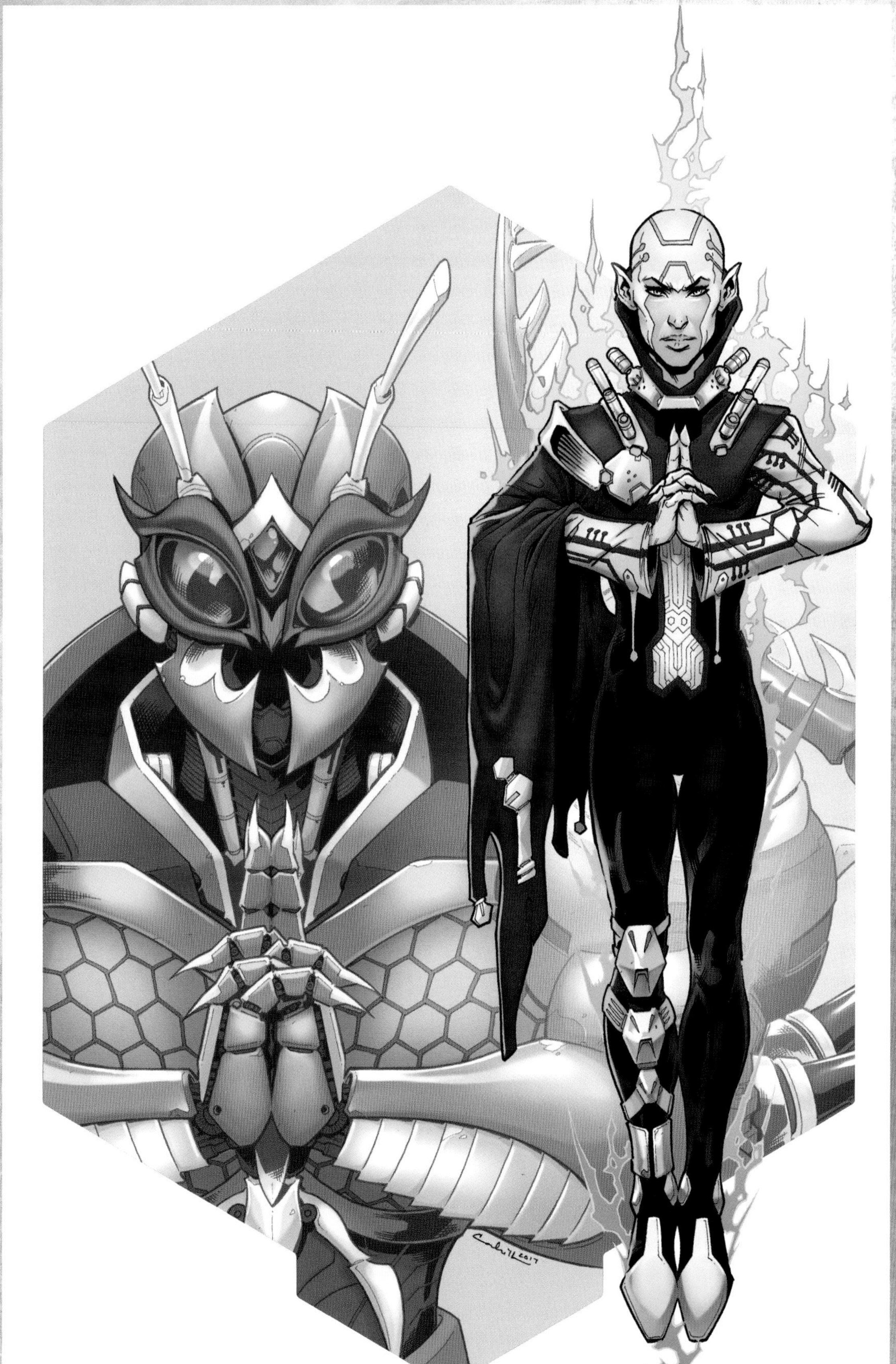

ART BY BRENDAN CAHILL
COLORS BY LAUREN BENNETT

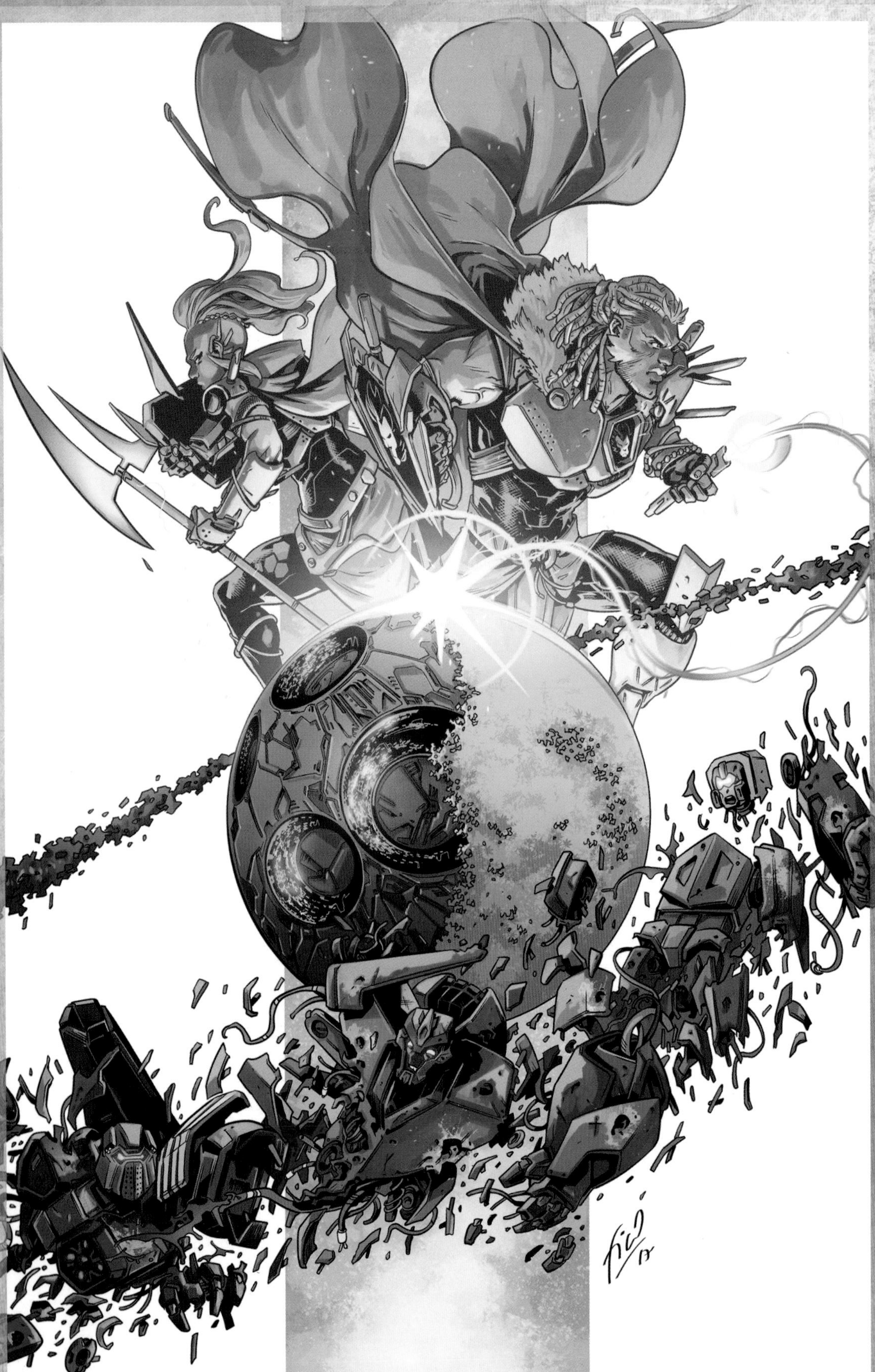

ART BY FICO OSSIO

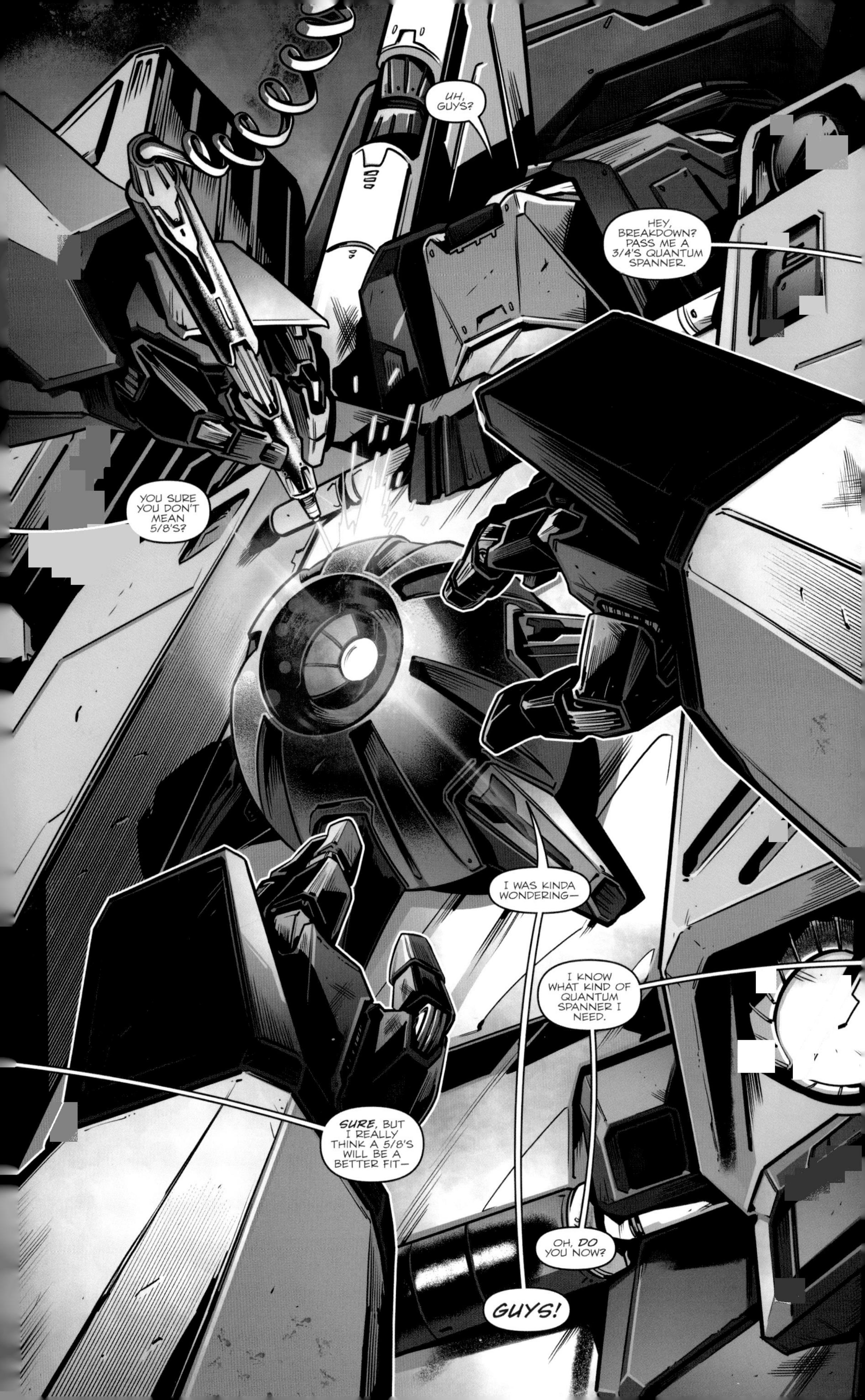
UH, GUYS?
HEY, BREAKDOWN? PASS ME A 3/4'S QUANTUM SPANNER.
YOU SURE YOU DON'T MEAN 5/8'S?
I WAS KINDA WONDERING—
I KNOW WHAT KIND OF QUANTUM SPANNER I NEED.
SURE, BUT I REALLY THINK A 5/8'S WILL BE A BETTER FIT—
OH, DO YOU NOW?
GUYS!

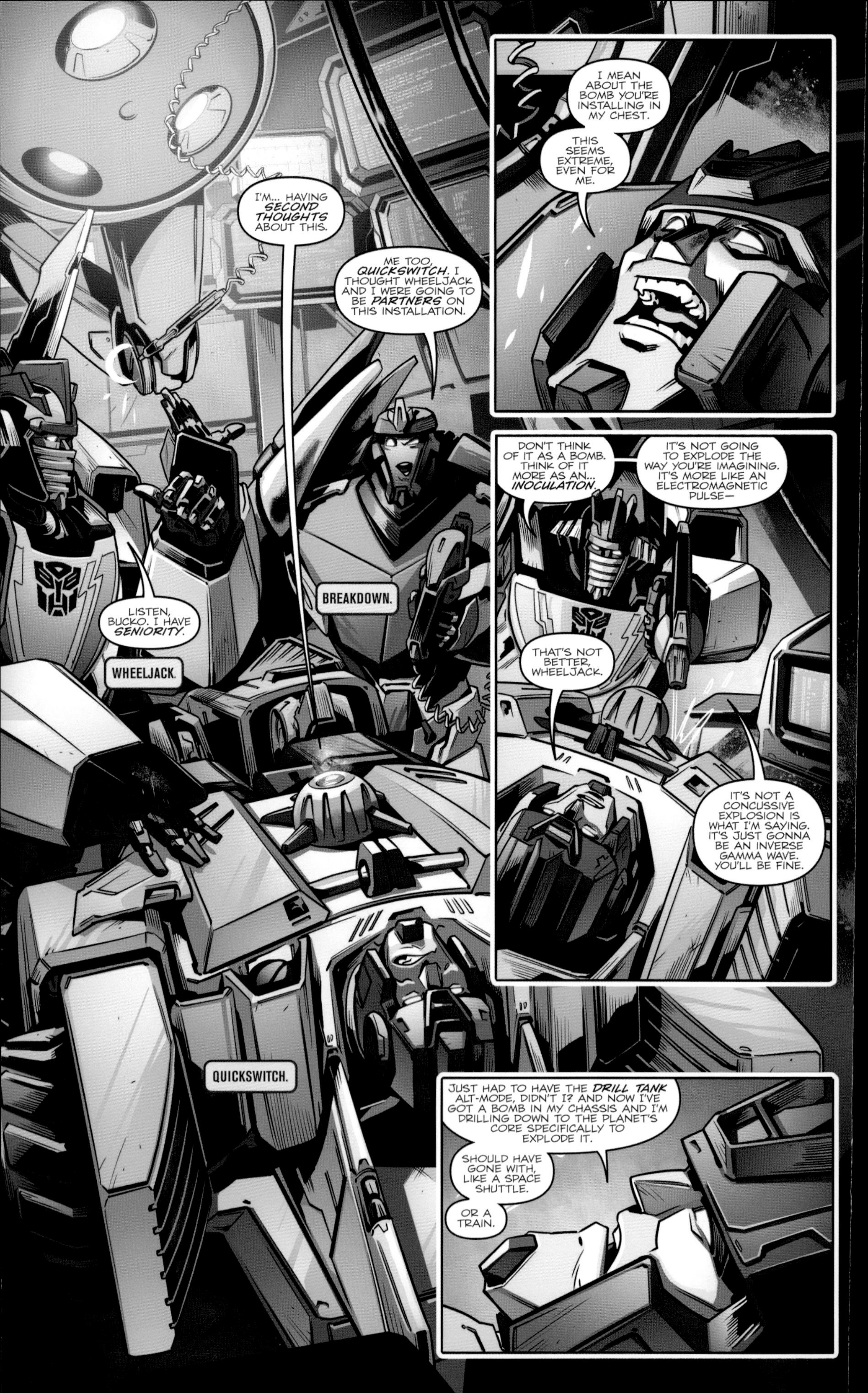
I'M... HAVING *SECOND THOUGHTS* ABOUT THIS.
ME TOO, *QUICKSWITCH*. I THOUGHT WHEELJACK AND I WERE GOING TO BE *PARTNERS* ON THIS INSTALLATION.
LISTEN, BUCKO. I HAVE *SENIORITY*.
BREAKDOWN.
WHEELJACK.
QUICKSWITCH.
I MEAN ABOUT THE BOMB YOU'RE INSTALLING IN MY CHEST.
THIS SEEMS EXTREME, EVEN FOR ME.
DON'T THINK OF IT AS A BOMB. THINK OF IT MORE AS AN... *INOCULATION*.
IT'S NOT GOING TO EXPLODE THE WAY YOU'RE IMAGINING. IT'S MORE LIKE AN ELECTROMAGNETIC PULSE—
THAT'S NOT BETTER, WHEELJACK.
IT'S NOT A CONCUSSIVE EXPLOSION IS WHAT I'M SAYING. IT'S JUST GONNA BE AN INVERSE GAMMA WAVE. YOU'LL BE FINE.
JUST HAD TO HAVE THE *DRILL TANK* ALT-MODE, DIDN'T I? AND NOW I'VE GOT A BOMB IN MY CHASSIS AND I'M DRILLING DOWN TO THE PLANET'S CORE SPECIFICALLY TO EXPLODE IT.
SHOULD HAVE GONE WITH, LIKE A SPACE SHUTTLE.
OR A TRAIN.

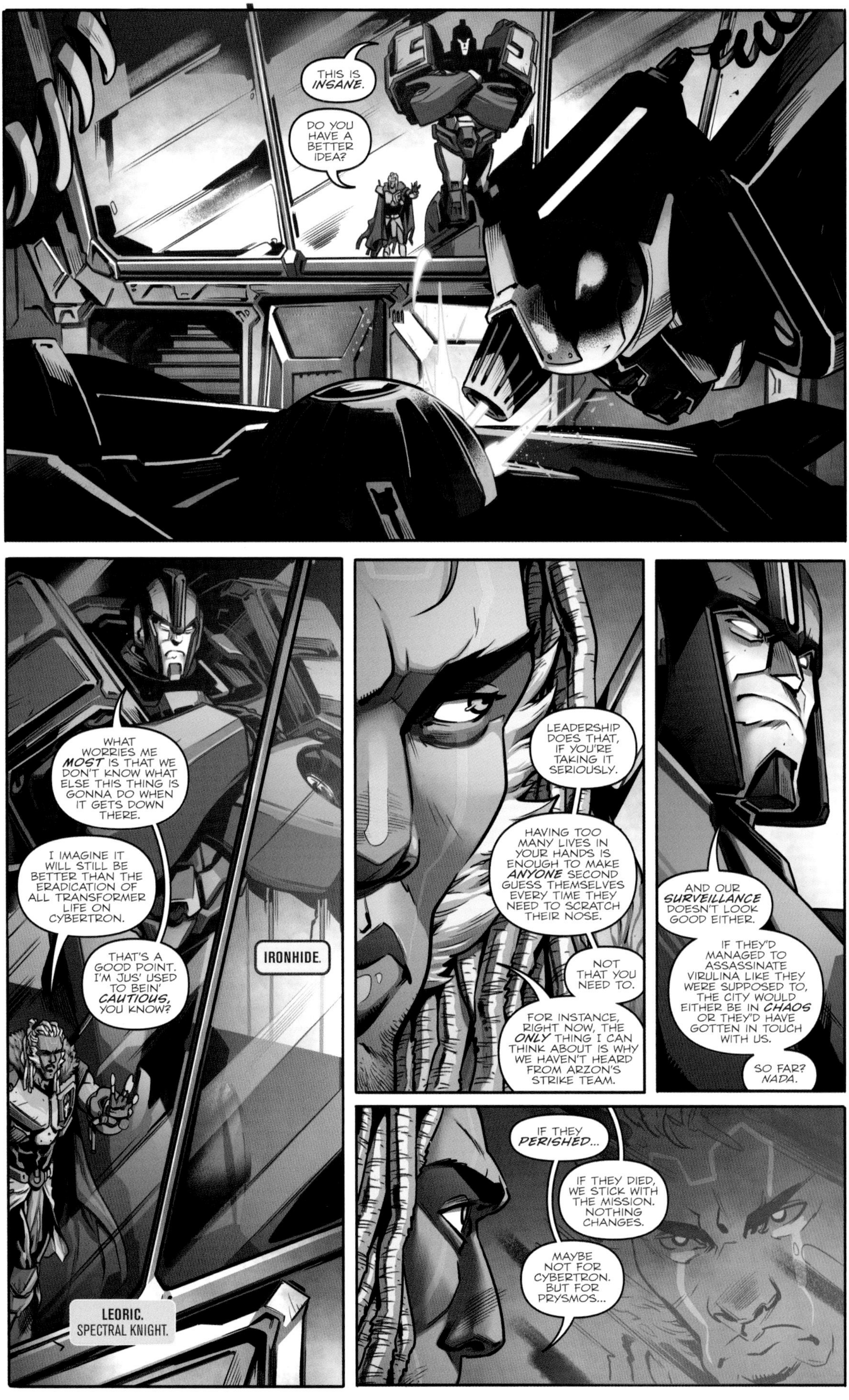
THIS IS *INSANE*.
DO YOU HAVE A BETTER IDEA?
WHAT WORRIES ME *MOST* IS THAT WE DON'T KNOW WHAT ELSE THIS THING IS GONNA DO WHEN IT GETS DOWN THERE.
I IMAGINE IT WILL STILL BE BETTER THAN THE ERADICATION OF ALL TRANSFORMER LIFE ON CYBERTRON.
THAT'S A GOOD POINT. I'M JUS' USED TO BEIN' *CAUTIOUS*, YOU KNOW?
IRONHIDE.
LEORIC. SPECTRAL KNIGHT.
LEADERSHIP DOES THAT, IF YOU'RE TAKING IT SERIOUSLY.
HAVING TOO MANY LIVES IN YOUR HANDS IS ENOUGH TO MAKE *ANYONE* SECOND GUESS THEMSELVES EVERY TIME THEY NEED TO SCRATCH THEIR NOSE.
NOT THAT YOU NEED TO.
FOR INSTANCE, RIGHT NOW, THE *ONLY* THING I CAN THINK ABOUT IS WHY WE HAVEN'T HEARD FROM ARZON'S STRIKE TEAM.
AND OUR *SURVEILLANCE* DOESN'T LOOK GOOD EITHER.
IF THEY'D MANAGED TO ASSASSINATE VIRULINA LIKE THEY WERE SUPPOSED TO, THE CITY WOULD EITHER BE IN *CHAOS* OR THEY'D HAVE GOTTEN IN TOUCH WITH US.
SO FAR? *NADA*.
IF THEY *PERISHED*...
IF THEY DIED, WE STICK WITH THE MISSION. NOTHING CHANGES.
MAYBE NOT FOR CYBERTRON. BUT FOR PRYSMOS...

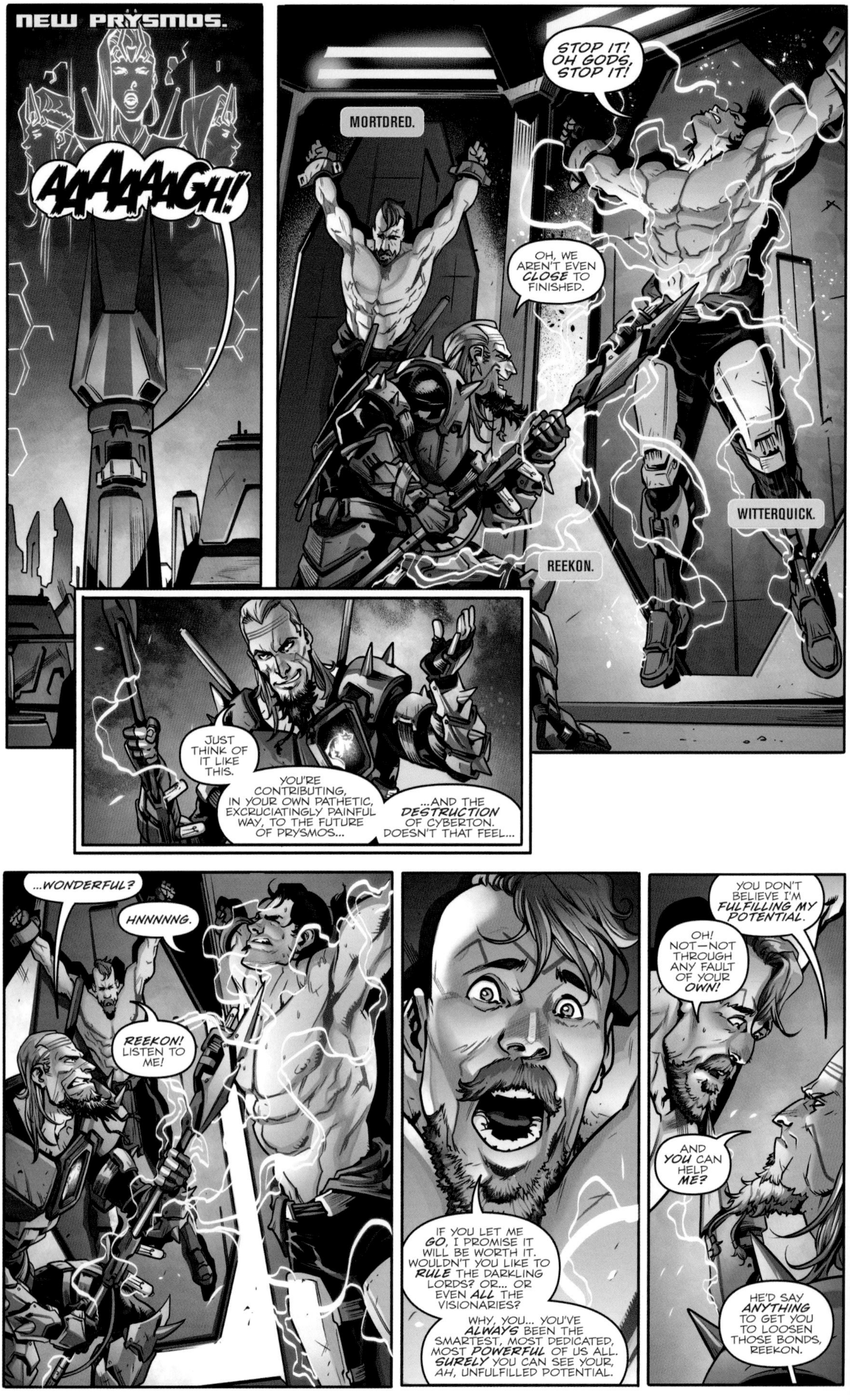
NEW PRYSMOS.
AAAAAAGH!
MORTDRED.
STOP IT! OH GODS, STOP IT!
OH, WE AREN'T EVEN CLOSE TO FINISHED.
REEKON.
WITTERQUICK.
JUST THINK OF IT LIKE THIS.
YOU'RE CONTRIBUTING, IN YOUR OWN PATHETIC, EXCRUCIATINGLY PAINFUL WAY, TO THE FUTURE OF PRYSMOS...
...AND THE DESTRUCTION OF CYBERTON. DOESN'T THAT FEEL...
...WONDERFUL?
HNNNNNG.
REEKON! LISTEN TO ME!
IF YOU LET ME GO, I PROMISE IT WILL BE WORTH IT. WOULDN'T YOU LIKE TO RULE THE DARKLING LORDS? OR... OR EVEN ALL THE VISIONARIES?
WHY, YOU... YOU'VE ALWAYS BEEN THE SMARTEST, MOST DEDICATED, MOST POWERFUL OF US ALL. SURELY YOU CAN SEE YOUR, AH, UNFULFILLED POTENTIAL.
YOU DON'T BELIEVE I'M FULFILLING MY POTENTIAL.
OH! NOT—NOT THROUGH ANY FAULT OF YOUR OWN!
AND YOU CAN HELP ME?
HE'D SAY ANYTHING TO GET YOU TO LOOSEN THOSE BONDS, REEKON.

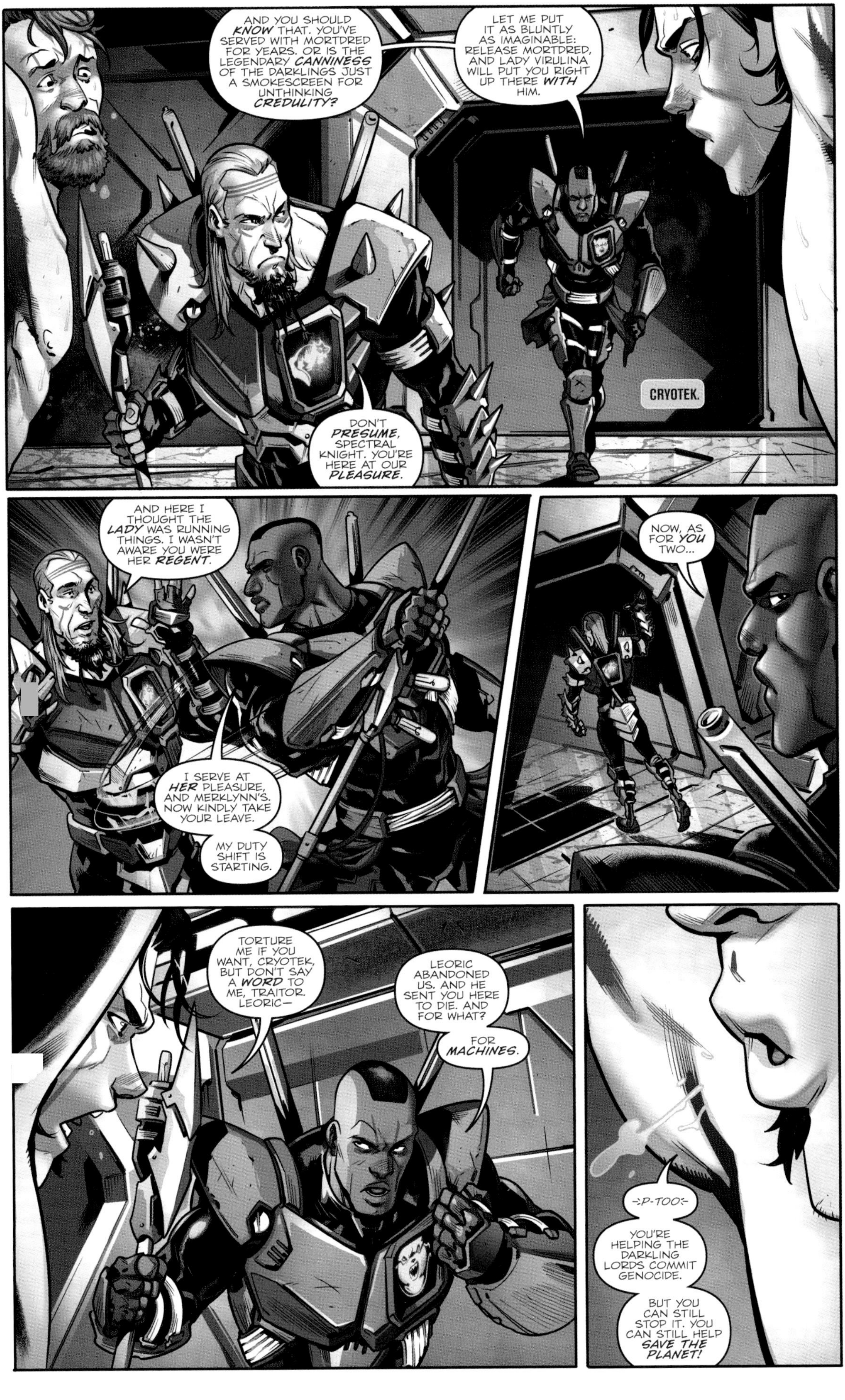
AND YOU SHOULD KNOW THAT. YOU'VE SERVED WITH MORTDRED FOR YEARS. OR IS THE LEGENDARY CANNINESS OF THE DARKLINGS JUST A SMOKESCREEN FOR UNTHINKING CREDULITY?
LET ME PUT IT AS BLUNTLY AS IMAGINABLE: RELEASE MORTDRED, AND LADY VIRULINA WILL PUT YOU RIGHT UP THERE WITH HIM.
CRYOTEK.
DON'T PRESUME, SPECTRAL KNIGHT. YOU'RE HERE AT OUR PLEASURE.
AND HERE I THOUGHT THE LADY WAS RUNNING THINGS. I WASN'T AWARE YOU WERE HER REGENT.
I SERVE AT HER PLEASURE, AND MERKLYNN'S. NOW KINDLY TAKE YOUR LEAVE.
MY DUTY SHIFT IS STARTING.
NOW, AS FOR YOU TWO...
TORTURE ME IF YOU WANT, CRYOTEK, BUT DON'T SAY A WORD TO ME, TRAITOR. LEORIC—
LEORIC ABANDONED US. AND HE SENT YOU HERE TO DIE. AND FOR WHAT?
FOR MACHINES.
P-TOO
YOU'RE HELPING THE DARKLING LORDS COMMIT GENOCIDE.
BUT YOU CAN STILL STOP IT. YOU CAN STILL HELP SAVE THE PLANET!

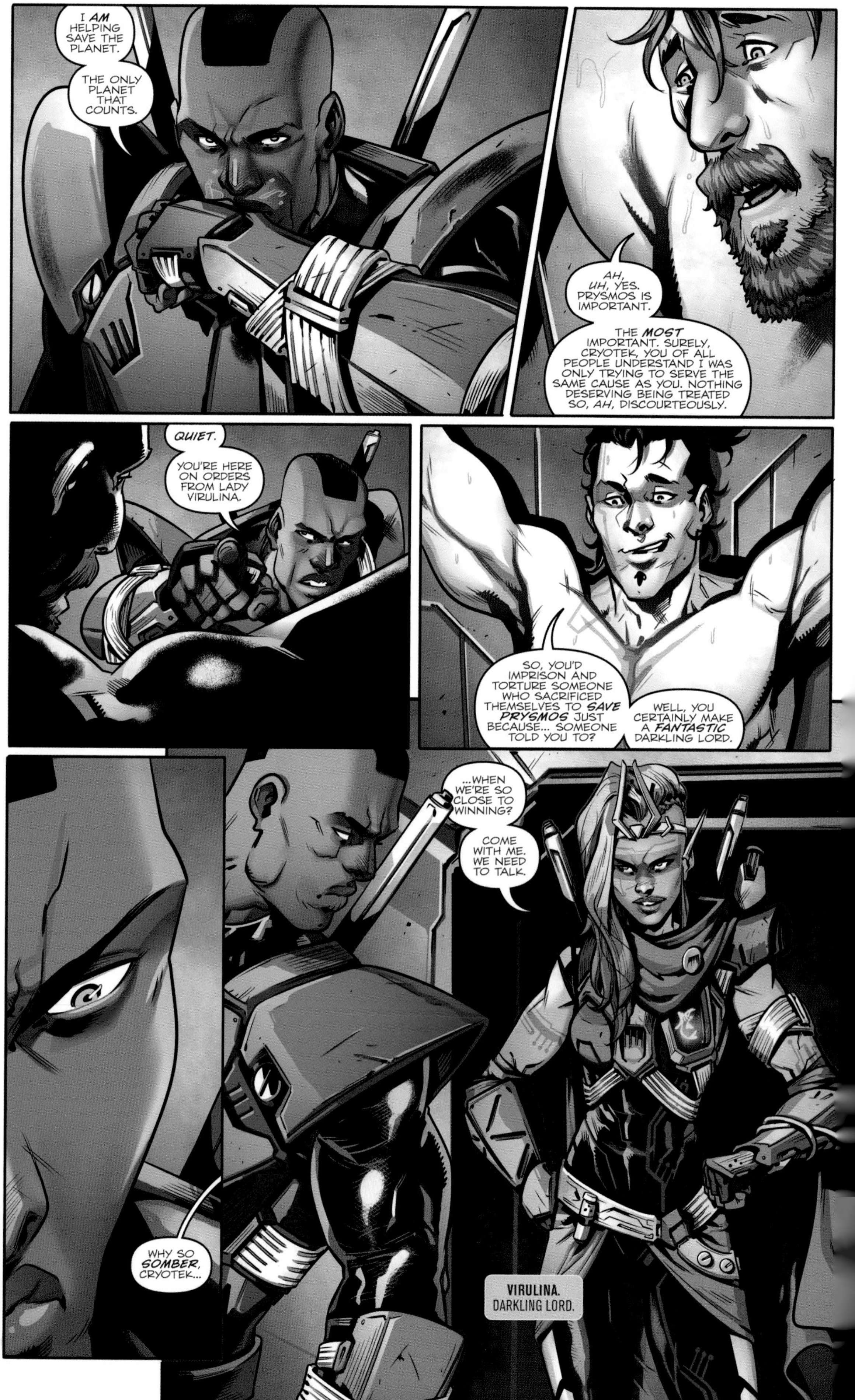
I *AM* HELPING SAVE THE PLANET.
THE ONLY PLANET THAT COUNTS.
AH, *UH,* YES. PRYSMOS IS IMPORTANT.
THE *MOST* IMPORTANT. SURELY, CRYOTEK, YOU OF ALL PEOPLE UNDERSTAND I WAS ONLY TRYING TO SERVE THE SAME CAUSE AS YOU. NOTHING DESERVING BEING TREATED SO, *AH,* DISCOURTEOUSLY.
QUIET.
YOU'RE HERE ON ORDERS FROM LADY VIRULINA.
SO, YOU'D IMPRISON AND TORTURE SOMEONE WHO SACRIFICED THEMSELVES TO *SAVE PRYSMOS* JUST BECAUSE... SOMEONE TOLD YOU TO?
WELL, YOU CERTAINLY MAKE A *FANTASTIC* DARKLING LORD.
WHY SO *SOMBER,* CRYOTEK...
...WHEN WE'RE SO CLOSE TO WINNING?
COME WITH ME. WE NEED TO TALK.
VIRULINA. DARKLING LORD.

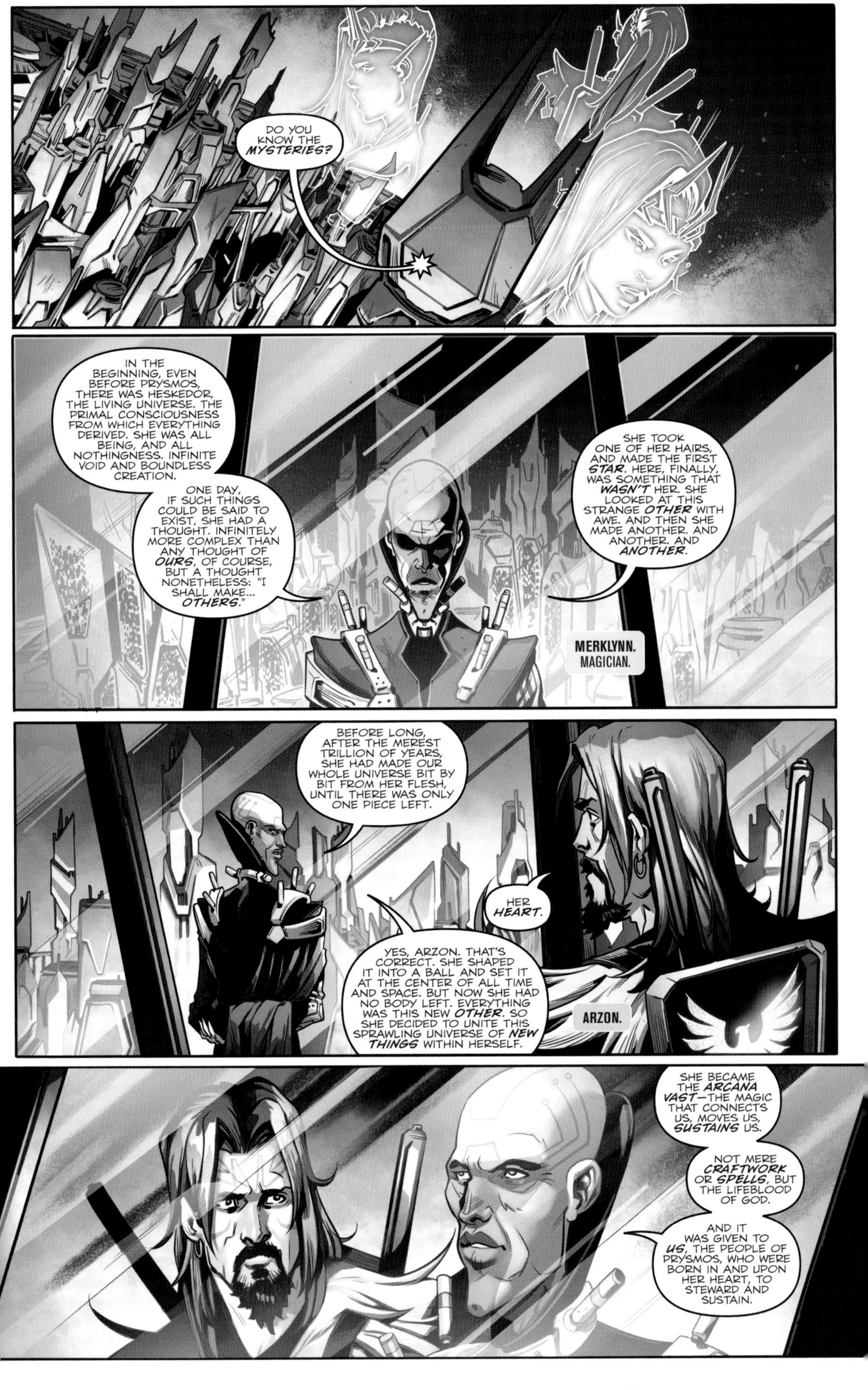
DO YOU KNOW THE MYSTERIES?
IN THE BEGINNING, EVEN BEFORE PRYSMOS, THERE WAS HESKEDOR, THE LIVING UNIVERSE. THE PRIMAL CONSCIOUSNESS FROM WHICH EVERYTHING DERIVED. SHE WAS ALL BEING, AND ALL NOTHINGNESS. INFINITE VOID AND BOUNDLESS CREATION.
ONE DAY, IF SUCH THINGS COULD BE SAID TO EXIST, SHE HAD A THOUGHT. INFINITELY MORE COMPLEX THAN ANY THOUGHT OF OURS, OF COURSE, BUT A THOUGHT NONETHELESS: "I SHALL MAKE... OTHERS."
SHE TOOK ONE OF HER HAIRS, AND MADE THE FIRST STAR. HERE, FINALLY, WAS SOMETHING THAT WASN'T HER. SHE LOOKED AT THIS STRANGE OTHER WITH AWE. AND THEN SHE MADE ANOTHER. AND ANOTHER. AND ANOTHER.
MERKLYNN. MAGICIAN.
BEFORE LONG, AFTER THE MEREST TRILLION OF YEARS, SHE HAD MADE OUR WHOLE UNIVERSE BIT BY BIT FROM HER FLESH, UNTIL THERE WAS ONLY ONE PIECE LEFT.
HER HEART.
YES, ARZON. THAT'S CORRECT. SHE SHAPED IT INTO A BALL AND SET IT AT THE CENTER OF ALL TIME AND SPACE. BUT NOW SHE HAD NO BODY LEFT. EVERYTHING WAS THIS NEW OTHER. SO SHE DECIDED TO UNITE THIS SPRAWLING UNIVERSE OF NEW THINGS WITHIN HERSELF.
ARZON.
SHE BECAME THE ARCANA VAST—THE MAGIC THAT CONNECTS US, MOVES US, SUSTAINS US.
NOT MERE CRAFTWORK OR SPELLS, BUT THE LIFEBLOOD OF GOD.
AND IT WAS GIVEN TO US, THE PEOPLE OF PRYSMOS, WHO WERE BORN IN AND UPON HER HEART, TO STEWARD AND SUSTAIN.

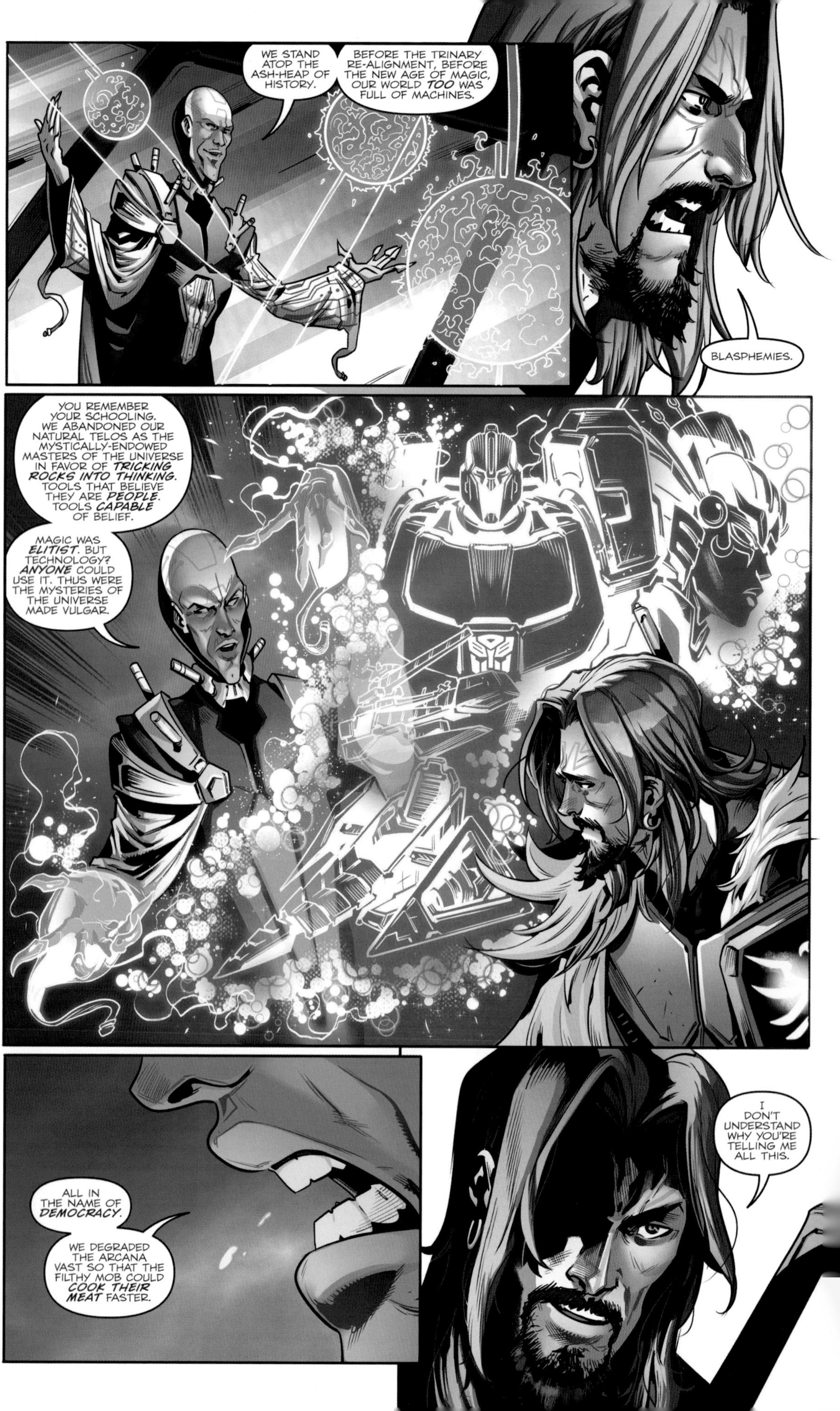

WE STAND ATOP THE ASH-HEAP OF HISTORY.
BEFORE THE TRINARY RE-ALIGNMENT, BEFORE THE NEW AGE OF MAGIC, OUR WORLD *TOO* WAS FULL OF MACHINES.
BLASPHEMIES.
YOU REMEMBER YOUR SCHOOLING. WE ABANDONED OUR NATURAL TELOS AS THE MYSTICALLY-ENDOWED MASTERS OF THE UNIVERSE IN FAVOR OF *TRICKING ROCKS INTO THINKING*. TOOLS THAT BELIEVE THEY ARE *PEOPLE*. TOOLS *CAPABLE* OF BELIEF.
MAGIC WAS *ELITIST*. BUT TECHNOLOGY? *ANYONE* COULD USE IT. THUS WERE THE MYSTERIES OF THE UNIVERSE MADE VULGAR.
ALL IN THE NAME OF *DEMOCRACY*.
WE DEGRADED THE ARCANA VAST SO THAT THE FILTHY MOB COULD *COOK THEIR MEAT* FASTER.
I DON'T UNDERSTAND WHY YOU'RE TELLING ME ALL THIS.

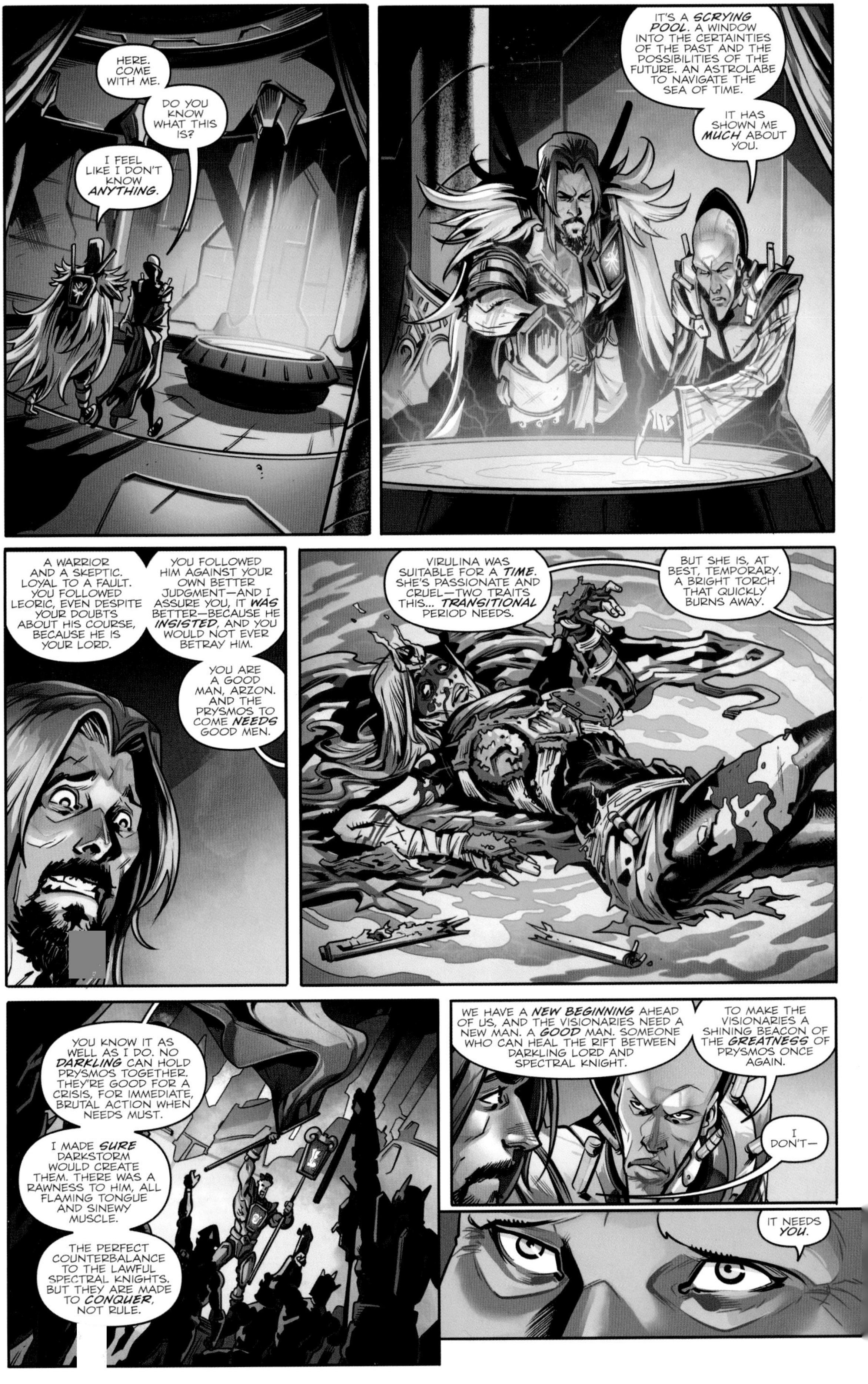
HERE. COME WITH ME.
DO YOU KNOW WHAT THIS IS?
I FEEL LIKE I DON'T KNOW ANYTHING.
IT'S A SCRYING POOL. A WINDOW INTO THE CERTAINTIES OF THE PAST AND THE POSSIBILITIES OF THE FUTURE. AN ASTROLABE TO NAVIGATE THE SEA OF TIME.
IT HAS SHOWN ME MUCH ABOUT YOU.
A WARRIOR AND A SKEPTIC. LOYAL TO A FAULT. YOU FOLLOWED LEORIC, EVEN DESPITE YOUR DOUBTS ABOUT HIS COURSE, BECAUSE HE IS YOUR LORD.
YOU FOLLOWED HIM AGAINST YOUR OWN BETTER JUDGMENT—AND I ASSURE YOU, IT WAS BETTER—BECAUSE HE INSISTED, AND YOU WOULD NOT EVER BETRAY HIM.
YOU ARE A GOOD MAN, ARZON. AND THE PRYSMOS TO COME NEEDS GOOD MEN.
VIRULINA WAS SUITABLE FOR A TIME. SHE'S PASSIONATE AND CRUEL—TWO TRAITS THIS... TRANSITIONAL PERIOD NEEDS.
BUT SHE IS, AT BEST, TEMPORARY. A BRIGHT TORCH THAT QUICKLY BURNS AWAY.
YOU KNOW IT AS WELL AS I DO. NO DARKLING CAN HOLD PRYSMOS TOGETHER. THEY'RE GOOD FOR A CRISIS, FOR IMMEDIATE, BRUTAL ACTION WHEN NEEDS MUST.
I MADE SURE DARKSTORM WOULD CREATE THEM. THERE WAS A RAWNESS TO HIM, ALL FLAMING TONGUE AND SINEWY MUSCLE.
THE PERFECT COUNTERBALANCE TO THE LAWFUL SPECTRAL KNIGHTS. BUT THEY ARE MADE TO CONQUER, NOT RULE.
WE HAVE A NEW BEGINNING AHEAD OF US, AND THE VISIONARIES NEED A NEW MAN. A GOOD MAN. SOMEONE WHO CAN HEAL THE RIFT BETWEEN DARKLING LORD AND SPECTRAL KNIGHT.
TO MAKE THE VISIONARIES A SHINING BEACON OF THE GREATNESS OF PRYSMOS ONCE AGAIN.
I DON'T—
IT NEEDS YOU.

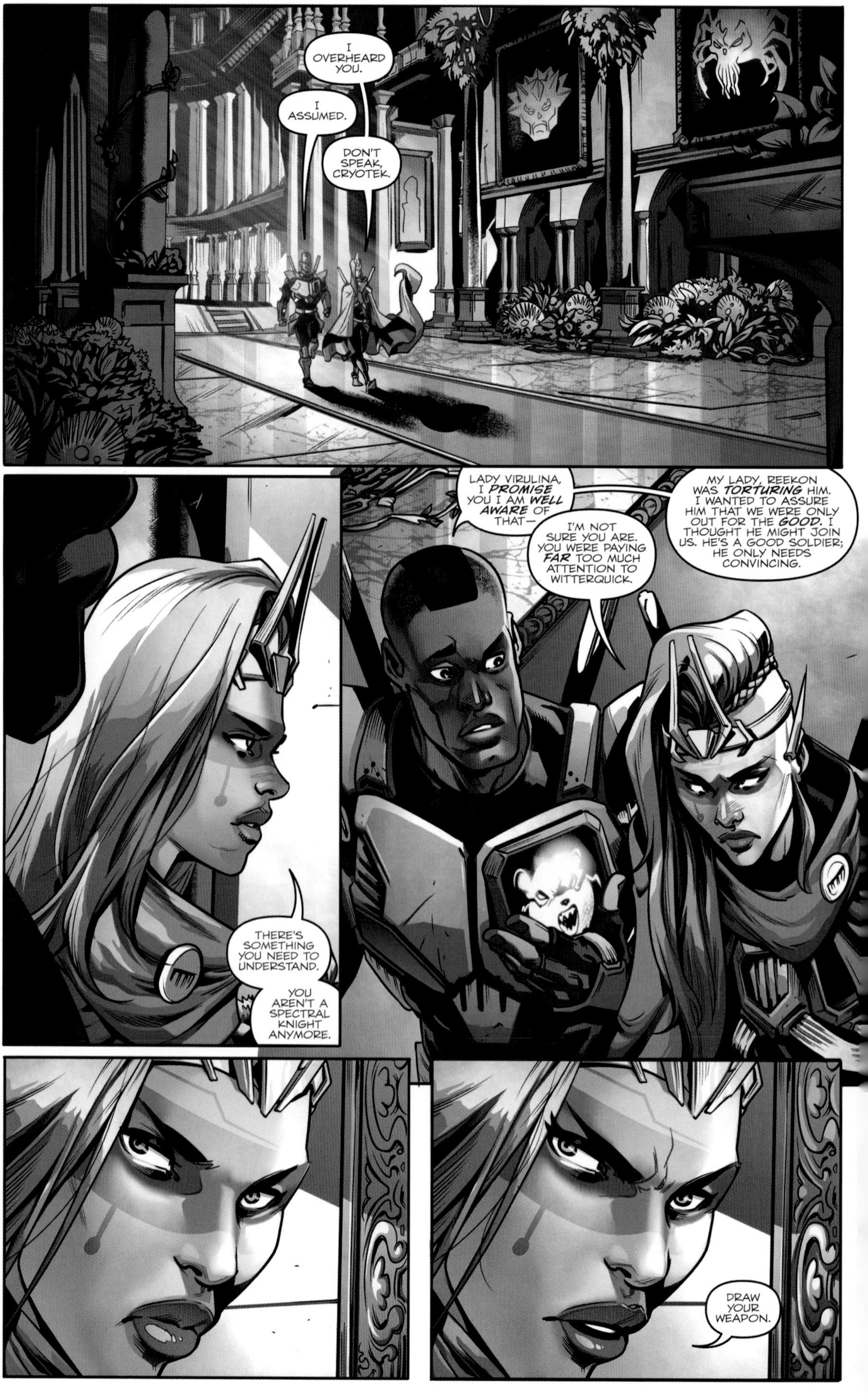
I OVERHEARD YOU.
I ASSUMED.
DON'T SPEAK, CRYOTEK.
LADY VIRULINA, I PROMISE YOU I AM WELL AWARE OF THAT—
I'M NOT SURE YOU ARE. YOU WERE PAYING FAR TOO MUCH ATTENTION TO WITTERQUICK.
MY LADY, REEKON WAS TORTURING HIM. I WANTED TO ASSURE HIM THAT WE WERE ONLY OUT FOR THE GOOD. I THOUGHT HE MIGHT JOIN US. HE'S A GOOD SOLDIER; HE ONLY NEEDS CONVINCING.
THERE'S SOMETHING YOU NEED TO UNDERSTAND.
YOU AREN'T A SPECTRAL KNIGHT ANYMORE.
DRAW YOUR WEAPON.

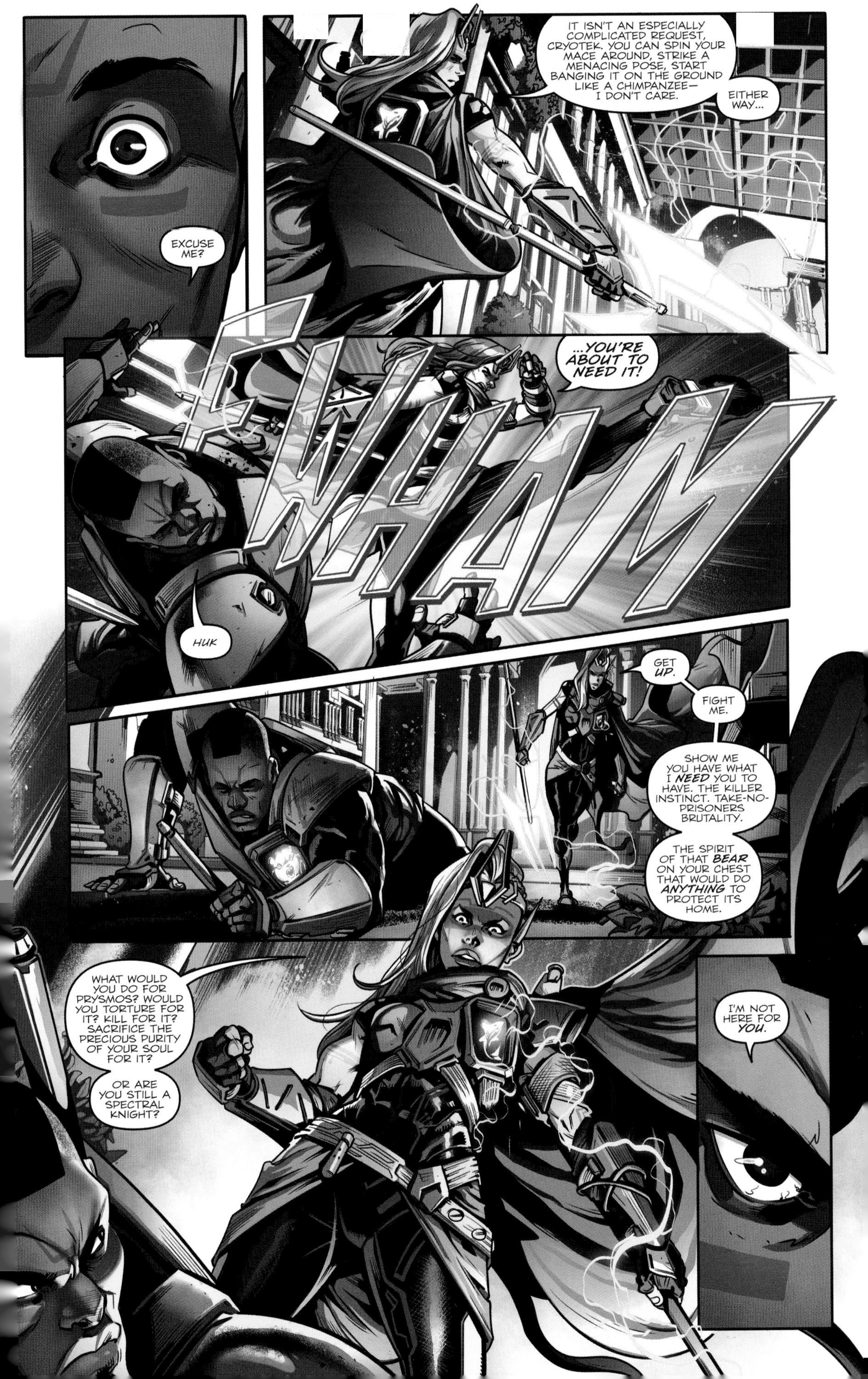
EXCUSE ME?
IT ISN'T AN ESPECIALLY COMPLICATED REQUEST, CRYOTEK. YOU CAN SPIN YOUR MACE AROUND, STRIKE A MENACING POSE, START BANGING IT ON THE GROUND LIKE A CHIMPANZEE— I DON'T CARE.
EITHER WAY...
...YOU'RE ABOUT TO NEED IT!
FWHAM
HUK
GET UP.
FIGHT ME.
SHOW ME YOU HAVE WHAT I NEED YOU TO HAVE. THE KILLER INSTINCT. TAKE-NO-PRISONERS BRUTALITY.
THE SPIRIT OF THAT BEAR ON YOUR CHEST THAT WOULD DO ANYTHING TO PROTECT ITS HOME.
WHAT WOULD YOU DO FOR PRYSMOS? WOULD YOU TORTURE FOR IT? KILL FOR IT? SACRIFICE THE PRECIOUS PURITY OF YOUR SOUL FOR IT?
OR ARE YOU STILL A SPECTRAL KNIGHT?
I'M NOT HERE FOR YOU.

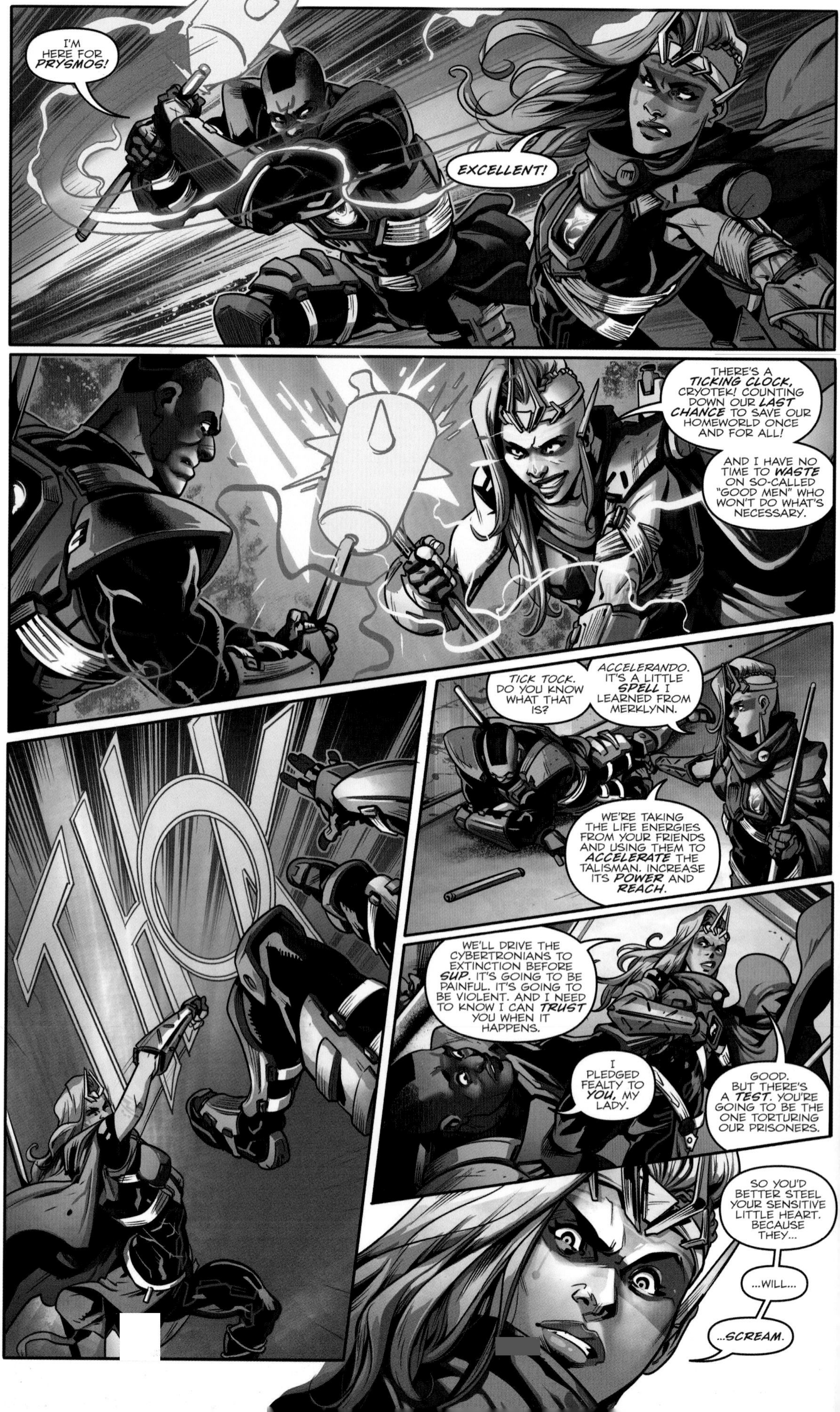

I'M HERE FOR PRYSMOS!
EXCELLENT!
THERE'S A TICKING CLOCK, CRYOTEK! COUNTING DOWN OUR LAST CHANCE TO SAVE OUR HOMEWORLD ONCE AND FOR ALL!
AND I HAVE NO TIME TO WASTE ON SO-CALLED "GOOD MEN" WHO WON'T DO WHAT'S NECESSARY.
TICK TOCK. DO YOU KNOW WHAT THAT IS?
ACCELERANDO. IT'S A LITTLE SPELL I LEARNED FROM MERKLYNN.
WE'RE TAKING THE LIFE ENERGIES FROM YOUR FRIENDS AND USING THEM TO ACCELERATE THE TALISMAN. INCREASE ITS POWER AND REACH.
WE'LL DRIVE THE CYBERTRONIANS TO EXTINCTION BEFORE SUP. IT'S GOING TO BE PAINFUL. IT'S GOING TO BE VIOLENT. AND I NEED TO KNOW I CAN TRUST YOU WHEN IT HAPPENS.
I PLEDGED FEALTY TO YOU, MY LADY.
GOOD. BUT THERE'S A TEST. YOU'RE GOING TO BE THE ONE TORTURING OUR PRISONERS.
SO YOU'D BETTER STEEL YOUR SENSITIVE LITTLE HEART. BECAUSE THEY...
...WILL...
...SCREAM.

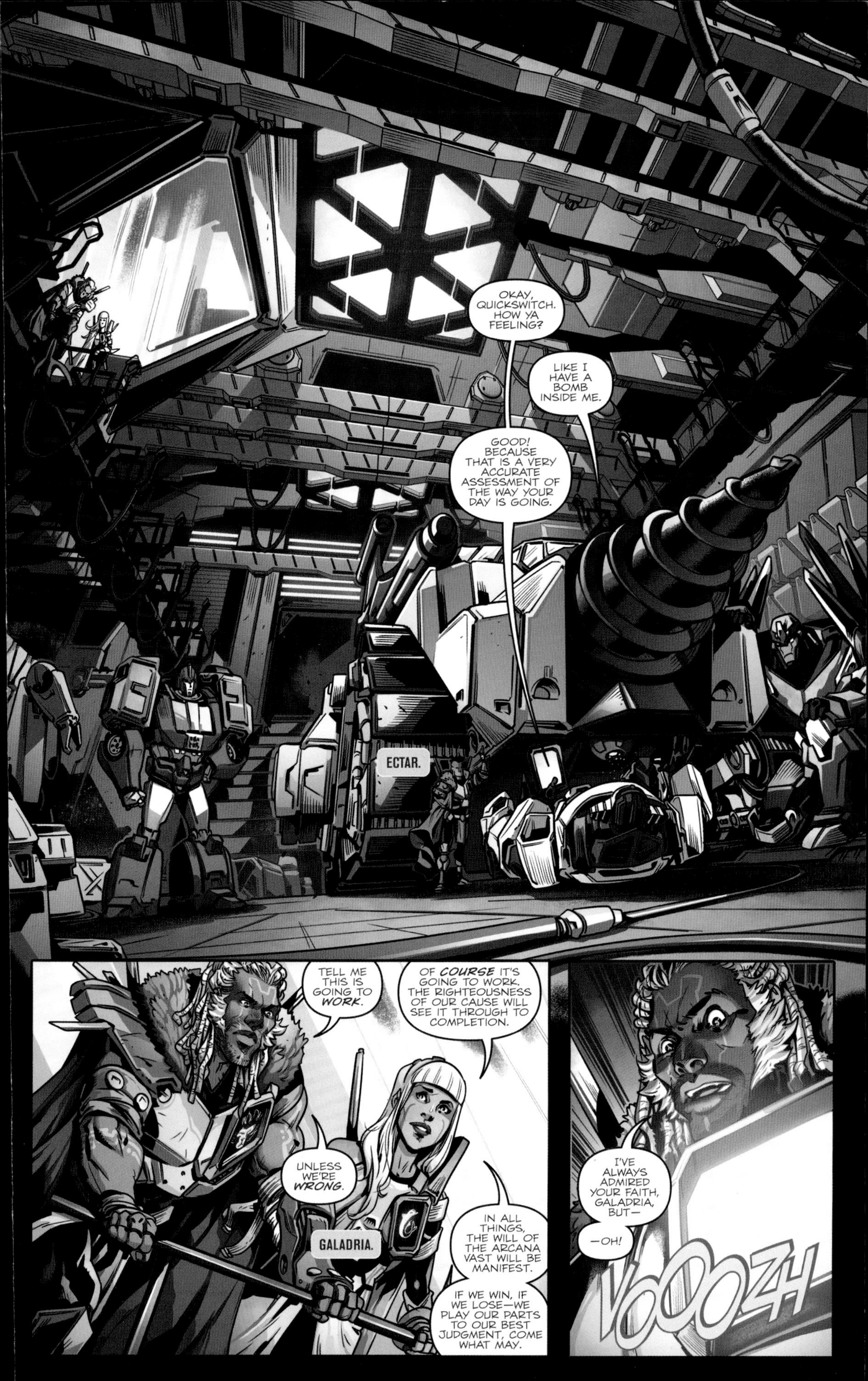
OKAY, QUICKSWITCH. HOW YA FEELING?
LIKE I HAVE A BOMB INSIDE ME.
GOOD! BECAUSE THAT IS A VERY ACCURATE ASSESSMENT OF THE WAY YOUR DAY IS GOING.
ECTAR.
TELL ME THIS IS GOING TO WORK.
OF COURSE IT'S GOING TO WORK. THE RIGHTEOUSNESS OF OUR CAUSE WILL SEE IT THROUGH TO COMPLETION.
UNLESS WE'RE WRONG.
GALADRIA.
IN ALL THINGS, THE WILL OF THE ARCANA VAST WILL BE MANIFEST.
IF WE WIN, IF WE LOSE—WE PLAY OUR PARTS TO OUR BEST JUDGMENT, COME WHAT MAY.
I'VE ALWAYS ADMIRED YOUR FAITH, GALADRIA, BUT—
—OH!
VOOOZH

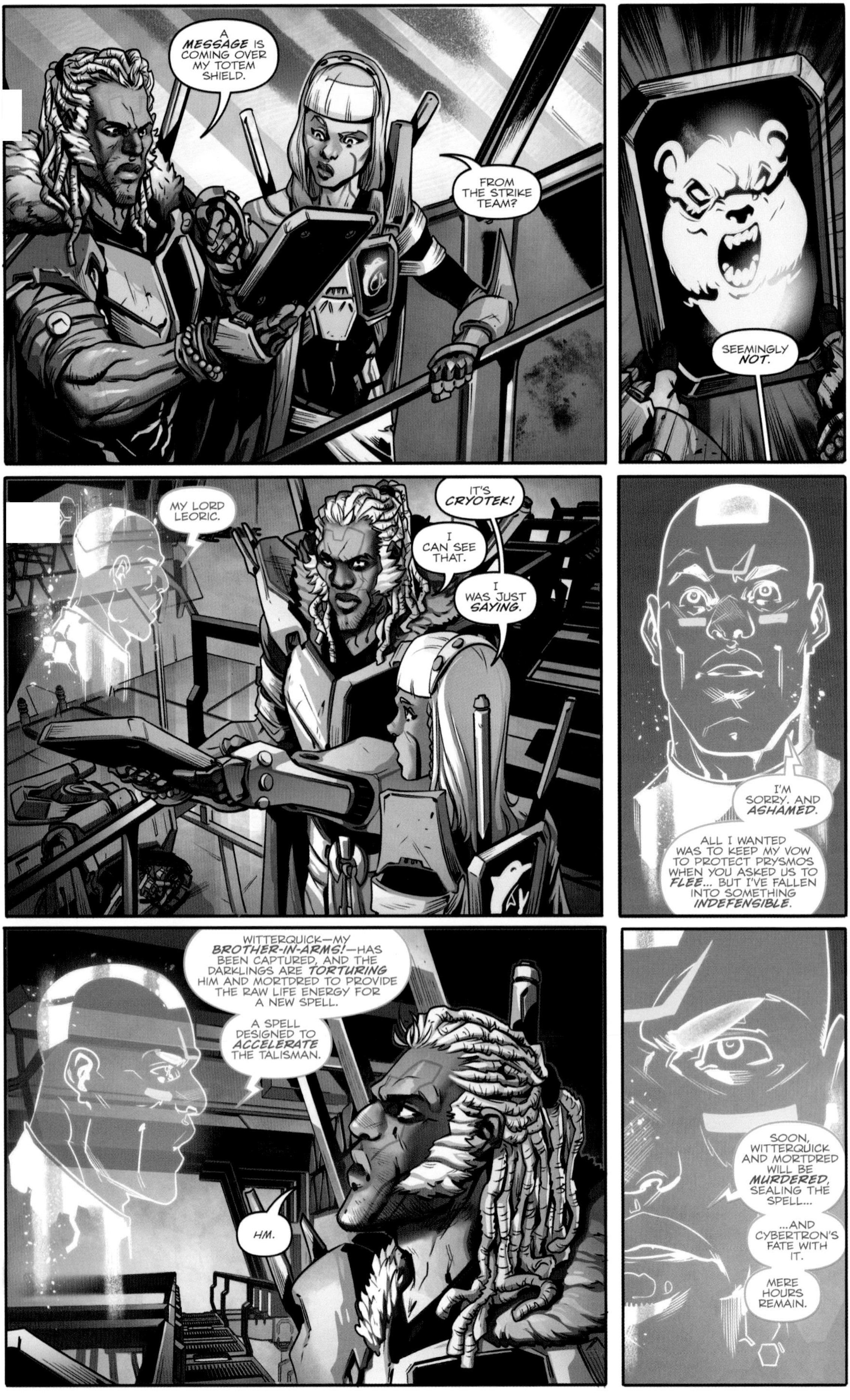

A MESSAGE IS COMING OVER MY TOTEM SHIELD.
FROM THE STRIKE TEAM?
SEEMINGLY NOT.
MY LORD LEORIC.
IT'S CRYOTEK!
I CAN SEE THAT.
I WAS JUST SAYING.
I'M SORRY. AND ASHAMED.
ALL I WANTED WAS TO KEEP MY VOW TO PROTECT PRYSMOS WHEN YOU ASKED US TO FLEE... BUT I'VE FALLEN INTO SOMETHING INDEFENSIBLE.
WITTERQUICK—MY BROTHER-IN-ARMS!—HAS BEEN CAPTURED, AND THE DARKLINGS ARE TORTURING HIM AND MORTDRED TO PROVIDE THE RAW LIFE ENERGY FOR A NEW SPELL.
A SPELL DESIGNED TO ACCELERATE THE TALISMAN.
HM.
SOON, WITTERQUICK AND MORTDRED WILL BE MURDERED, SEALING THE SPELL...
...AND CYBERTRON'S FATE WITH IT.
MERE HOURS REMAIN.

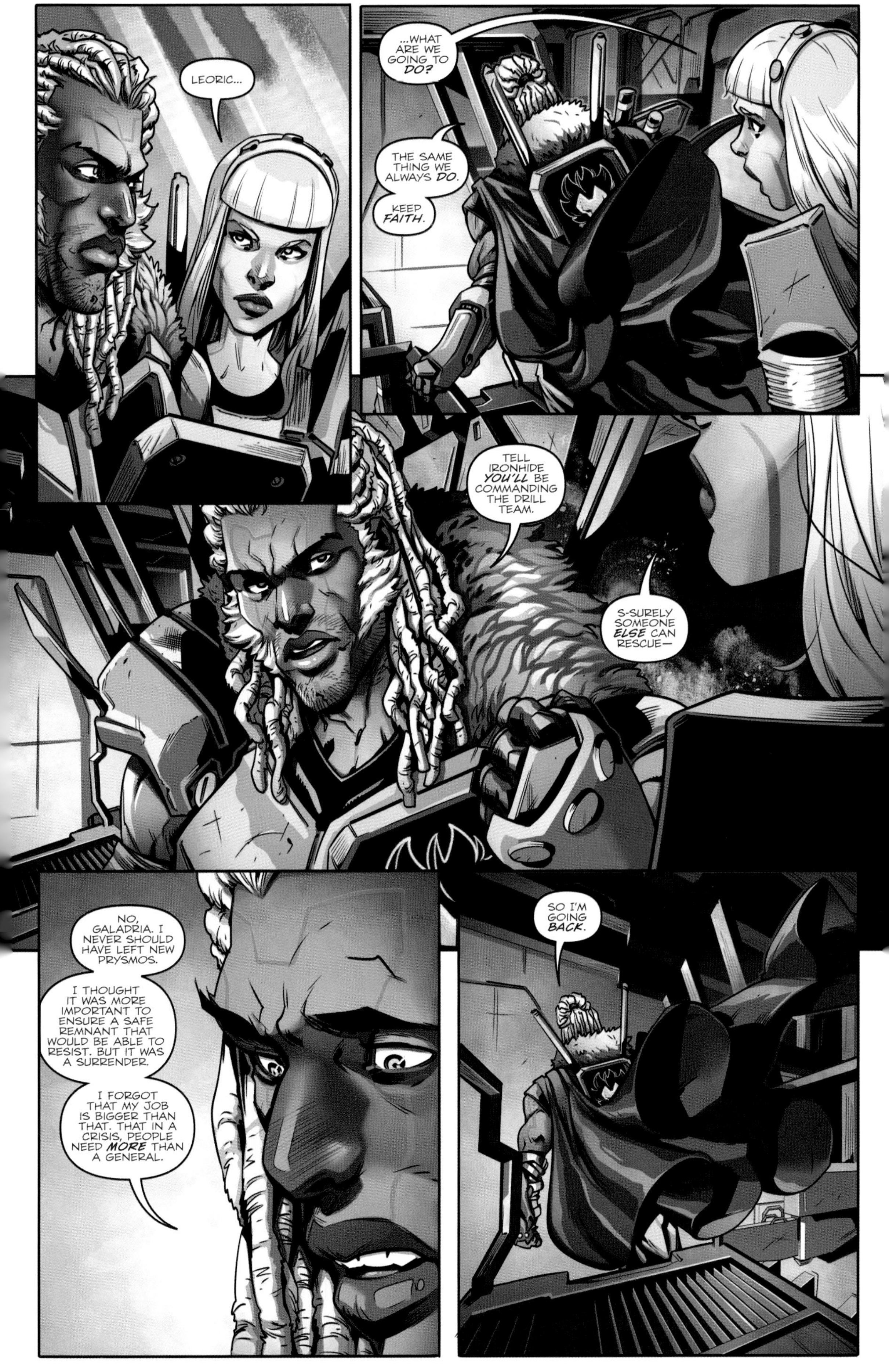
LEORIC...
...WHAT ARE WE GOING TO DO?
THE SAME THING WE ALWAYS DO.
KEEP FAITH.
TELL IRONHIDE YOU'LL BE COMMANDING THE DRILL TEAM.
S-SURELY SOMEONE ELSE CAN RESCUE—
NO, GALADRIA. I NEVER SHOULD HAVE LEFT NEW PRYSMOS.
I THOUGHT IT WAS MORE IMPORTANT TO ENSURE A SAFE REMNANT THAT WOULD BE ABLE TO RESIST. BUT IT WAS A SURRENDER.
I FORGOT THAT MY JOB IS BIGGER THAN THAT. THAT IN A CRISIS, PEOPLE NEED MORE THAN A GENERAL.
SO I'M GOING BACK.

ALRIGHT EVERYBODY!

LET'S MOVE!

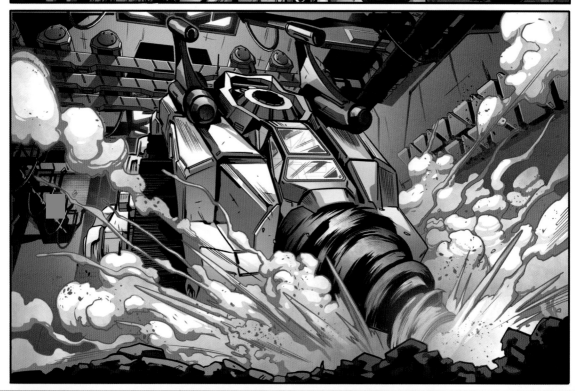

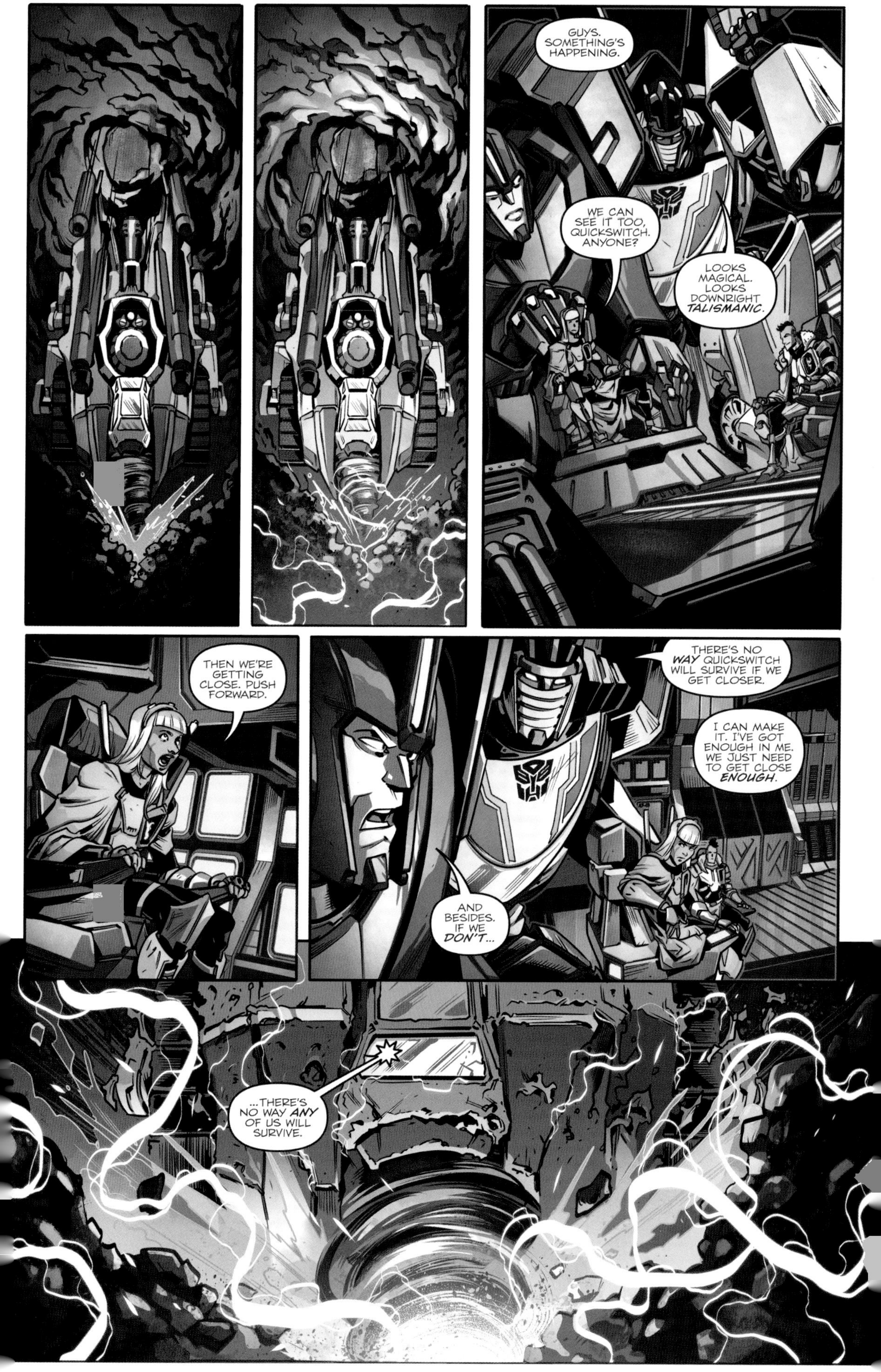
GUYS. SOMETHING'S HAPPENING.
WE CAN SEE IT TOO, QUICKSWITCH. ANYONE?
LOOKS MAGICAL. LOOKS DOWNRIGHT *TALISMANIC*.
THEN WE'RE GETTING CLOSE. PUSH FORWARD.
THERE'S NO *WAY* QUICKSWITCH WILL SURVIVE IF WE GET CLOSER.
I CAN MAKE IT. I'VE GOT ENOUGH IN ME. WE JUST NEED TO GET CLOSE *ENOUGH*.
AND BESIDES. IF WE *DON'T*...
...THERE'S NO WAY *ANY* OF US WILL SURVIVE.

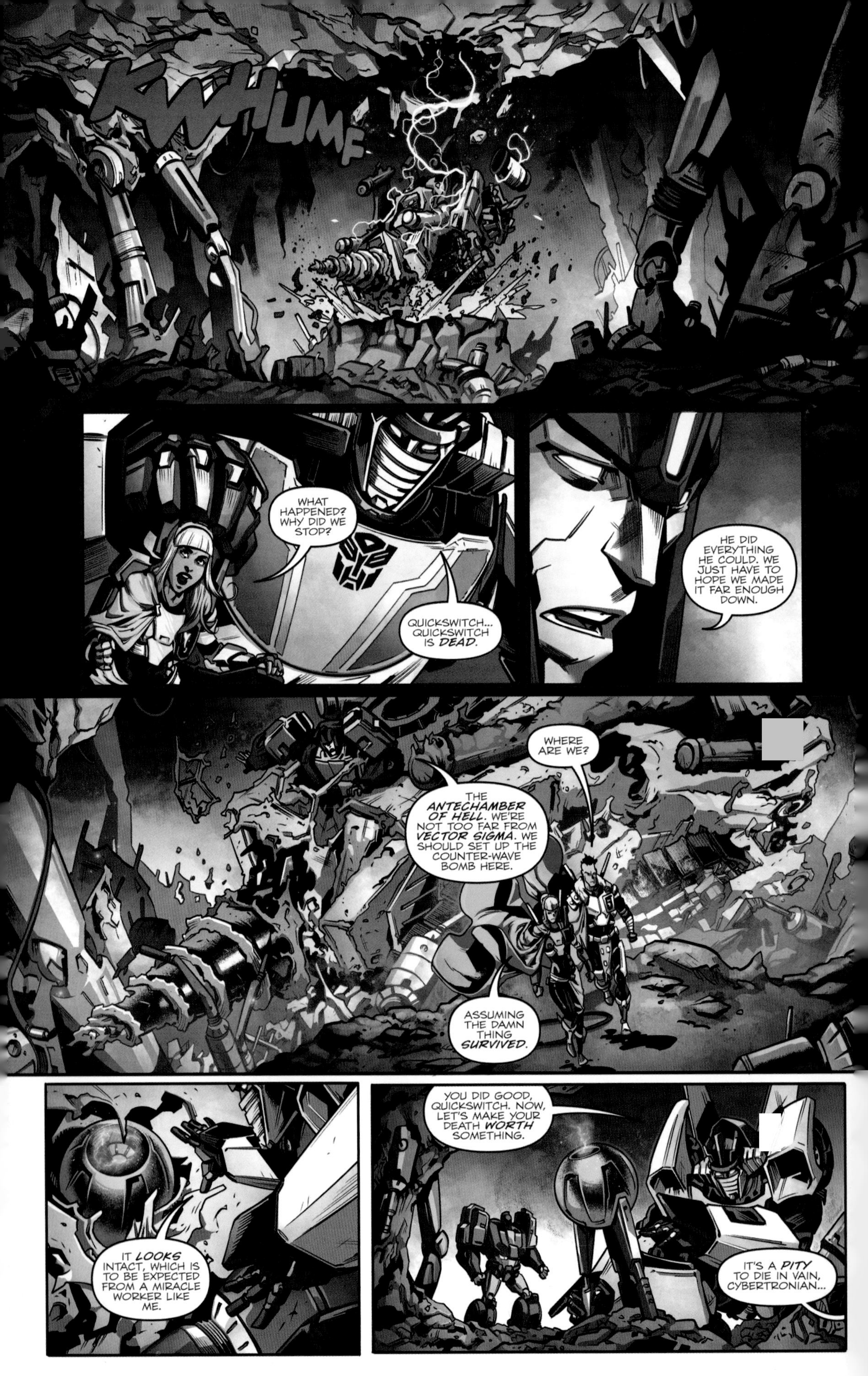
KWHUMF
WHAT HAPPENED? WHY DID WE STOP?
QUICKSWITCH... QUICKSWITCH IS *DEAD*.
HE DID EVERYTHING HE COULD. WE JUST HAVE TO HOPE WE MADE IT FAR ENOUGH DOWN.
WHERE ARE WE?
THE *ANTECHAMBER OF HELL*. WE'RE NOT TOO FAR FROM *VECTOR SIGMA*. WE SHOULD SET UP THE COUNTER-WAVE BOMB HERE.
ASSUMING THE DAMN THING *SURVIVED*.
IT *LOOKS* INTACT, WHICH IS TO BE EXPECTED FROM A MIRACLE WORKER LIKE ME.
YOU DID GOOD, QUICKSWITCH. NOW, LET'S MAKE YOUR DEATH *WORTH* SOMETHING.
IT'S A *PITY* TO DIE IN VAIN, CYBERTRONIAN...

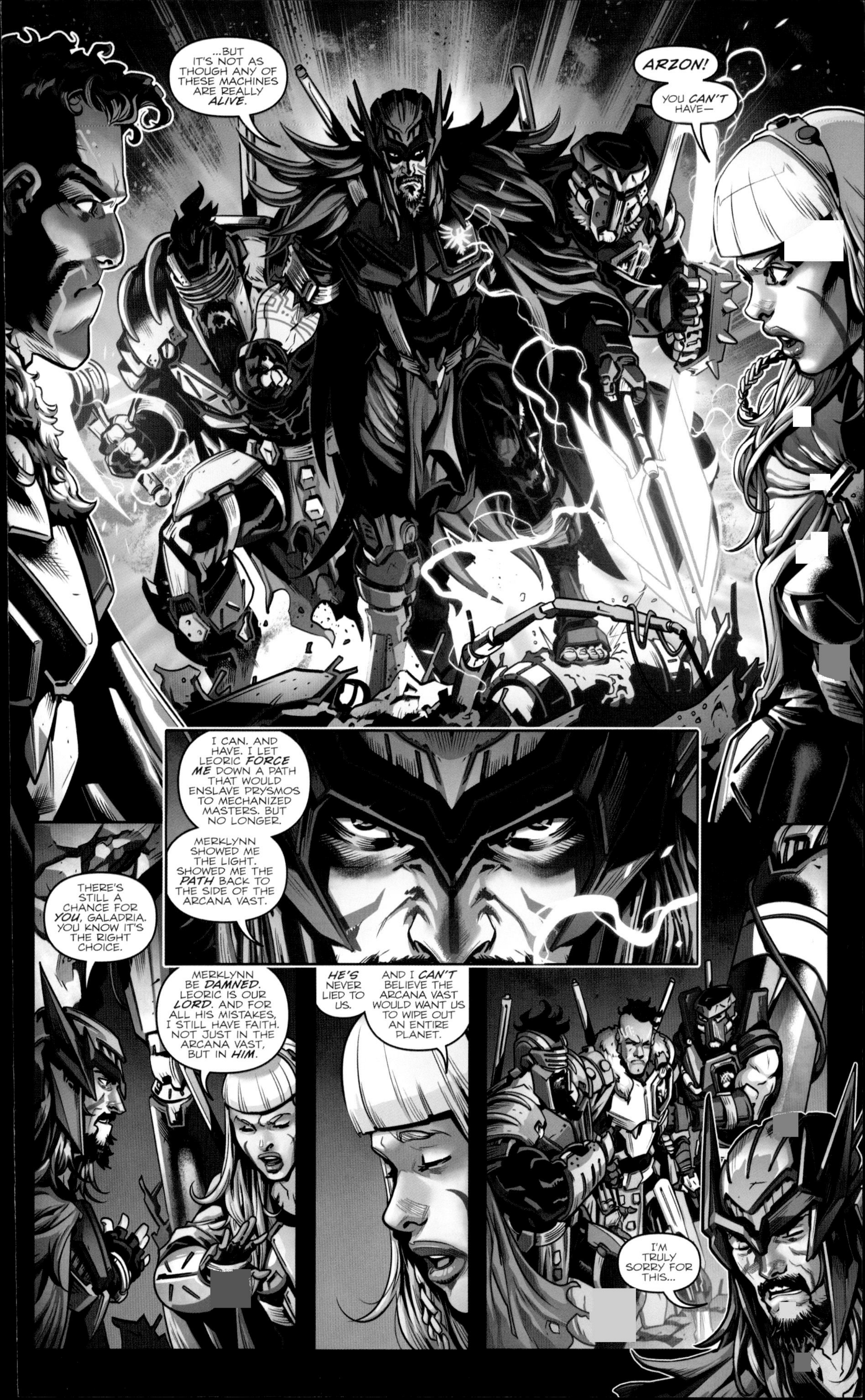
...BUT IT'S NOT AS THOUGH ANY OF THESE MACHINES ARE REALLY ALIVE.
ARZON!
YOU CAN'T HAVE—
I CAN. AND HAVE. I LET LEORIC FORCE ME DOWN A PATH THAT WOULD ENSLAVE PRYSMOS TO MECHANIZED MASTERS. BUT NO LONGER.
MERKLYNN SHOWED ME THE LIGHT. SHOWED ME THE PATH BACK TO THE SIDE OF THE ARCANA VAST.
THERE'S STILL A CHANCE FOR YOU, GALADRIA. YOU KNOW IT'S THE RIGHT CHOICE.
MERKLYNN BE DAMNED. LEORIC IS OUR LORD. AND FOR ALL HIS MISTAKES, I STILL HAVE FAITH. NOT JUST IN THE ARCANA VAST, BUT IN HIM.
HE'S NEVER LIED TO US.
AND I CAN'T BELIEVE THE ARCANA VAST WOULD WANT US TO WIPE OUT AN ENTIRE PLANET.
I'M TRULY SORRY FOR THIS...

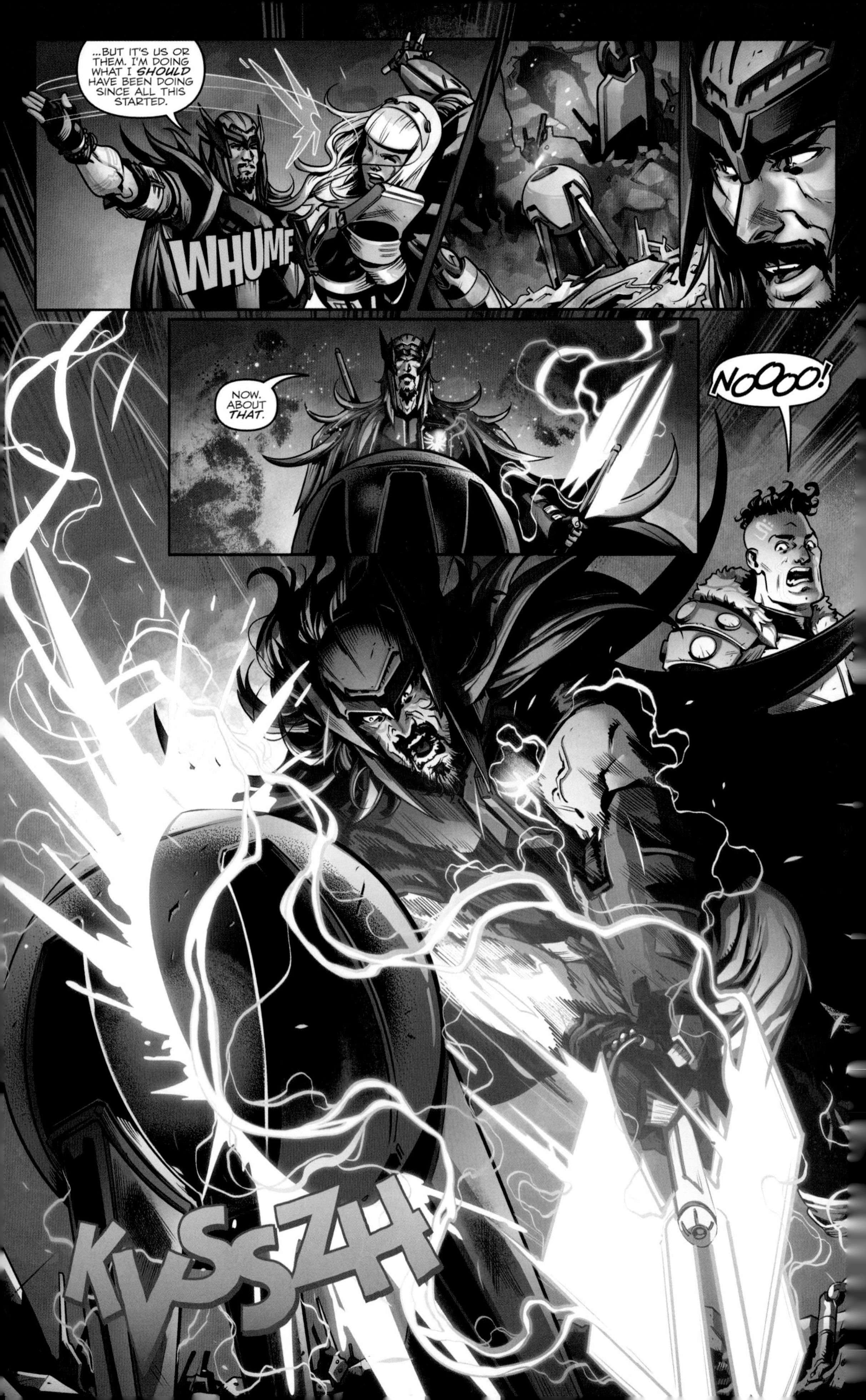
...BUT IT'S US OR THEM. I'M DOING WHAT I SHOULD HAVE BEEN DOING SINCE ALL THIS STARTED.
WHUMF
NOW. ABOUT THAT.
NOOOO!
KVSSZH

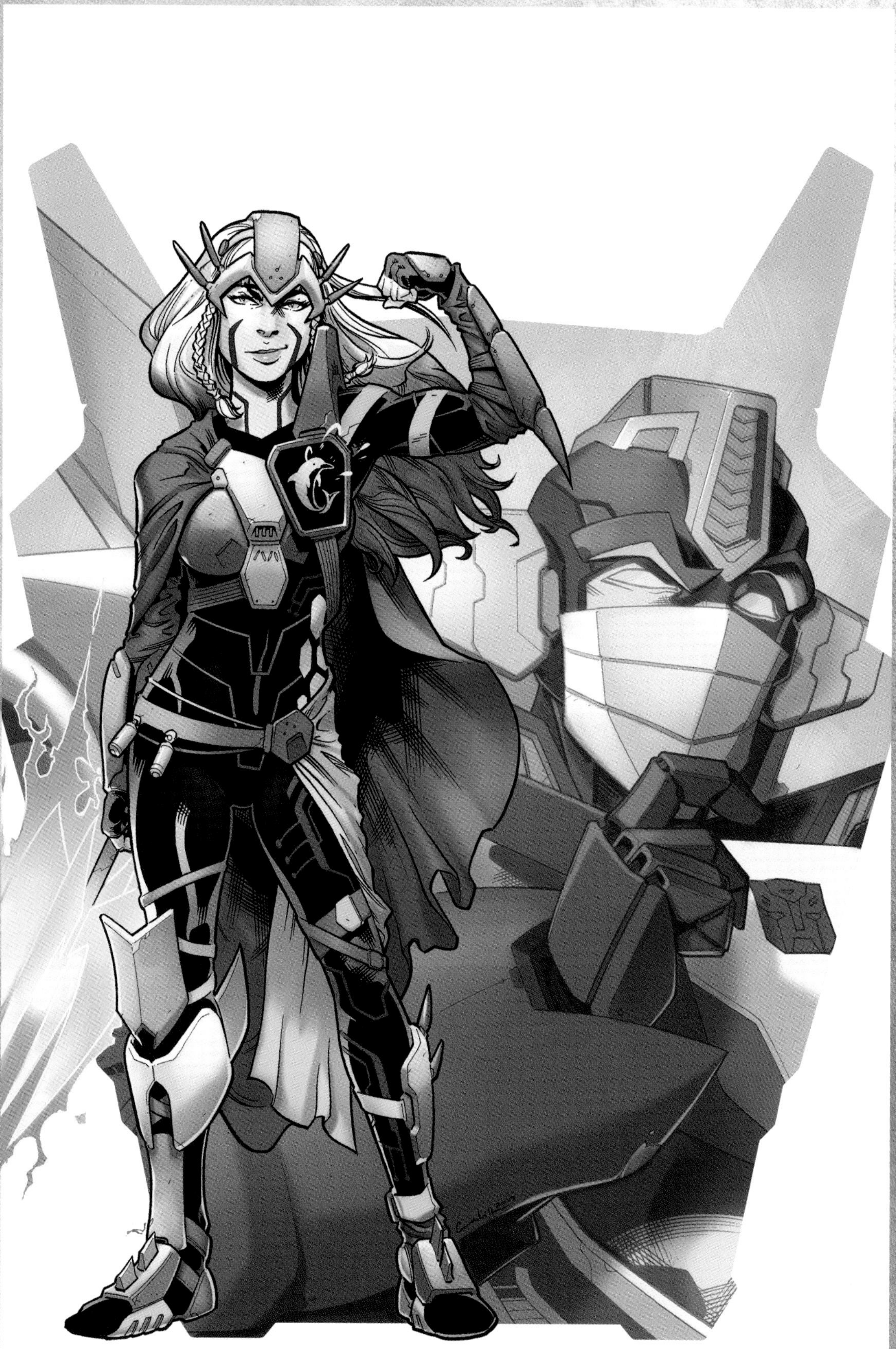

ART BY BRENDAN CAHILL
COLORS BY LAUREN BENNETT

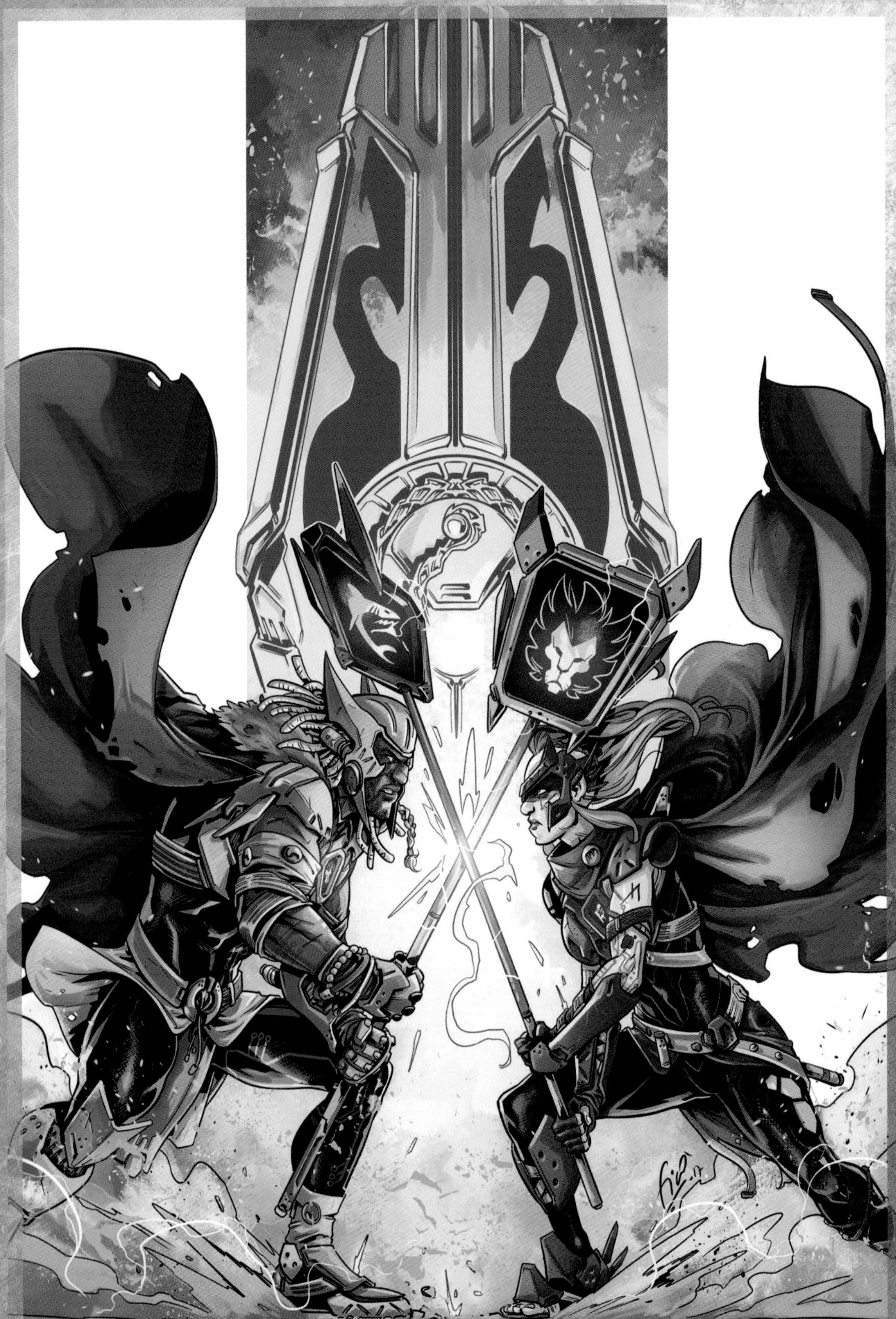

ART BY **FICO OSSIO**

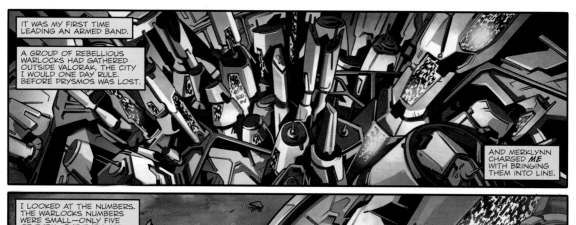

IT WAS MY FIRST TIME LEADING AN ARMED BAND.

A GROUP OF REBELLIOUS WARLOCKS HAD GATHERED OUTSIDE VALORAK, THE CITY I WOULD ONE DAY RULE. BEFORE PRYSMOS WAS LOST.

AND MERKLYNN CHARGED *ME* WITH BRINGING THEM INTO LINE.

I LOOKED AT THE NUMBERS. THE WARLOCKS NUMBERS WERE SMALL—ONLY FIVE OF THEM—BUT THEY HAD MANAGED TO WREAK SOME HAVOC ON VALORAK.

SET NEIGHBOR AGAINST NEIGHBOR. THE PETTIEST SLIGHTS BECAME BLOOD FEUDS. THEY NEEDED TO BE STOPPED.

I TOOK A SMALL PARTY CONSISTING OF MYSELF, DARKSTORM, A FEW OTHERS. MORE THAN ENOUGH, I SUPPOSED.

I SUPPOSED WRONG. WE INITIALLY PROVED UNABLE TO RESIST THEIR MAGICS, AND BATTLED AMONG OURSELVES.

AND EVEN AFTER WE OVERCAME THE SPELL AND SLAUGHTERED THE WARLOCKS TO A MAN, STILL WE CLASHED.

THAT WAS WHEN DARKSTORM LEFT, TAKING HALF THE VISIONARIES WITH HIM.

THE VISIONARIES WERE RENT IN TWO.

ALL BECAUSE I FAILED.

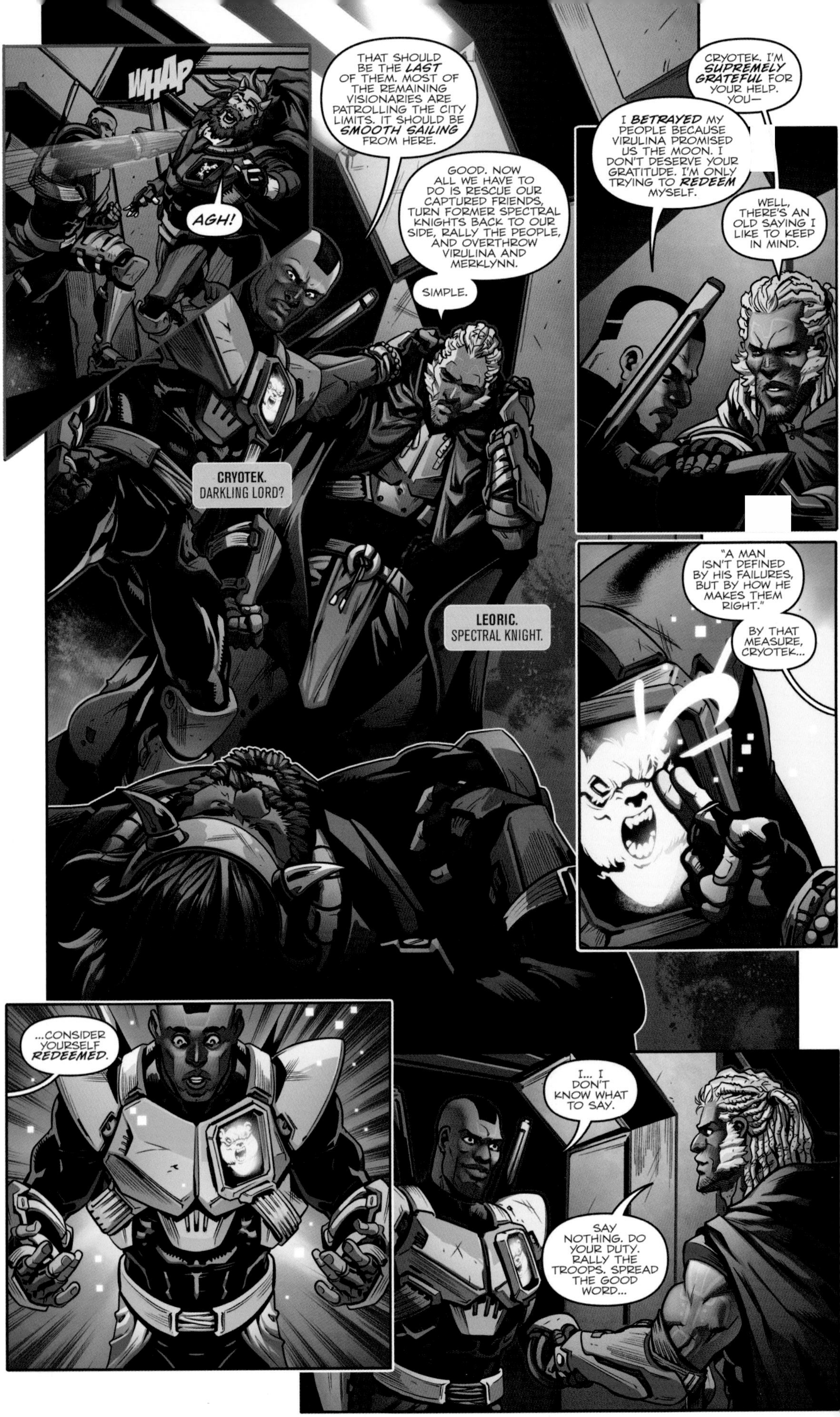
WHAP
AGH!
THAT SHOULD BE THE LAST OF THEM. MOST OF THE REMAINING VISIONARIES ARE PATROLLING THE CITY LIMITS. IT SHOULD BE SMOOTH SAILING FROM HERE.
GOOD. NOW ALL WE HAVE TO DO IS RESCUE OUR CAPTURED FRIENDS, TURN FORMER SPECTRAL KNIGHTS BACK TO OUR SIDE, RALLY THE PEOPLE, AND OVERTHROW VIRULINA AND MERKLYNN.
SIMPLE.
CRYOTEK. DARKLING LORD?
LEORIC. SPECTRAL KNIGHT.
CRYOTEK. I'M SUPREMELY GRATEFUL FOR YOUR HELP. YOU—
I BETRAYED MY PEOPLE BECAUSE VIRULINA PROMISED US THE MOON. I DON'T DESERVE YOUR GRATITUDE. I'M ONLY TRYING TO REDEEM MYSELF.
WELL, THERE'S AN OLD SAYING I LIKE TO KEEP IN MIND.
"A MAN ISN'T DEFINED BY HIS FAILURES, BUT BY HOW HE MAKES THEM RIGHT."
BY THAT MEASURE, CRYOTEK...
...CONSIDER YOURSELF REDEEMED.
I... I DON'T KNOW WHAT TO SAY.
SAY NOTHING. DO YOUR DUTY. RALLY THE TROOPS. SPREAD THE GOOD WORD...

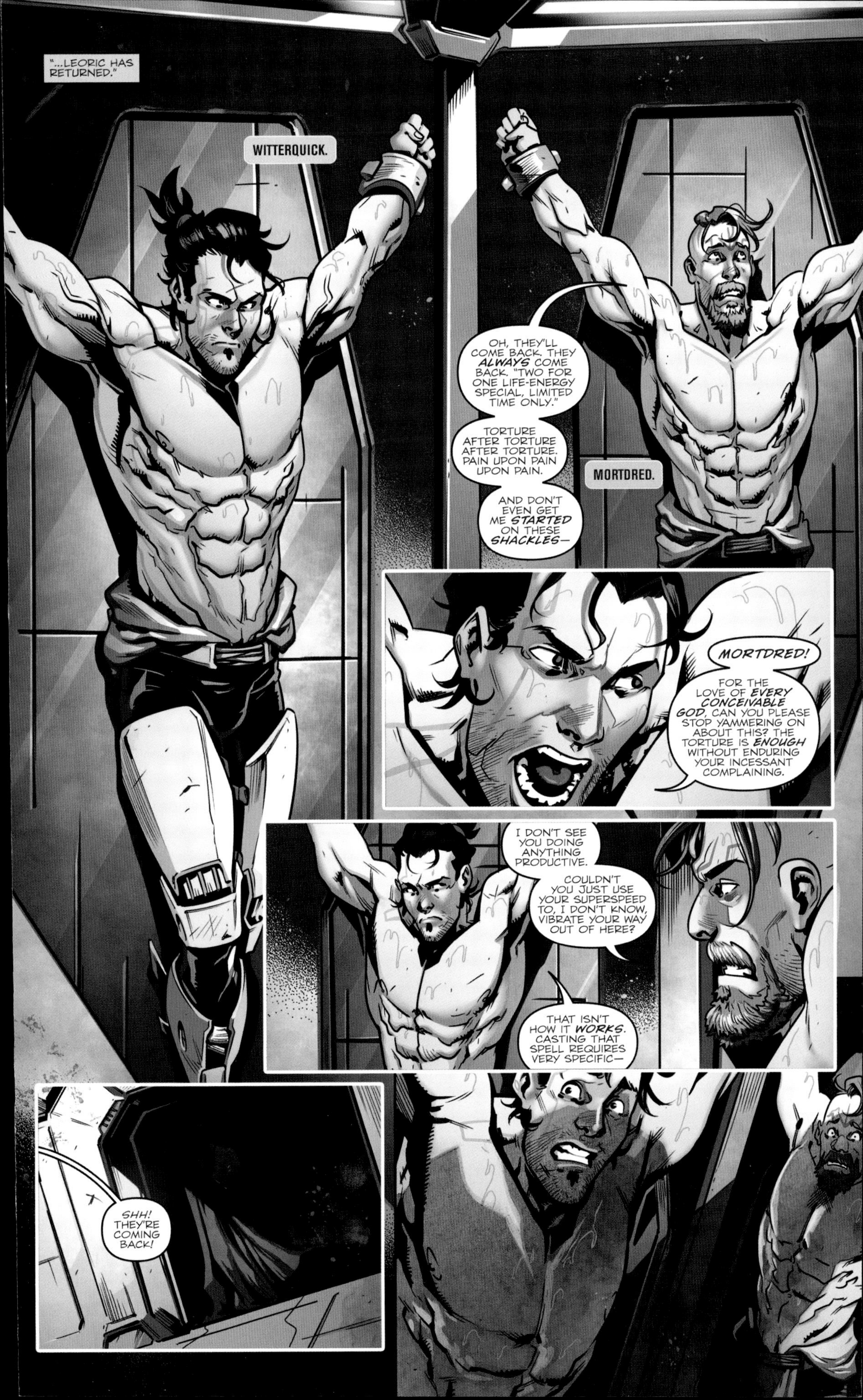
"...LEORIC HAS RETURNED."
WITTERQUICK.
OH, THEY'LL COME BACK. THEY ALWAYS COME BACK. "TWO FOR ONE LIFE-ENERGY SPECIAL, LIMITED TIME ONLY."
TORTURE AFTER TORTURE AFTER TORTURE. PAIN UPON PAIN UPON PAIN.
AND DON'T EVEN GET ME STARTED ON THESE SHACKLES—
MORTDRED.
MORTDRED!
FOR THE LOVE OF EVERY CONCEIVABLE GOD, CAN YOU PLEASE STOP YAMMERING ON ABOUT THIS? THE TORTURE IS ENOUGH WITHOUT ENDURING YOUR INCESSANT COMPLAINING.
I DON'T SEE YOU DOING ANYTHING PRODUCTIVE.
COULDN'T YOU JUST USE YOUR SUPERSPEED TO, I DON'T KNOW, VIBRATE YOUR WAY OUT OF HERE?
THAT ISN'T HOW IT WORKS. CASTING THAT SPELL REQUIRES VERY SPECIFIC—
SHH! THEY'RE COMING BACK!

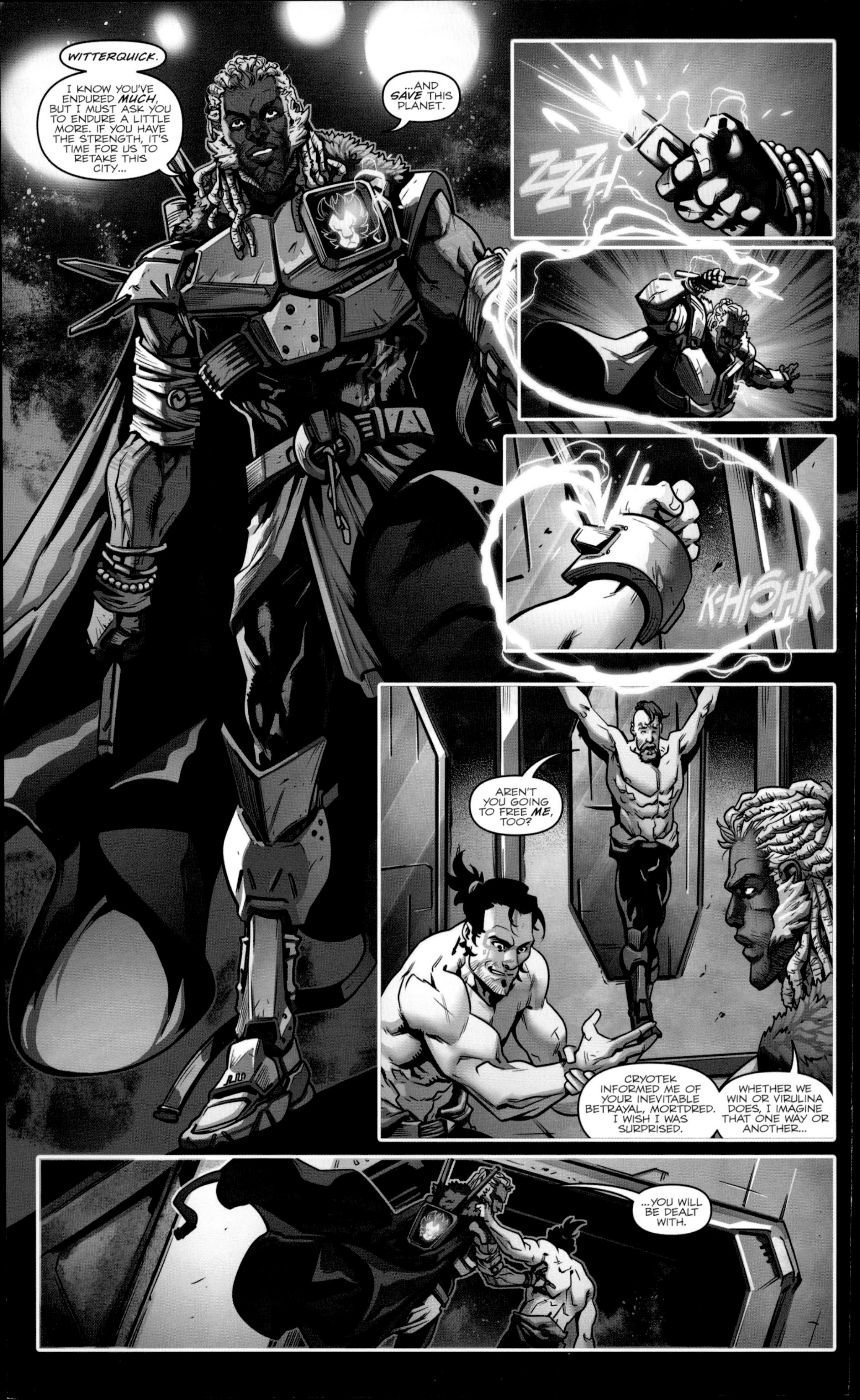
WITTERQUICK.
I KNOW YOU'VE ENDURED MUCH, BUT I MUST ASK YOU TO ENDURE A LITTLE MORE. IF YOU HAVE THE STRENGTH, IT'S TIME FOR US TO RETAKE THIS CITY...
...AND SAVE THIS PLANET.
ZZZH
K-HISHK
AREN'T YOU GOING TO FREE ME, TOO?
CRYOTEK INFORMED ME OF YOUR INEVITABLE BETRAYAL, MORTDRED. I WISH I WAS SURPRISED.
WHETHER WE WIN OR VIRULINA DOES, I IMAGINE THAT ONE WAY OR ANOTHER...
...YOU WILL BE DEALT WITH.

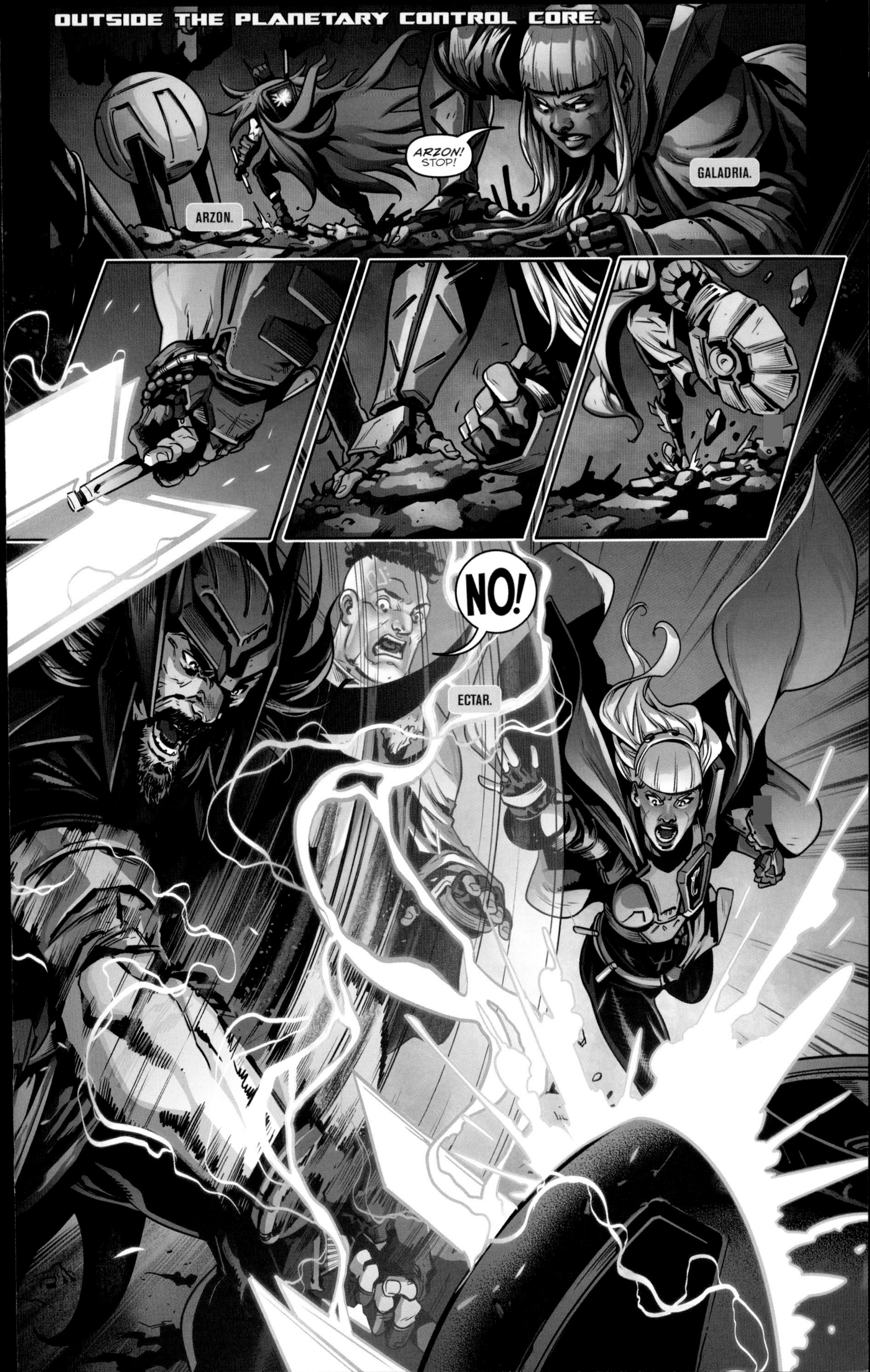
OUTSIDE THE PLANETARY CONTROL CORE.
ARZON! STOP!
GALADRIA.
ARZON.
NO!
ECTAR.

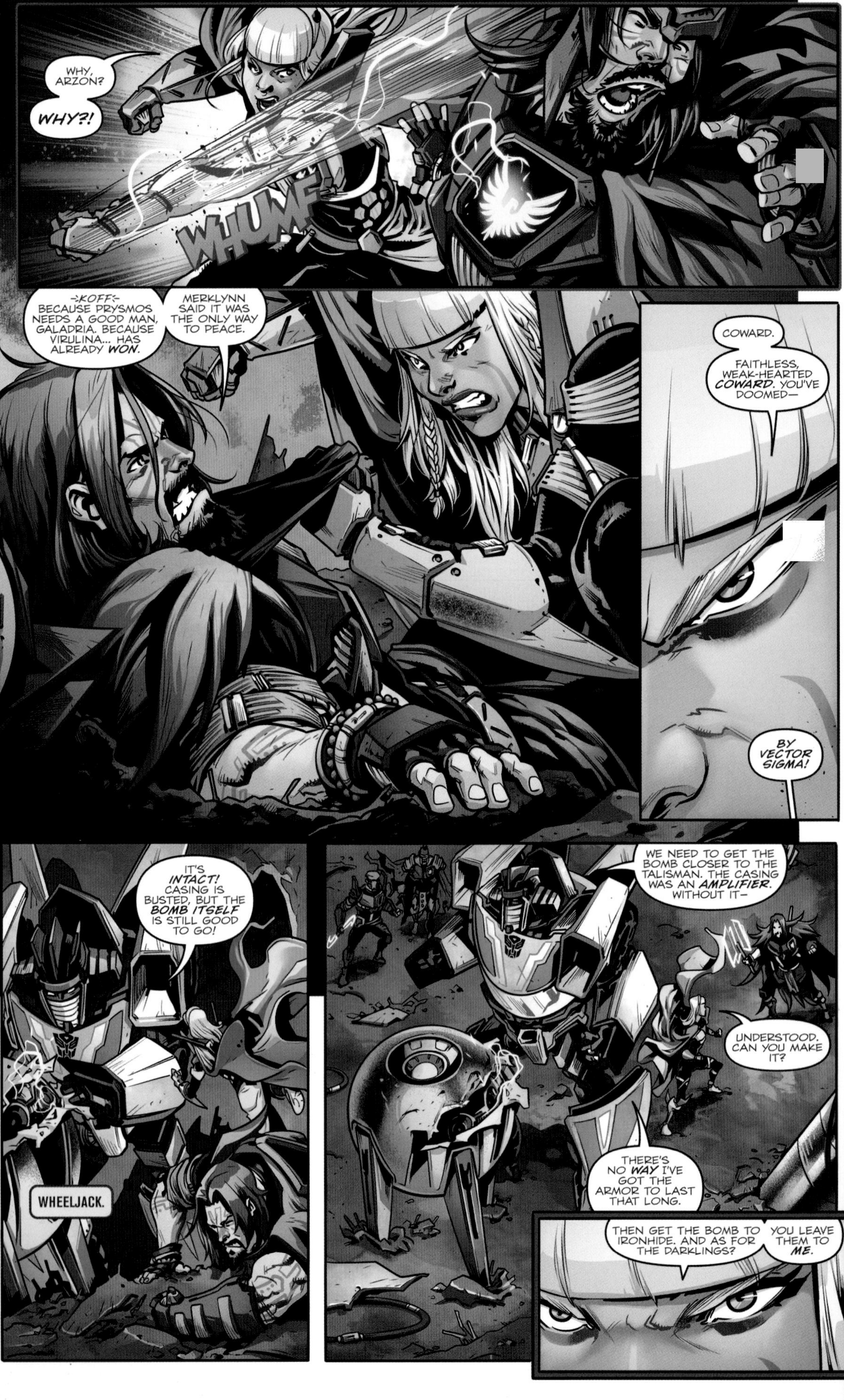

WHY, ARZON?
WHY?!
WHUMF
-KOFF- BECAUSE PRYSMOS NEEDS A GOOD MAN, GALADRIA. BECAUSE VIRULINA... HAS ALREADY WON.
MERKLYNN SAID IT WAS THE ONLY WAY TO PEACE.
COWARD.
FAITHLESS, WEAK-HEARTED COWARD. YOU'VE DOOMED—
BY VECTOR SIGMA!
IT'S INTACT! CASING IS BUSTED, BUT THE BOMB ITSELF IS STILL GOOD TO GO!
WHEELJACK.
WE NEED TO GET THE BOMB CLOSER TO THE TALISMAN. THE CASING WAS AN AMPLIFIER. WITHOUT IT—
UNDERSTOOD. CAN YOU MAKE IT?
THERE'S NO WAY I'VE GOT THE ARMOR TO LAST THAT LONG.
THEN GET THE BOMB TO IRONHIDE. AND AS FOR THE DARKLINGS?
YOU LEAVE THEM TO ME.

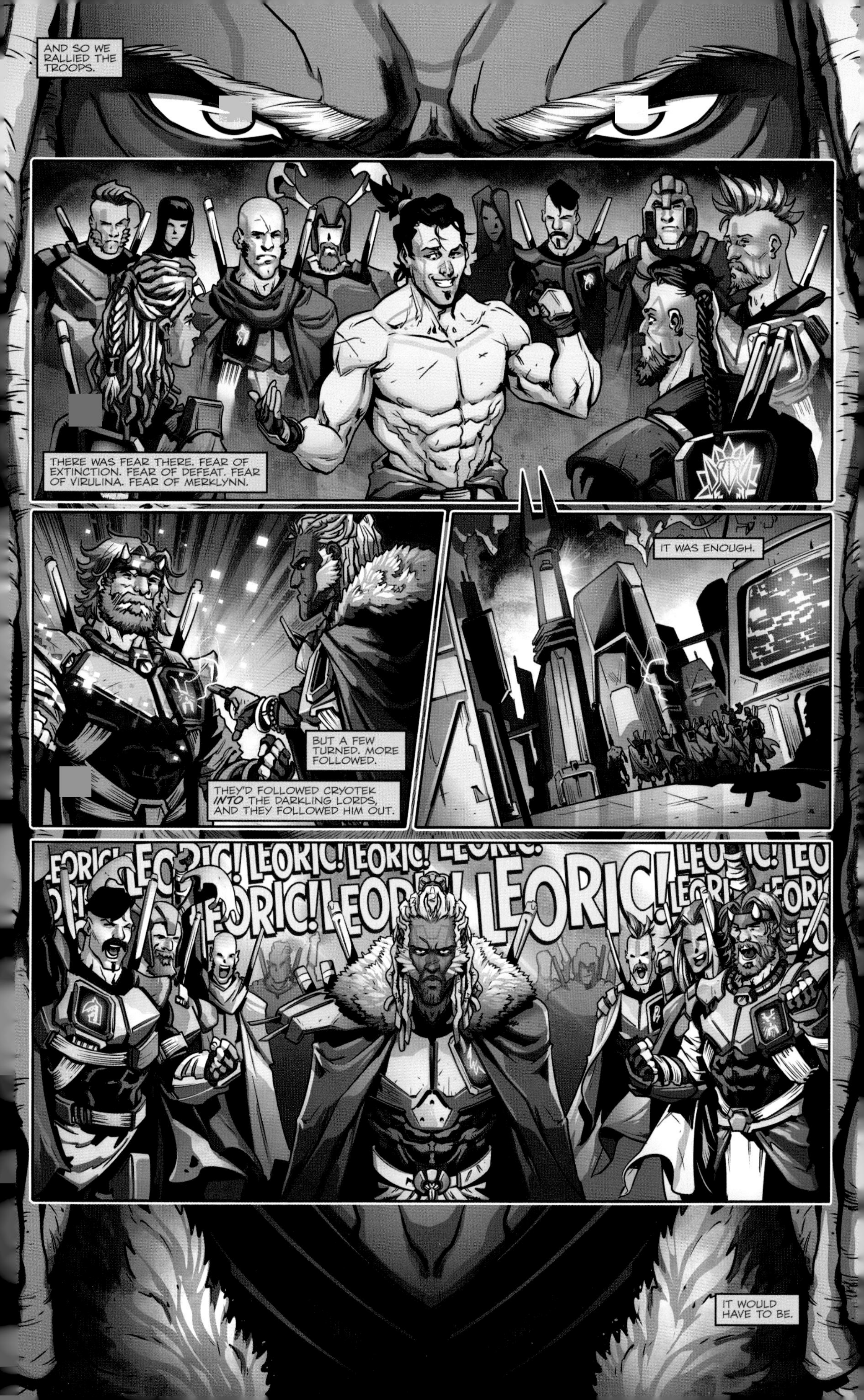
AND SO WE RALLIED THE TROOPS.
THERE WAS FEAR THERE. FEAR OF EXTINCTION. FEAR OF DEFEAT. FEAR OF VIRULINA. FEAR OF MERKLYNN.
BUT A FEW TURNED. MORE FOLLOWED.
THEY'D FOLLOWED CRYOTEK *INTO* THE DARKLING LORDS, AND THEY FOLLOWED HIM OUT.
IT WAS ENOUGH.
LEORIC! LEORIC! LEORIC! LEORIC! LEORIC!
IT WOULD HAVE TO BE.

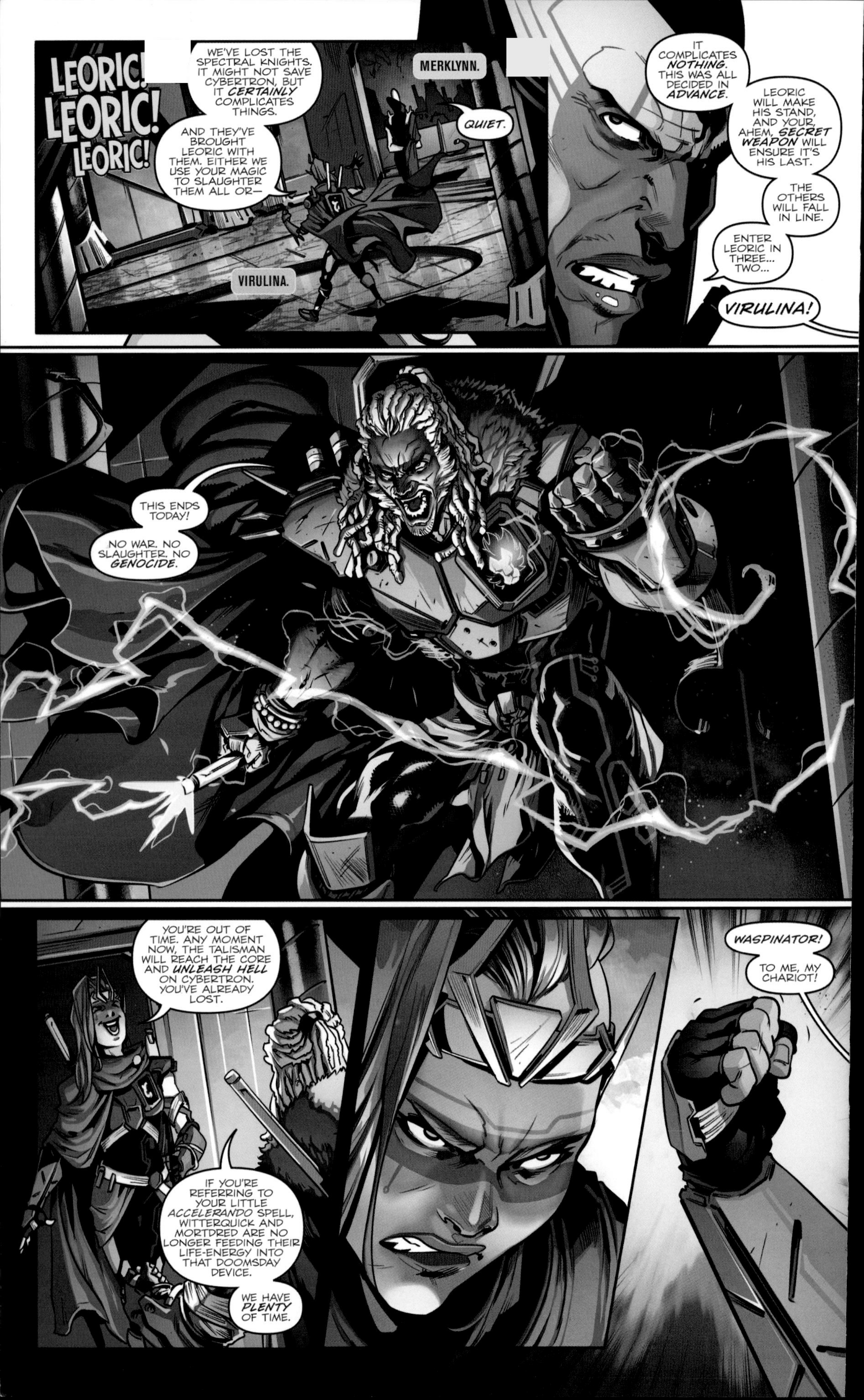
LEORIC! LEORIC! LEORIC!
WE'VE LOST THE SPECTRAL KNIGHTS. IT MIGHT NOT SAVE CYBERTRON, BUT IT CERTAINLY COMPLICATES THINGS.
AND THEY'VE BROUGHT LEORIC WITH THEM. EITHER WE USE YOUR MAGIC TO SLAUGHTER THEM ALL OR—
VIRULINA.
MERKLYNN.
QUIET.
IT COMPLICATES NOTHING. THIS WAS ALL DECIDED IN ADVANCE.
LEORIC WILL MAKE HIS STAND, AND YOUR, AHEM, SECRET WEAPON WILL ENSURE IT'S HIS LAST.
THE OTHERS WILL FALL IN LINE.
ENTER LEORIC IN THREE... TWO...
VIRULINA!
THIS ENDS TODAY!
NO WAR. NO SLAUGHTER. NO GENOCIDE.
YOU'RE OUT OF TIME. ANY MOMENT NOW, THE TALISMAN WILL REACH THE CORE AND UNLEASH HELL ON CYBERTRON. YOU'VE ALREADY LOST.
IF YOU'RE REFERRING TO YOUR LITTLE ACCELERANDO SPELL, WITTERQUICK AND MORTDRED ARE NO LONGER FEEDING THEIR LIFE-ENERGY INTO THAT DOOMSDAY DEVICE.
WE HAVE PLENTY OF TIME.
WASPINATOR!
TO ME, MY CHARIOT!

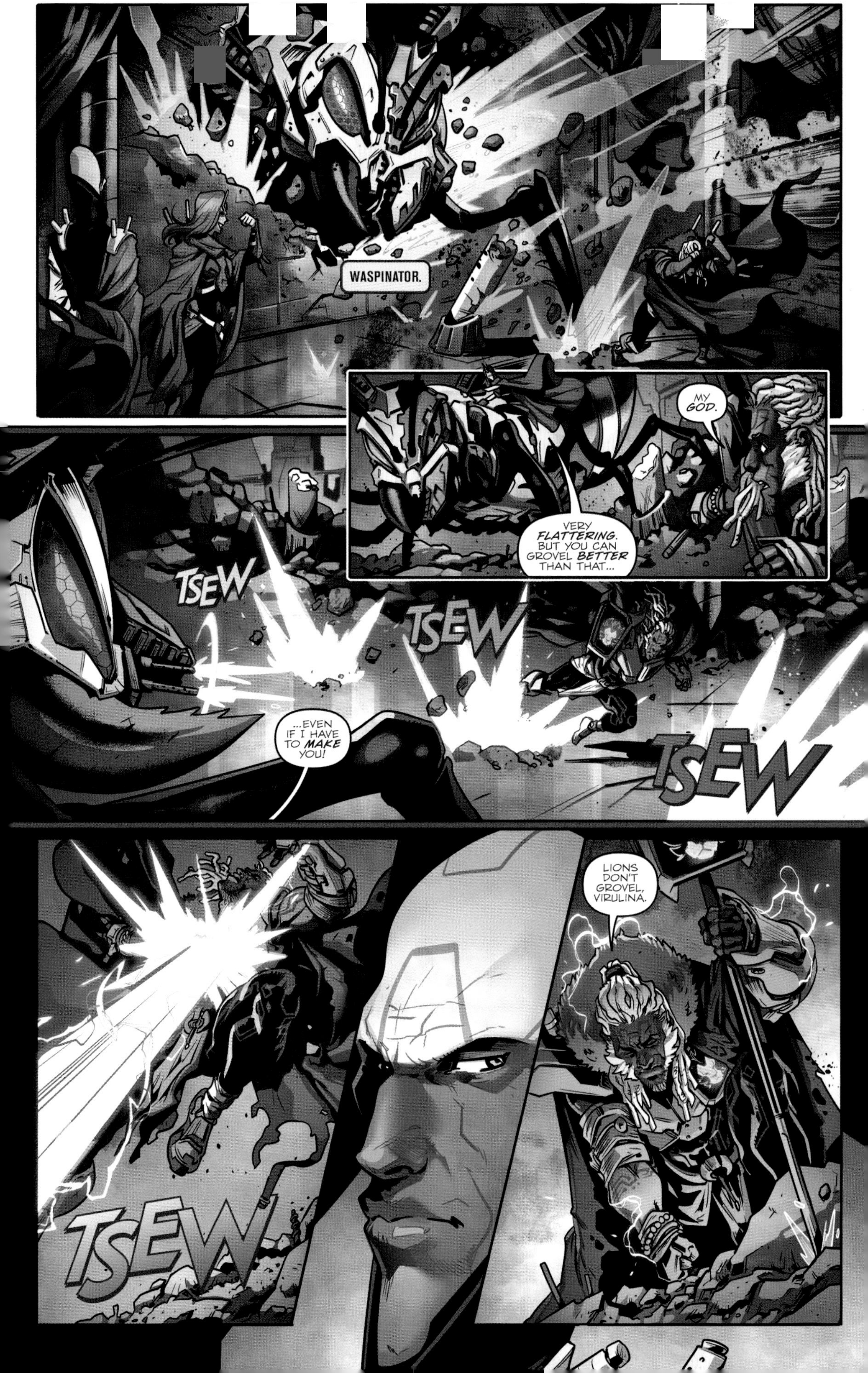
WASPINATOR.
MY GOD.
VERY FLATTERING. BUT YOU CAN GROVEL BETTER THAN THAT...
TSEW
TSEW
...EVEN IF I HAVE TO MAKE YOU!
TSEW
LIONS DON'T GROVEL, VIRULINA.
TSEW

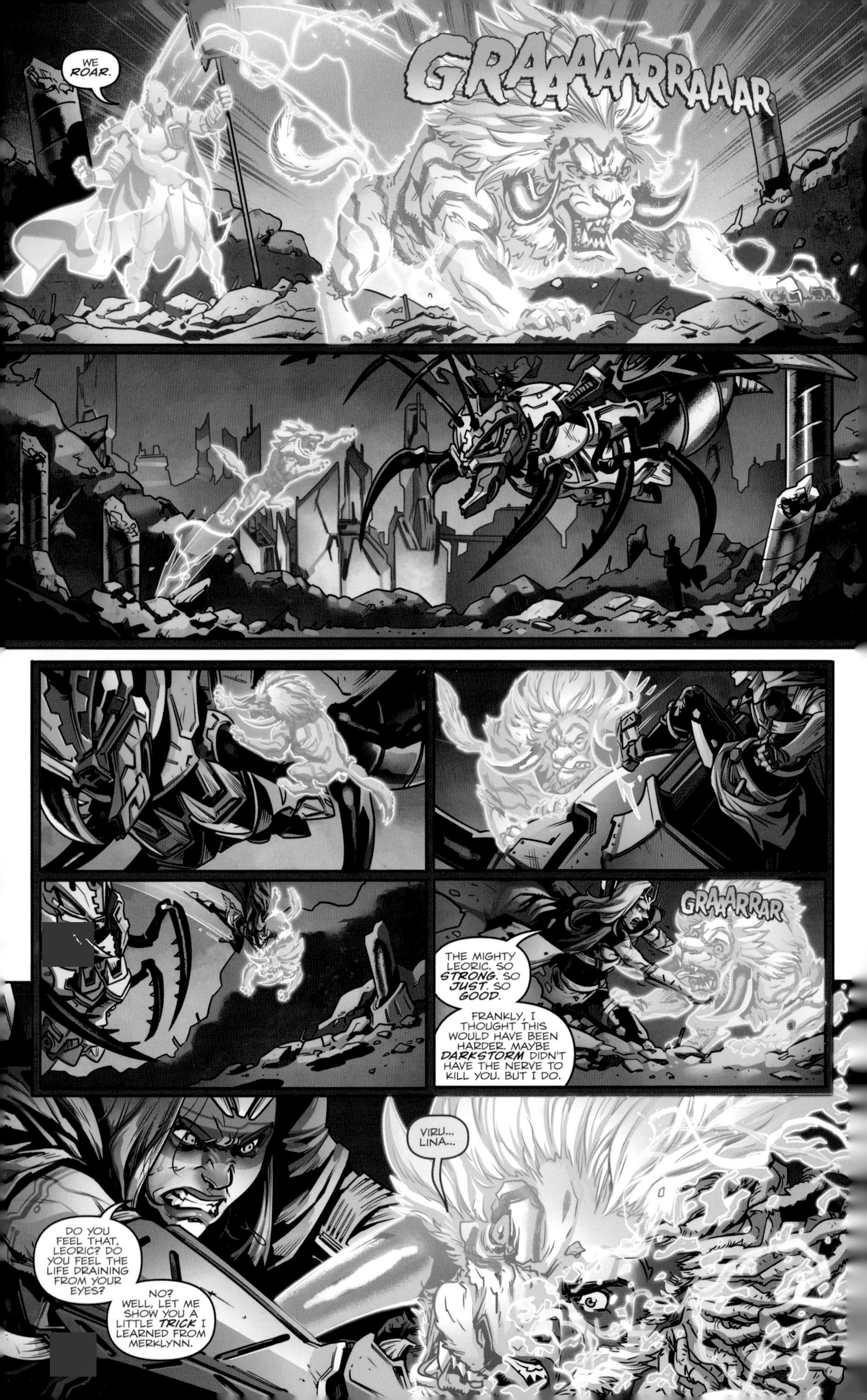
WE ROAR.
GRAAAAARRAAAR
GRAAARRAR
THE MIGHTY LEORIC. SO STRONG. SO JUST. SO GOOD.
FRANKLY, I THOUGHT THIS WOULD HAVE BEEN HARDER. MAYBE DARKSTORM DIDN'T HAVE THE NERVE TO KILL YOU. BUT I DO.
VIRU... LINA...
DO YOU FEEL THAT, LEORIC? DO YOU FEEL THE LIFE DRAINING FROM YOUR EYES?
NO? WELL, LET ME SHOW YOU A LITTLE TRICK I LEARNED FROM MERKLYNN.

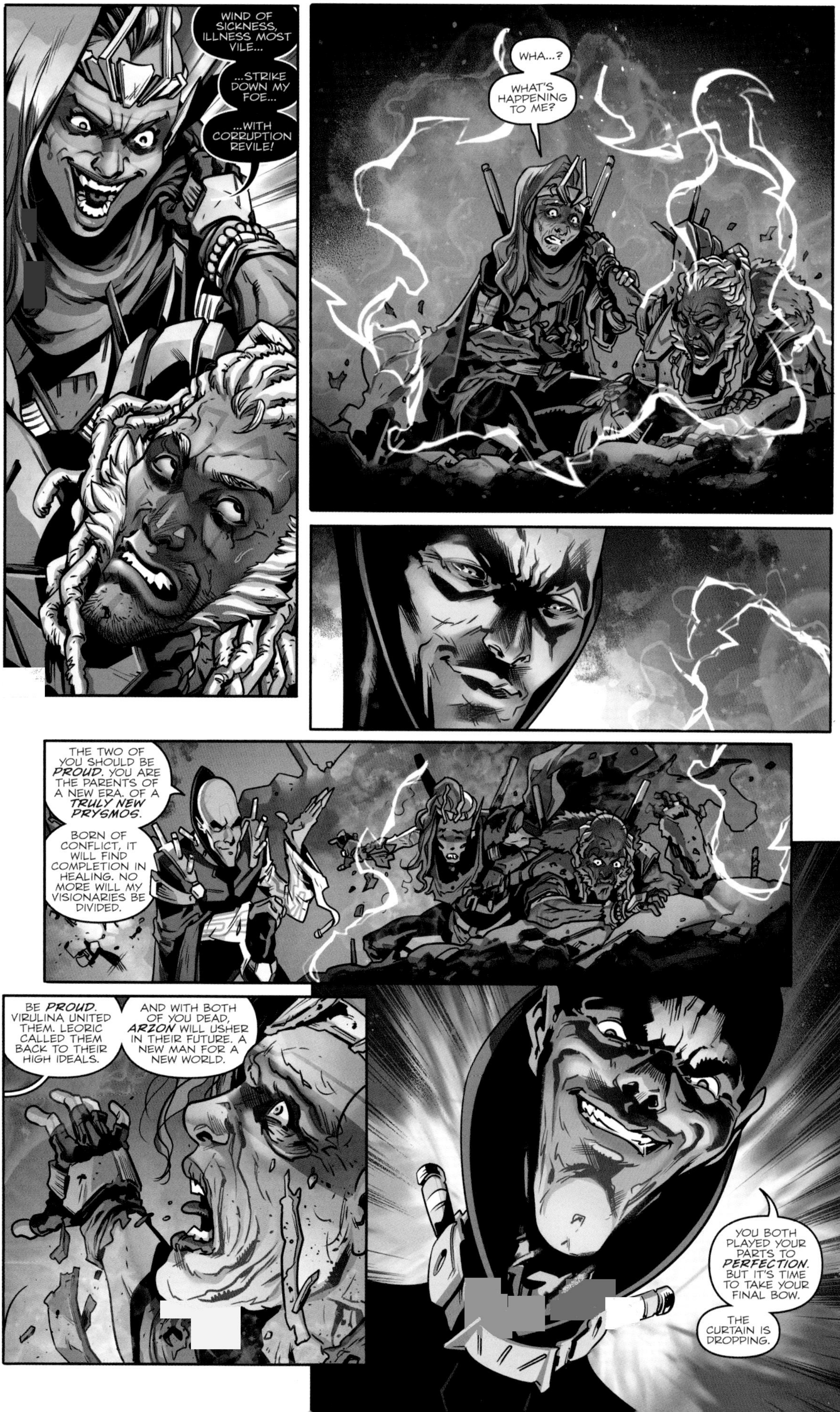
WIND OF SICKNESS, ILLNESS MOST VILE...
...STRIKE DOWN MY FOE...
...WITH CORRUPTION REVILE!
WHA...?
WHAT'S HAPPENING TO ME?
THE TWO OF YOU SHOULD BE PROUD. YOU ARE THE PARENTS OF A NEW ERA. OF A TRULY NEW PRYSMOS.
BORN OF CONFLICT, IT WILL FIND COMPLETION IN HEALING. NO MORE WILL MY VISIONARIES BE DIVIDED.
BE PROUD. VIRULINA UNITED THEM. LEORIC CALLED THEM BACK TO THEIR HIGH IDEALS.
AND WITH BOTH OF YOU DEAD, ARZON WILL USHER IN THEIR FUTURE. A NEW MAN FOR A NEW WORLD.
YOU BOTH PLAYED YOUR PARTS TO PERFECTION. BUT IT'S TIME TO TAKE YOUR FINAL BOW.
THE CURTAIN IS DROPPING.

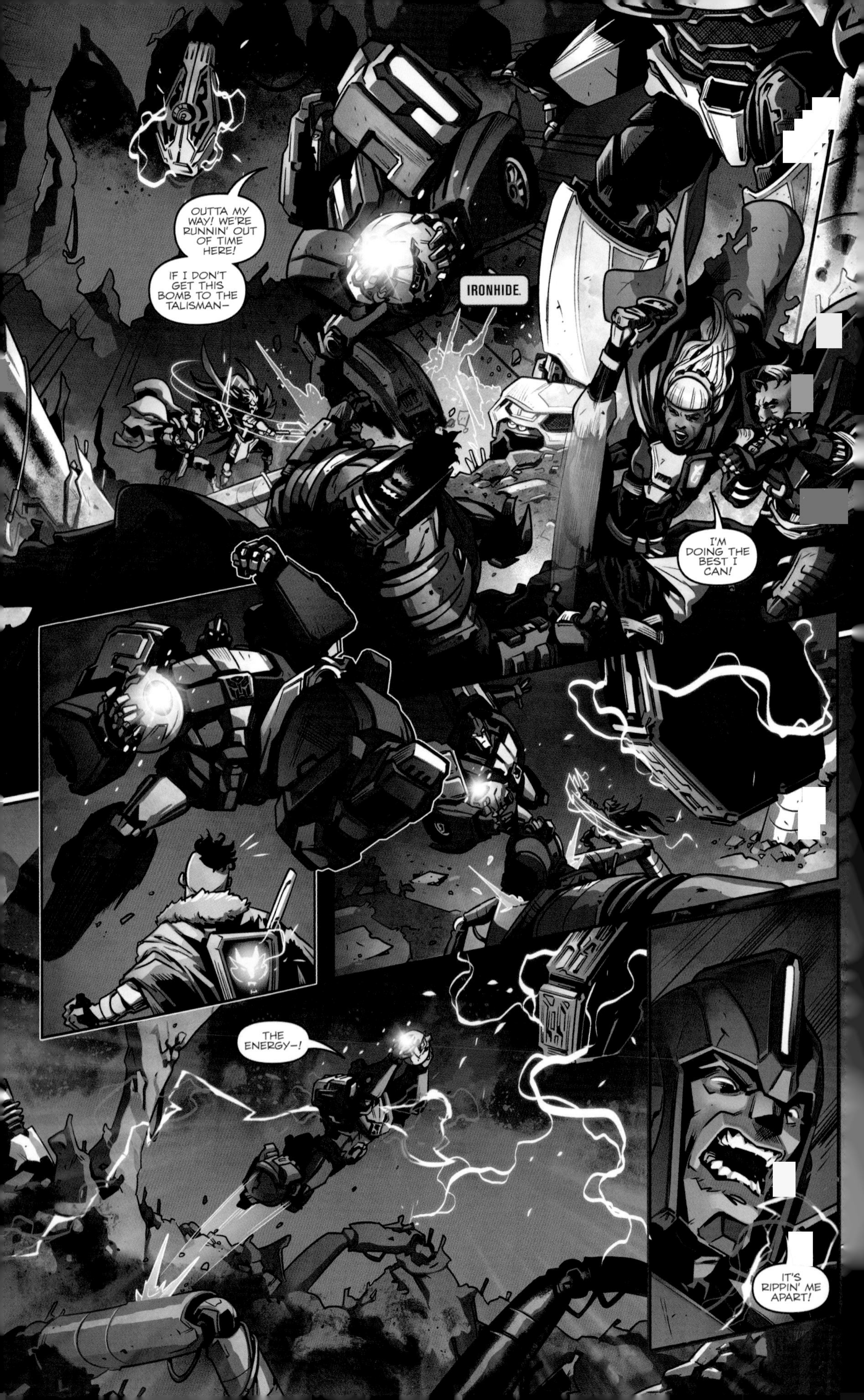
OUTTA MY WAY! WE'RE RUNNIN' OUT OF TIME HERE!
IF I DON'T GET THIS BOMB TO THE TALISMAN—
IRONHIDE.
I'M DOING THE BEST I CAN!
THE ENERGY—!
IT'S RIPPIN' ME APART!

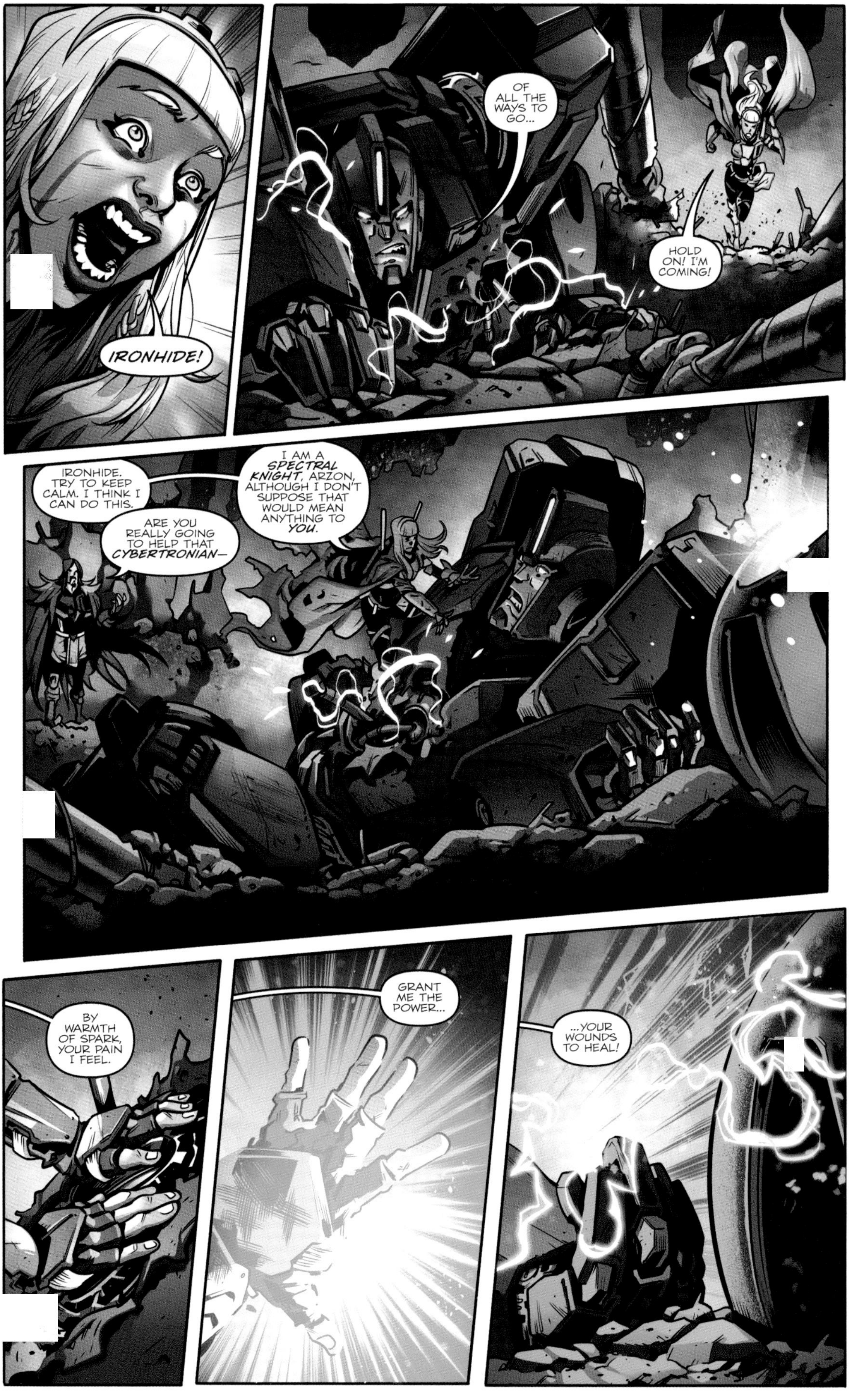
IRONHIDE!
OF ALL THE WAYS TO GO...
HOLD ON! I'M COMING!
IRONHIDE. TRY TO KEEP CALM. I THINK I CAN DO THIS.
ARE YOU REALLY GOING TO HELP THAT CYBERTRONIAN—
I AM A SPECTRAL KNIGHT, ARZON, ALTHOUGH I DON'T SUPPOSE THAT WOULD MEAN ANYTHING TO YOU.
BY WARMTH OF SPARK, YOUR PAIN I FEEL.
GRANT ME THE POWER...
...YOUR WOUNDS TO HEAL!

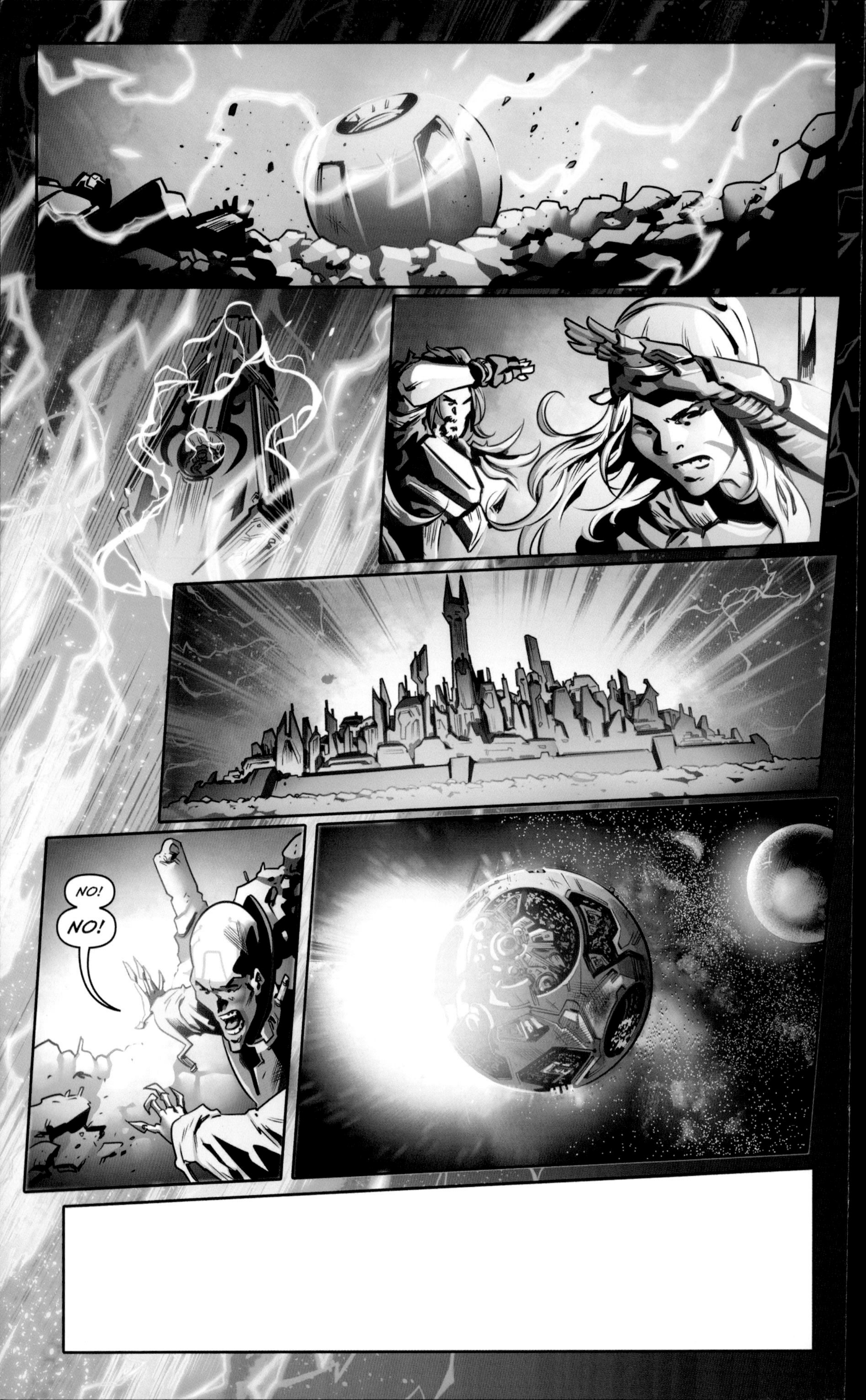
NO!
NO!

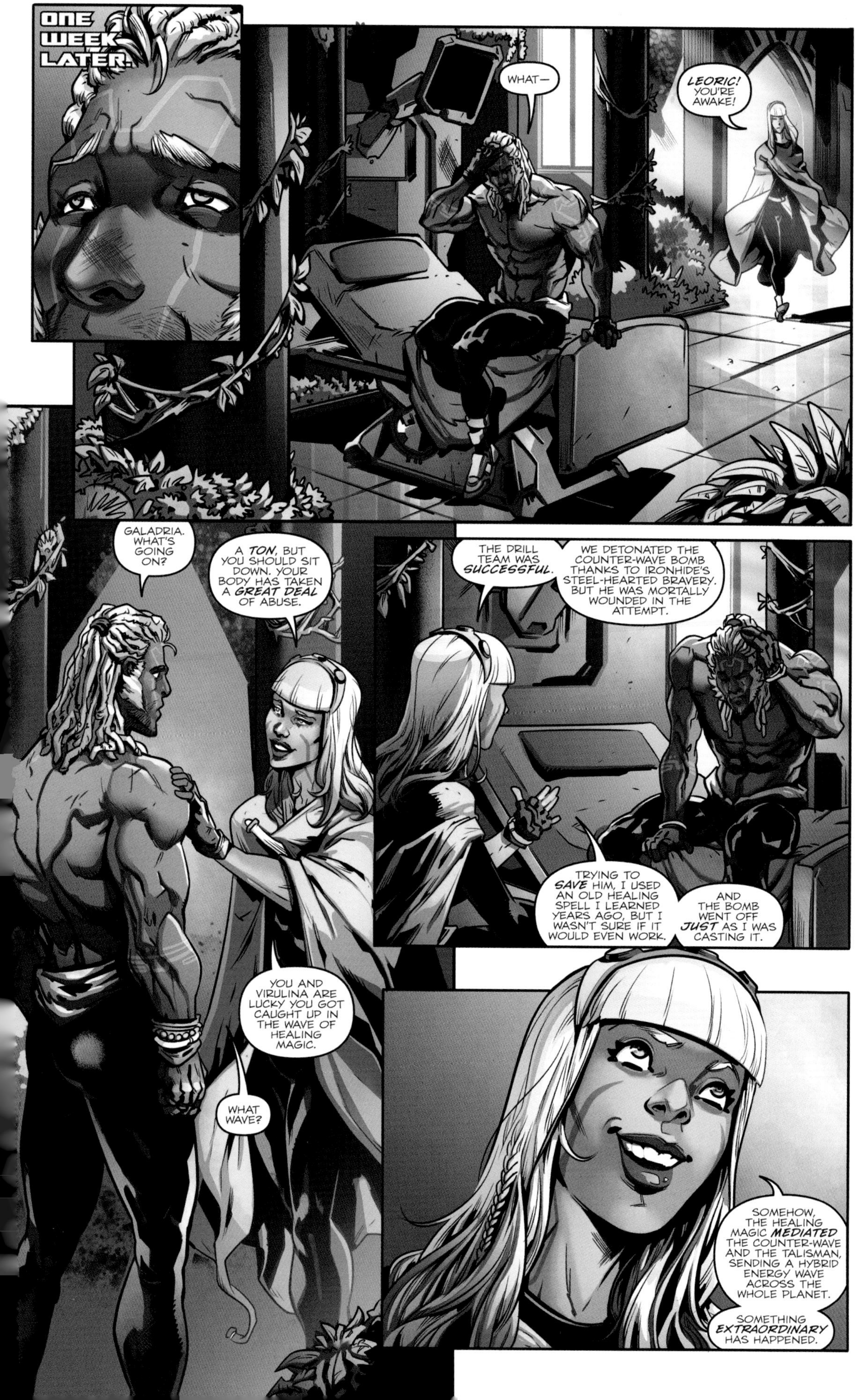
ONE WEEK LATER...
WHAT—
LEORIC! YOU'RE AWAKE!
GALADRIA. WHAT'S GOING ON?
A TON, BUT YOU SHOULD SIT DOWN. YOUR BODY HAS TAKEN A GREAT DEAL OF ABUSE.
THE DRILL TEAM WAS SUCCESSFUL.
WE DETONATED THE COUNTER-WAVE BOMB THANKS TO IRONHIDE'S STEEL-HEARTED BRAVERY. BUT HE WAS MORTALLY WOUNDED IN THE ATTEMPT.
TRYING TO SAVE HIM, I USED AN OLD HEALING SPELL I LEARNED YEARS AGO, BUT I WASN'T SURE IF IT WOULD EVEN WORK.
AND THE BOMB WENT OFF JUST AS I WAS CASTING IT.
YOU AND VIRULINA ARE LUCKY YOU GOT CAUGHT UP IN THE WAVE OF HEALING MAGIC.
WHAT WAVE?
SOMEHOW, THE HEALING MAGIC MEDIATED THE COUNTER-WAVE AND THE TALISMAN, SENDING A HYBRID ENERGY WAVE ACROSS THE WHOLE PLANET.
SOMETHING EXTRAORDINARY HAS HAPPENED.

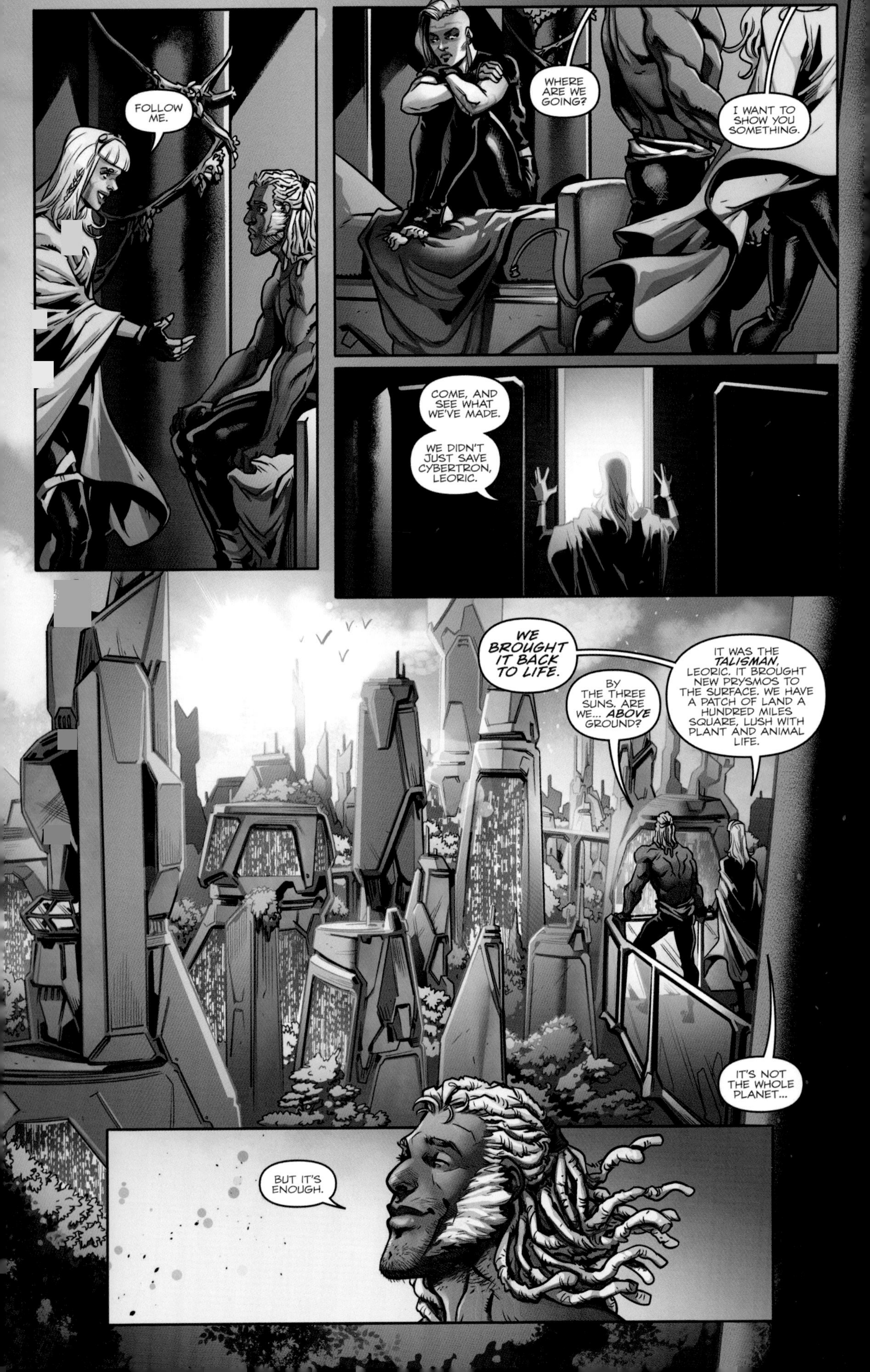
FOLLOW ME.
WHERE ARE WE GOING?
I WANT TO SHOW YOU SOMETHING.
COME, AND SEE WHAT WE'VE MADE.
WE DIDN'T JUST SAVE CYBERTRON, LEORIC.
WE BROUGHT IT BACK TO LIFE.
BY THE THREE SUNS. ARE WE... ABOVE GROUND?
IT WAS THE TALISMAN, LEORIC. IT BROUGHT NEW PRYSMOS TO THE SURFACE. WE HAVE A PATCH OF LAND A HUNDRED MILES SQUARE, LUSH WITH PLANT AND ANIMAL LIFE.
IT'S NOT THE WHOLE PLANET...
BUT IT'S ENOUGH.

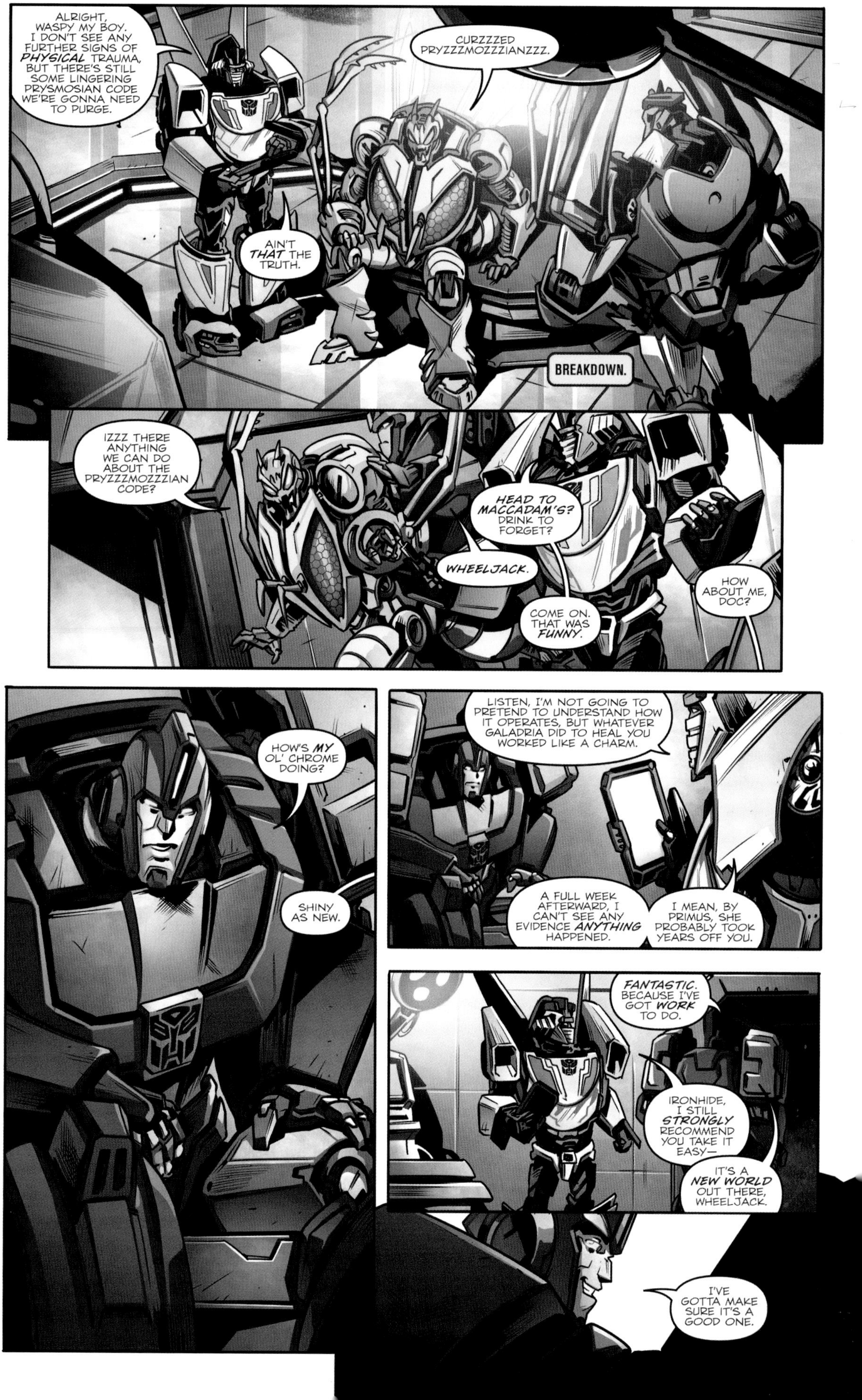

ALRIGHT, WASPY MY BOY. I DON'T SEE ANY FURTHER SIGNS OF PHYSICAL TRAUMA, BUT THERE'S STILL SOME LINGERING PRYSMOSIAN CODE WE'RE GONNA NEED TO PURGE.
CURZZZED PRYZZZMOZZZIANZZZ.
AIN'T THAT THE TRUTH.
BREAKDOWN.
IZZZ THERE ANYTHING WE CAN DO ABOUT THE PRYZZZMOZZZIAN CODE?
HEAD TO MACCADAM'S? DRINK TO FORGET?
WHEELJACK.
COME ON. THAT WAS FUNNY.
HOW ABOUT ME, DOC?
HOW'S MY OL' CHROME DOING?
SHINY AS NEW.
LISTEN, I'M NOT GOING TO PRETEND TO UNDERSTAND HOW IT OPERATES, BUT WHATEVER GALADRIA DID TO HEAL YOU WORKED LIKE A CHARM.
A FULL WEEK AFTERWARD, I CAN'T SEE ANY EVIDENCE ANYTHING HAPPENED.
I MEAN, BY PRIMUS, SHE PROBABLY TOOK YEARS OFF YOU.
FANTASTIC. BECAUSE I'VE GOT WORK TO DO.
IRONHIDE, I STILL STRONGLY RECOMMEND YOU TAKE IT EASY—
IT'S A NEW WORLD OUT THERE, WHEELJACK.
I'VE GOTTA MAKE SURE IT'S A GOOD ONE.

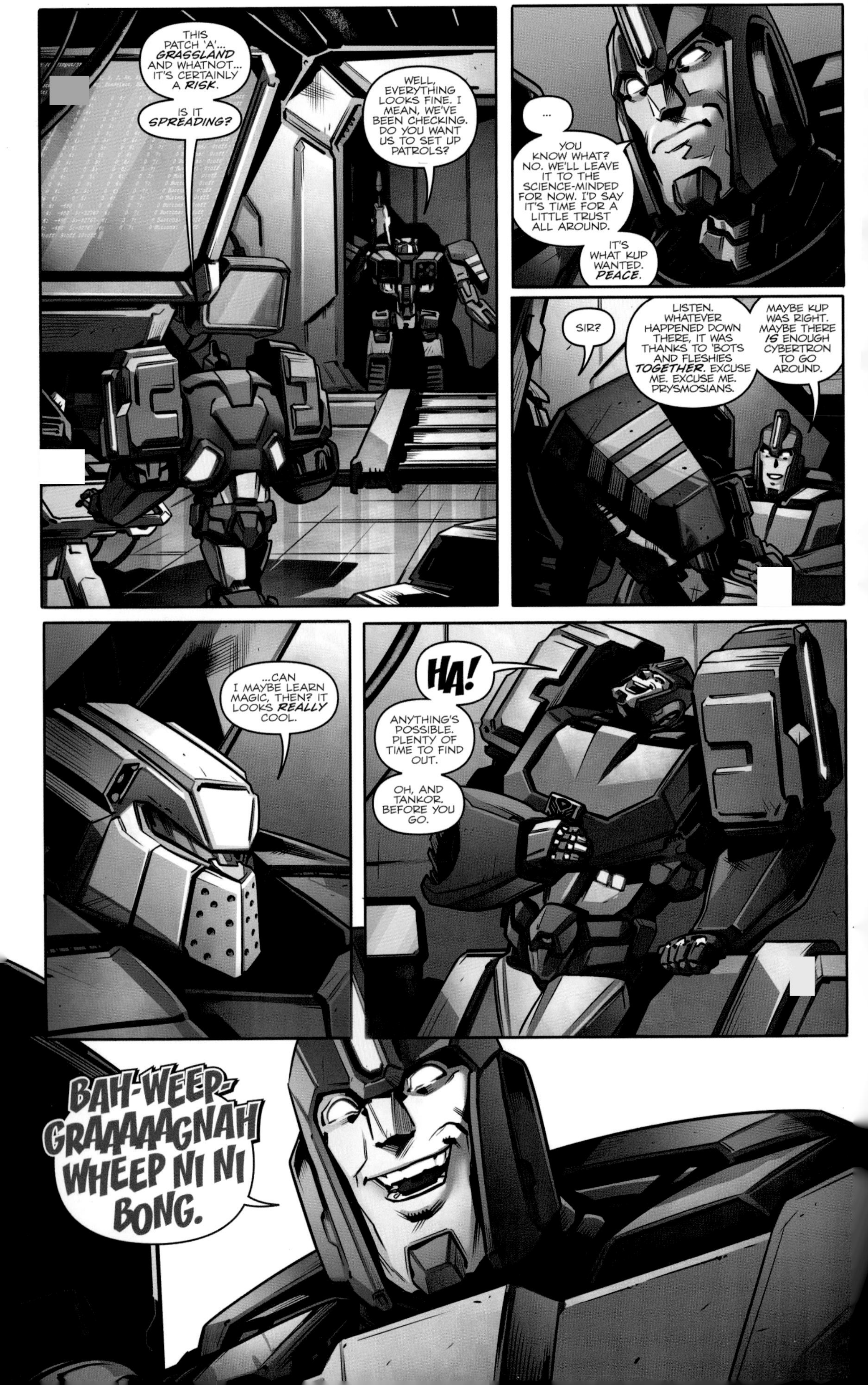
THIS PATCH 'A'... GRASSLAND AND WHATNOT... IT'S CERTAINLY A RISK.
IS IT SPREADING?
WELL, EVERYTHING LOOKS FINE. I MEAN, WE'VE BEEN CHECKING. DO YOU WANT US TO SET UP PATROLS?
...
YOU KNOW WHAT? NO. WE'LL LEAVE IT TO THE SCIENCE-MINDED FOR NOW. I'D SAY IT'S TIME FOR A LITTLE TRUST ALL AROUND.
IT'S WHAT KUP WANTED. PEACE.
SIR?
LISTEN. WHATEVER HAPPENED DOWN THERE, IT WAS THANKS TO 'BOTS AND FLESHIES TOGETHER. EXCUSE ME. EXCUSE ME. PRYSMOSIANS.
MAYBE KUP WAS RIGHT. MAYBE THERE IS ENOUGH CYBERTRON TO GO AROUND.
...CAN I MAYBE LEARN MAGIC, THEN? IT LOOKS REALLY COOL.
HA!
ANYTHING'S POSSIBLE. PLENTY OF TIME TO FIND OUT.
OH, AND TANKOR. BEFORE YOU GO.
BAH-WEEP-GRAAAAAGNAH WHEEP NI NI BONG.

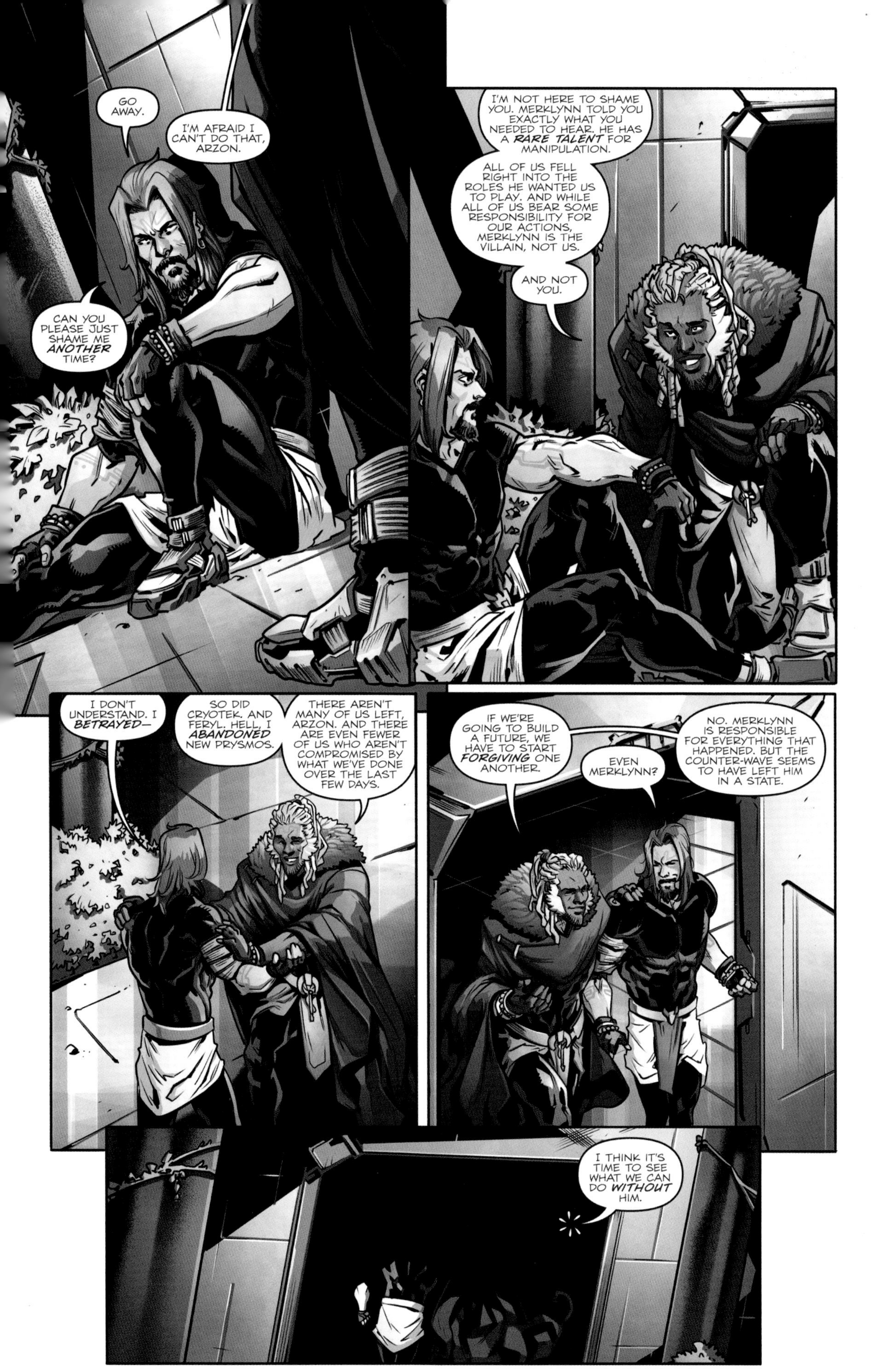
GO AWAY.
I'M AFRAID I CAN'T DO THAT, ARZON.
CAN YOU PLEASE JUST SHAME ME *ANOTHER* TIME?
I'M NOT HERE TO SHAME YOU. MERKLYNN TOLD YOU EXACTLY WHAT YOU NEEDED TO HEAR. HE HAS A *RARE TALENT* FOR MANIPULATION.
ALL OF US FELL RIGHT INTO THE ROLES HE WANTED US TO PLAY. AND WHILE ALL OF US BEAR SOME RESPONSIBILITY FOR OUR ACTIONS, MERKLYNN IS THE VILLAIN, NOT US.
AND NOT YOU.
I DON'T UNDERSTAND. I *BETRAYED*—
SO DID CRYOTEK. AND FERYL. HELL, I *ABANDONED* NEW PRYSMOS.
THERE AREN'T MANY OF US LEFT, ARZON. AND THERE ARE EVEN FEWER OF US WHO AREN'T COMPROMISED BY WHAT WE'VE DONE OVER THE LAST FEW DAYS.
IF WE'RE GOING TO BUILD A FUTURE, WE HAVE TO START *FORGIVING* ONE ANOTHER.
EVEN MERKLYNN?
NO. MERKLYNN IS RESPONSIBLE FOR EVERYTHING THAT HAPPENED. BUT THE COUNTER-WAVE SEEMS TO HAVE LEFT HIM IN A STATE.
I THINK IT'S TIME TO SEE WHAT WE CAN DO *WITHOUT* HIM.

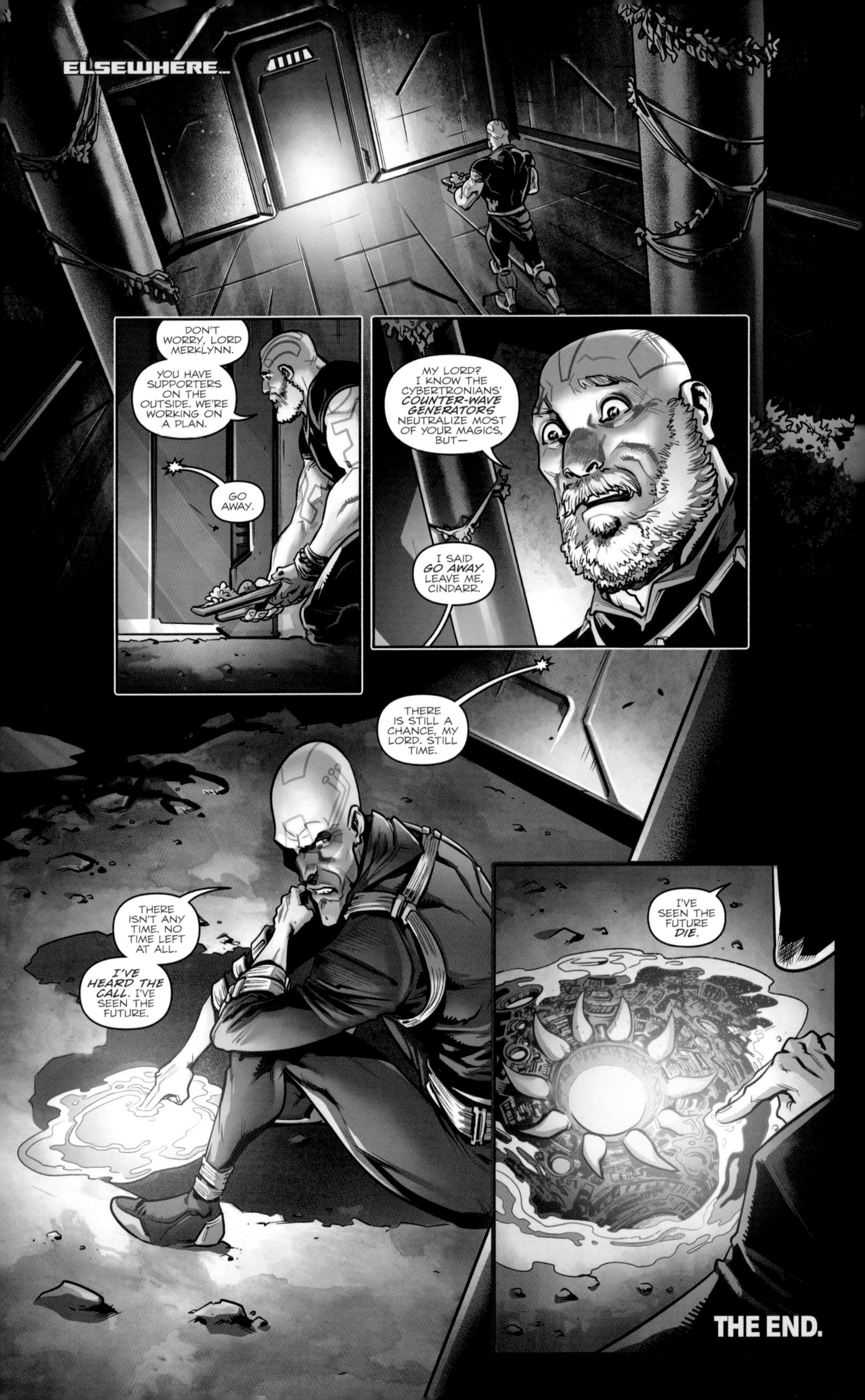
ELSEWHERE...
DON'T WORRY, LORD MERKLYNN.
YOU HAVE SUPPORTERS ON THE OUTSIDE. WE'RE WORKING ON A PLAN.
GO AWAY.
MY LORD? I KNOW THE CYBERTRONIANS' COUNTER-WAVE GENERATORS NEUTRALIZE MOST OF YOUR MAGICS, BUT—
I SAID GO AWAY. LEAVE ME, CINDARR.
THERE IS STILL A CHANCE, MY LORD. STILL TIME.
THERE ISN'T ANY TIME. NO TIME LEFT AT ALL.
I'VE HEARD THE CALL. I'VE SEEN THE FUTURE.
I'VE SEEN THE FUTURE DIE.
THE END.

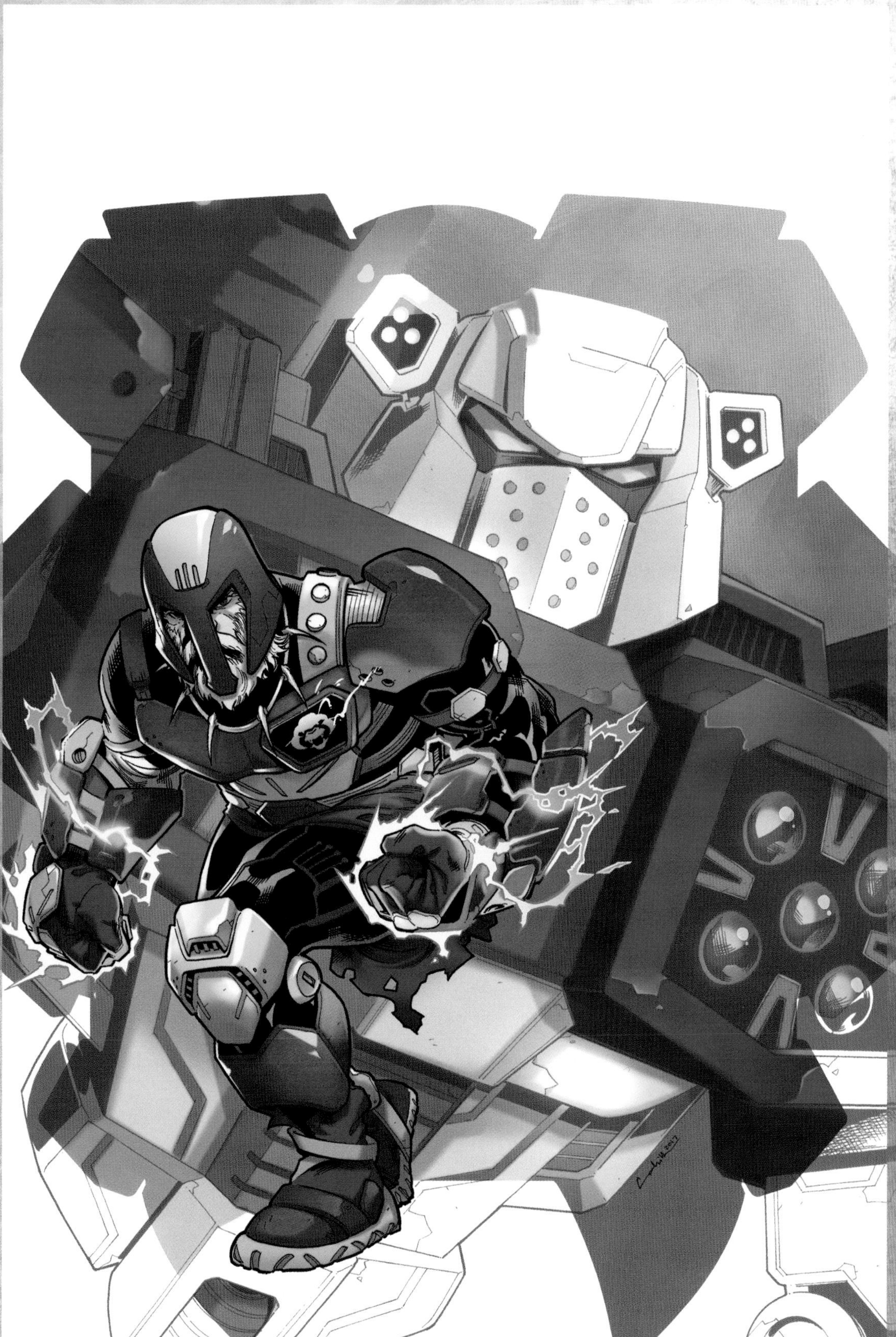

ART BY **BRENDAN CAHILL**
COLORS BY **LAUREN BENNETT**

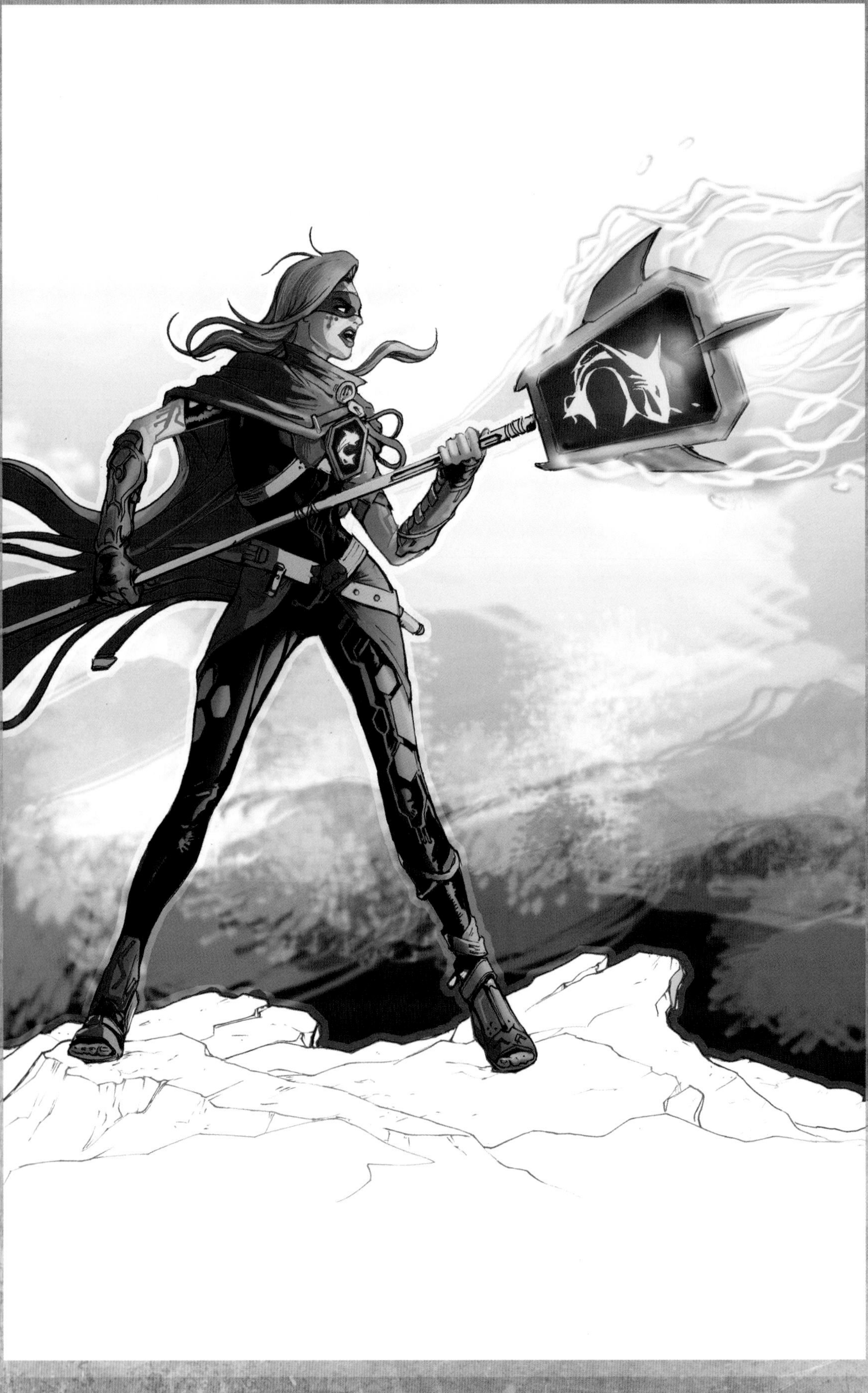

ART BY ANDREW GRIFFITH

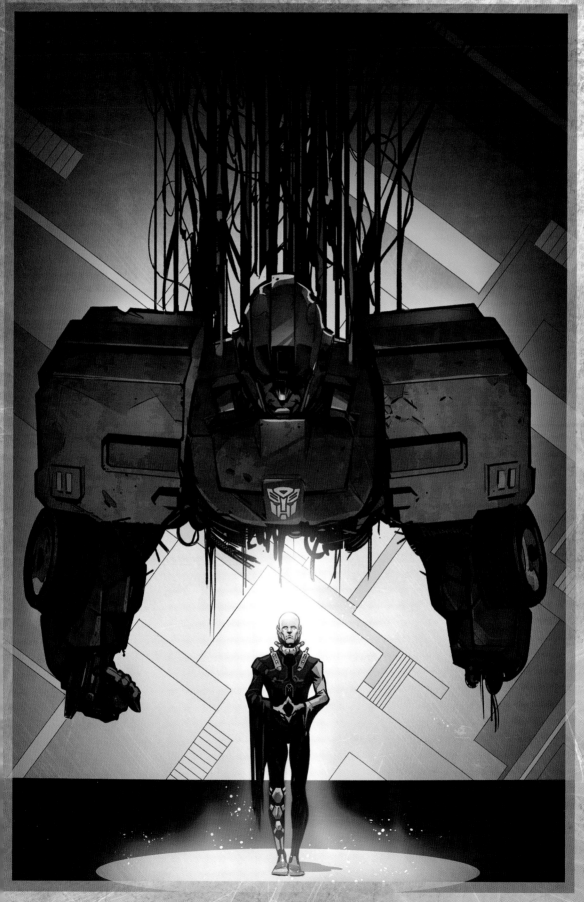

ART BY **ANGEL HERNANDEZ**
COLORS BY **ESTHER SANZ**

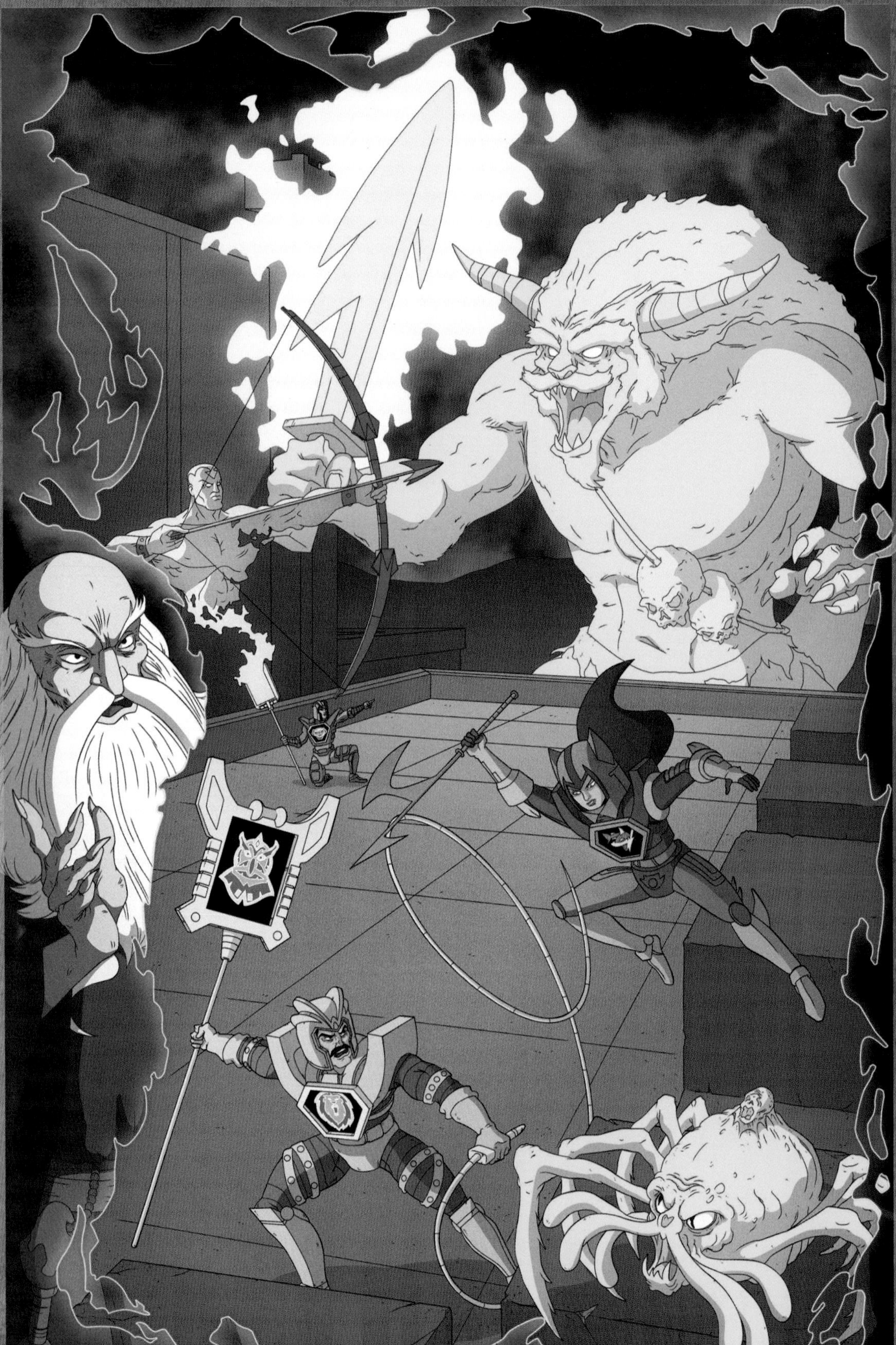

ART BY **PHILIP MURPHY**

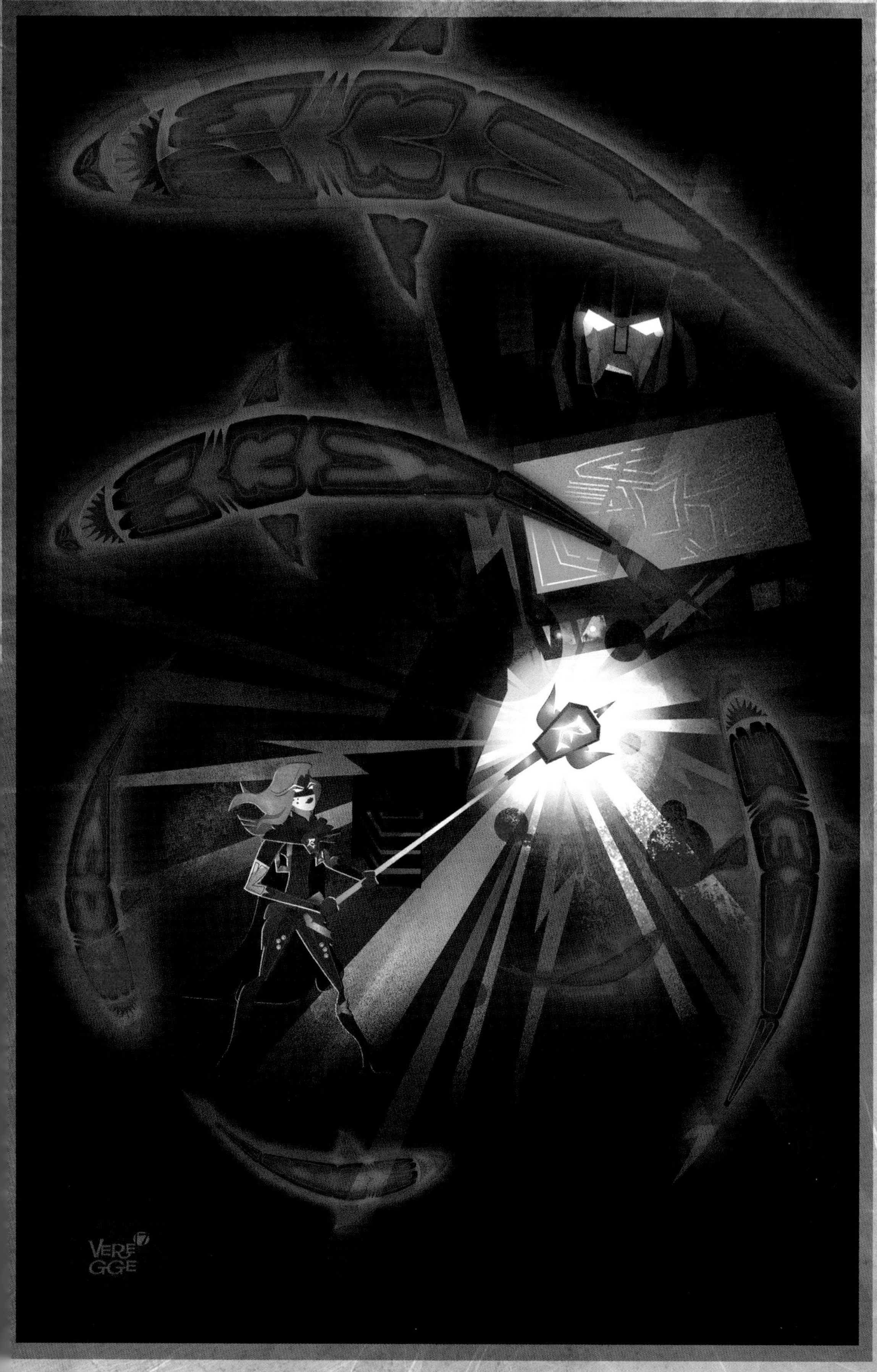
VEREGGE

ART BY **JEFFREY VEREGGE**

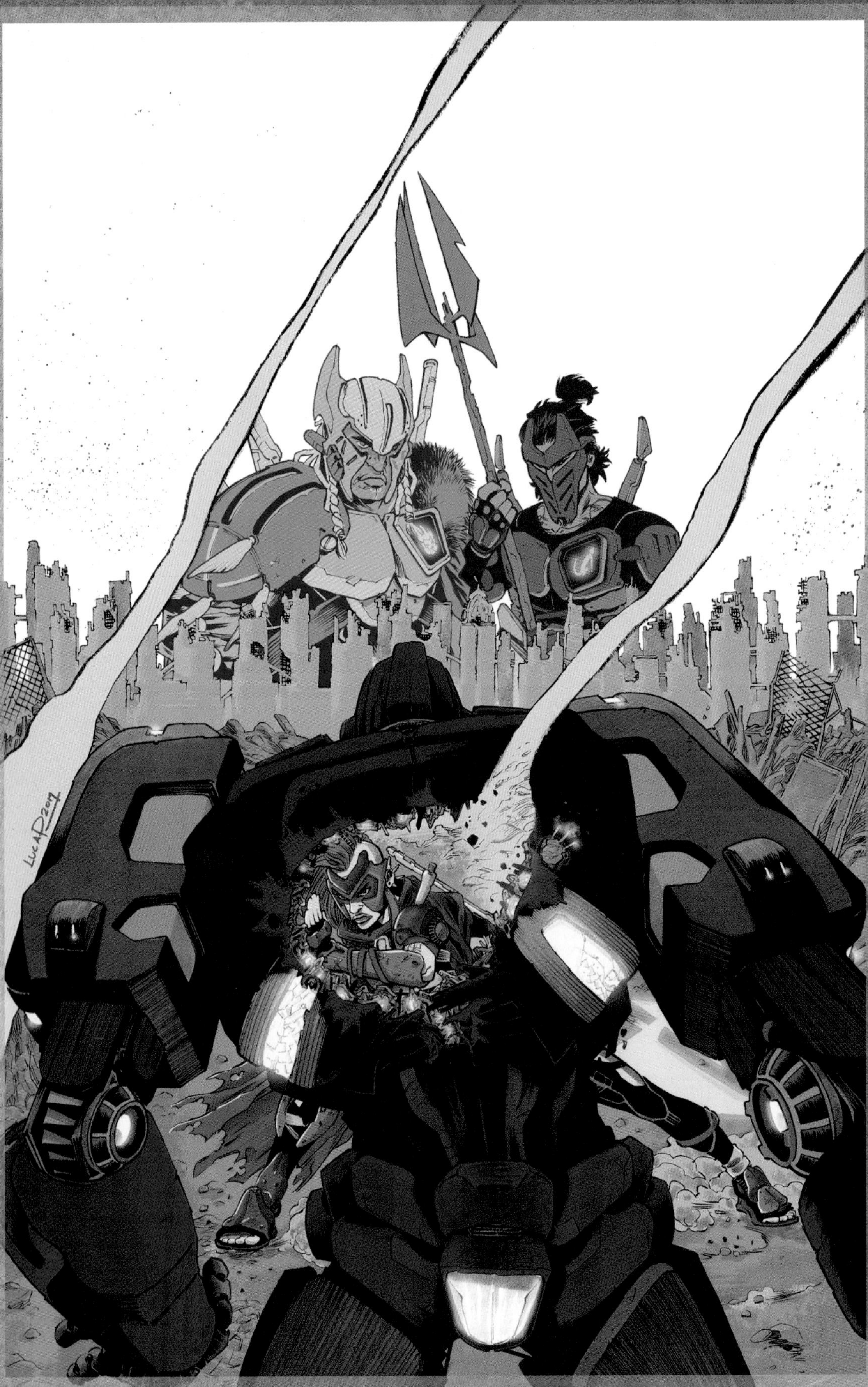

ART BY **LUCA PIZZARI**

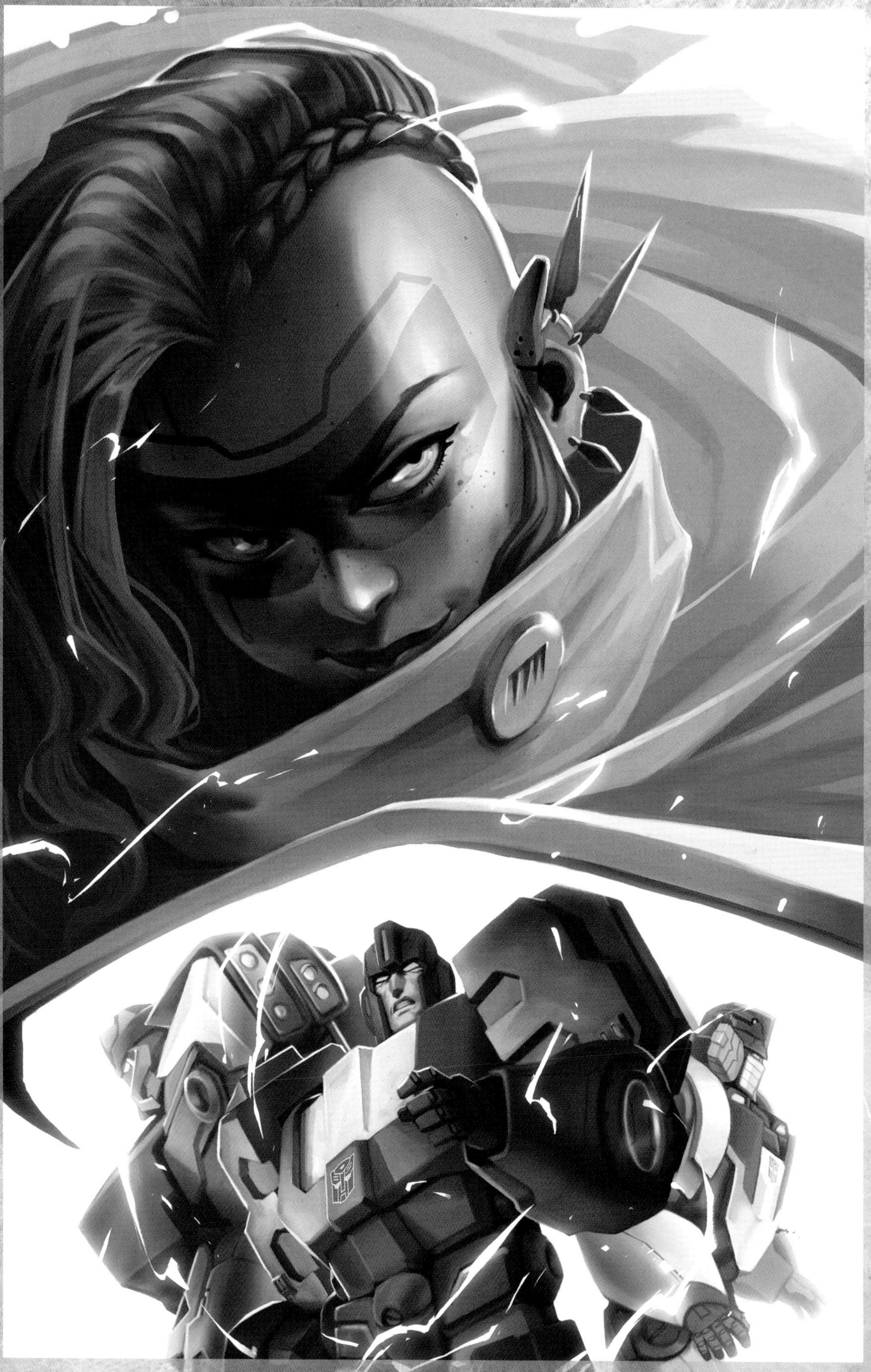

ART BY **SARA PITRE-DUROCHER**

THE ART OF THE PROCESS

TRANSFORMERS VS VISIONARIES #2 "CYBERTRON NO MORE"

ONE

Panel 1: Wide shot. New Prysmos from the air. In the largely-empty streets, we see a red form racing. It's IRONHIDE's alt-mode.

1. CAPTION: New Prysmos. Miles beneath the surface of Cybertron.

Panel 2: Interior, a winding staircase in Merklynn's tower. VIRULINA is leading CRAVEX up the stairs, triumphant. CRAVEX is hauling KUP's head; he's a big guy. Maybe its strapped to his back.

2. VIRULINA: <u>Faster</u>, Cravex.

3. VIRULINA: This is our <u>moment</u>.

Panel 3: Close on IRONHIDE's alt-form, exiting the energy barrier through TANKOR's checkpoint at breakneck speed, nearly hitting him in the process.

4. TANKOR: <u>Whoa</u>!

5. IRONHIDE: Ironhide to <u>Cybertron Command</u>! Kup is <u>dead</u>!

6. IRONHIDE: Repeat, the Prysmosians have <u>killed Kup</u>!

Panel 4: Interior, the staircase. LEORIC is chasing VIRULINA and CRAVEX up the stairs, furious.

7. LEORIC: <u>Virulina</u>! Stop!

8. LEORIC: Do you have any idea what you've done?

Panel 5: VIRULINA turns her head.

9. VIRULINA: Saved us, Leoric.

10. VIRULINA: I've <u>saved</u> us.

TRANSFORMERS VS VISIONARIES #2 / Magdalene Visaggio

TWO

Panel 1: MERKLYNN's sanctum. VIRULINA enters triumphantly, CRAVEX and LEORIC behind her. MERKLYNN, still restrained, in the foreground, his back to the door.

1. MERKLYNN: I knew I could trust you to <u>take the hint</u>.

2. VIRULINA: My Lord. The Cybertronian died like <u>swine</u>.

Panel 2: MERKLYNN turns to face the camera. His two guards have also been destroyed, and the wreckage lies on either side of him. MERKLYNN is perfectly neutral as he breaks his <u>own</u> bonds with a crackle of magical energy.

3. MERKLYNN: Yes.

4. MERKLYNN: It is characteristic of them.

5. SFX: KSSH

Panel 3: LEORIC, eyes wide in horror.

6. LEORIC: Merklynn!

7. LEORIC: You can't tell me you <u>condone</u>...

8. LEORIC: ...We were trying to make <u>peace</u> with them. An accommodation. You said—

Panel 4: MERKLYNN, VIRULINA, and CRAVEX walk toward the balcony away from LEORIC.

9. MERKLYNN: I said that we must place <u>our survival first</u>, child. Had the Cybertronians been willing to respect us, perhaps none of this would have come to pass.

10. MERKLYNN: But as they have <u>not</u>...

Panel 5: LEORIC, alone.

1. MERKLYNN (OP): ...I see <u>few other options</u> for us.

TRANSFORMERS VS VISIONARIES #2 / Magdalene Visaggio

THREE

Panel 1: Inset panel. MERKLYNN, VIRULINA, and CRAVEX exit onto the balcony; beneath them, we see the *entire population* of New Prysmos gathered, waiting.

1. MERKLYNN: Now, Virulina...

2. MERKLYNN: ...your people await you.

Panel 2: SPLASH! From below, looking up at the balcony of the tower, we can see CRAVEX holding up Kup's head in victory. VIRULINA takes the lead, standing in the most visible position, her cape waving dramatically in the wind.

3. VIRULINA (BL): Citizens! Remnant of Prysmos!

4. VIRULINA (BL): We are no longer <u>prisoners</u>! Our destinies can be ours once again!

5. VIRLINA (BL): Our magic is <u>strong</u>! The Cybertronians can be <u>beaten</u>! And this planet will be...

6. VIRULINA (TITLE): CYBERTRON NO MORE!

TRANSFORMERS VS VISIONARIES #2 / Magdalene Visaggio

FOUR

Panel 1: Exterior, the Redoubt, the fortress HQ of the Spectral Knights. It's classical and heroic, with columns and a large dome straight out of *Star Trek*, gleaming pure white.

1. CAPTION: The <u>Redoubt</u>.

2. CAPTION: Fortress of the Spectral Knights.

Panel 2: Interior, the war room. No large conference table here; the room is covered in maps of the city marking strategic points, and each of the VISIONARIES – ARZON, ECTAR, WITTERQUICK, and GALADRIA – are standing, frustrated and hopeless as LEORIC harangues them.

3. LEORIC: We're facing an <u>existential threat</u>, brethren. An <u>entire planet</u> marshaled against our transplanted city. An entire planet of <u>thirty-foot monsters</u> who will want us dead...all because Virulina couldn't be patient.

4. LEORIC: If we can't <u>stop this from escalating</u>, the whole weight of Cybertron will fall on us. Peace <u>has</u> to be our way forward.

5. ARZON: But first, <u>war</u>. Right?

Panel 3: LEORIC, solemnly.

6. LEORIC: The quicker we can neutralize the Darkling Lords, the quicker—

Panel 4: ARZON, skeptical.

7. ARZON: I'm not sure about that. How many Prysmosians are left? Ten-thousand? Eleven?

8. ARZON: We're not exactly suffering from an embarrassment of independence at the moment.

Panel 5: LEORIC, angry and disappointed, glares offpanel.

9. ARZON (OP): Is it possible that Virulina's <u>right</u>?

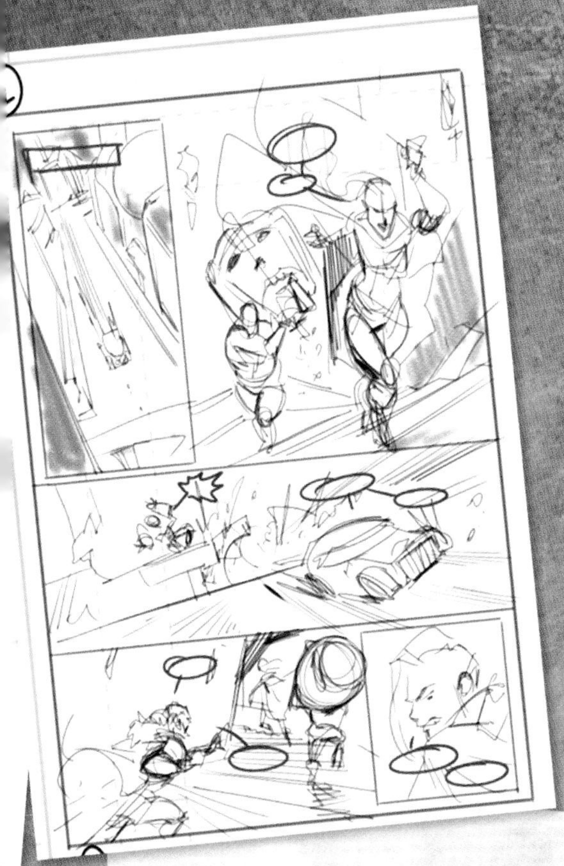

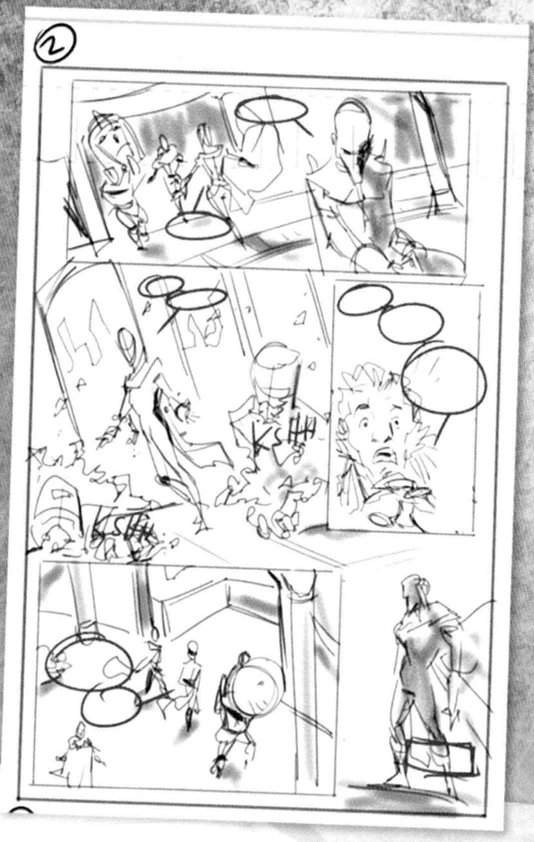
2
KSHH
KSHH

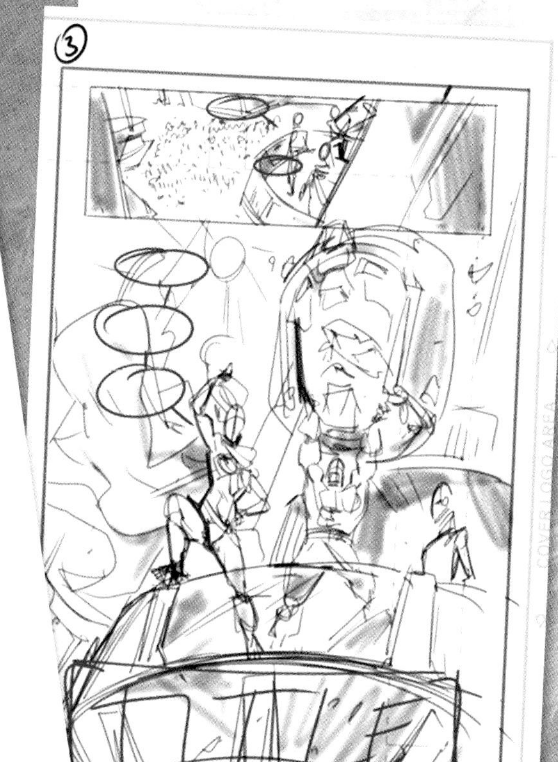
3
TITLE

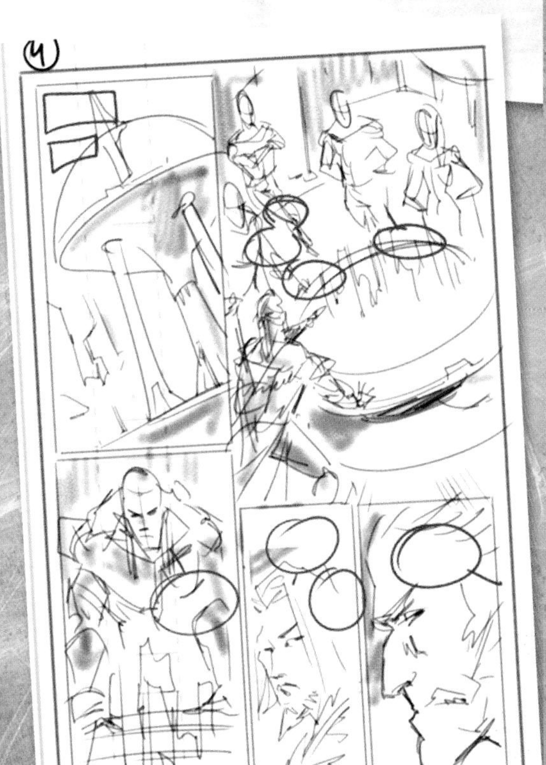
4

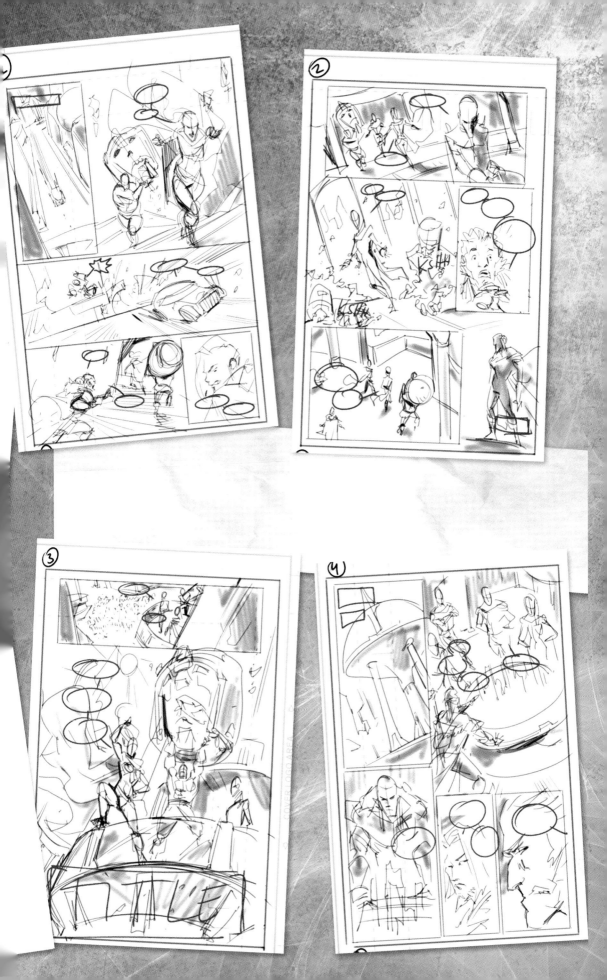

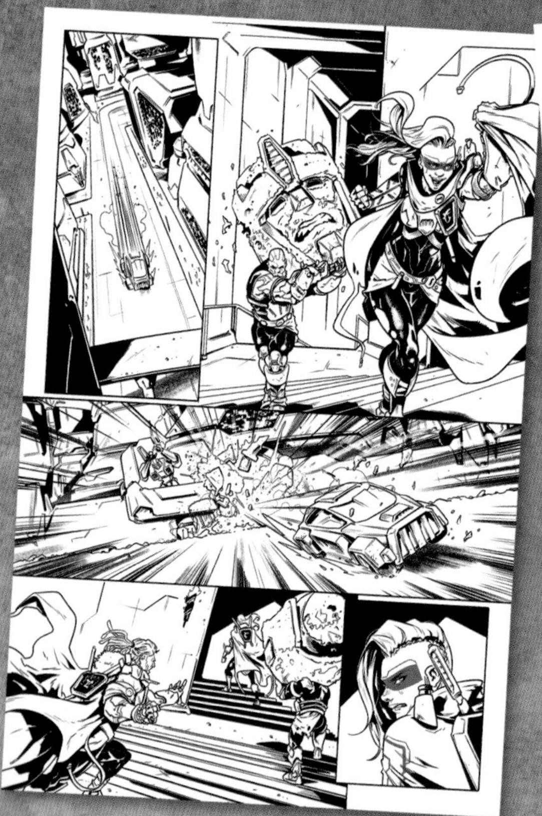

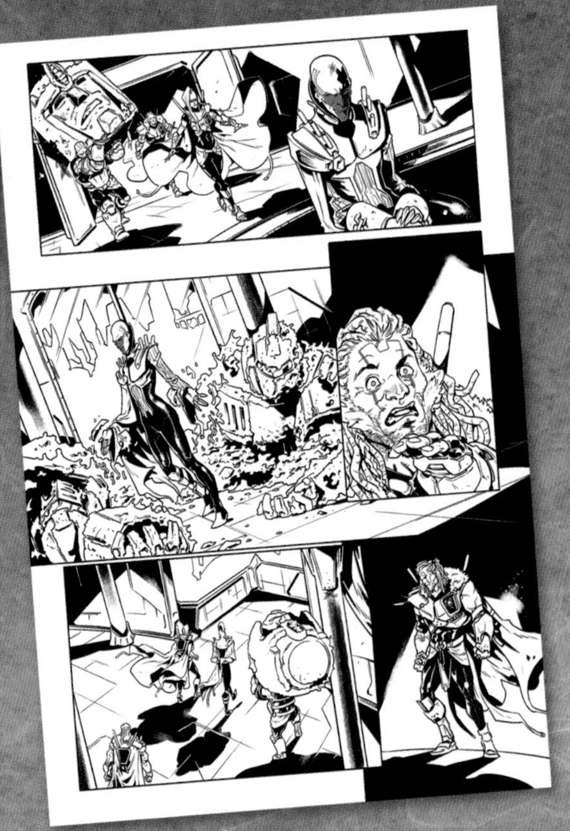

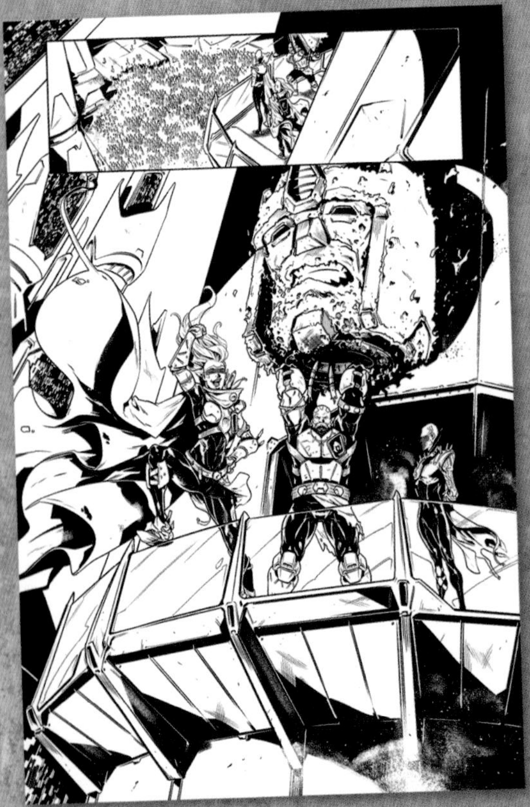

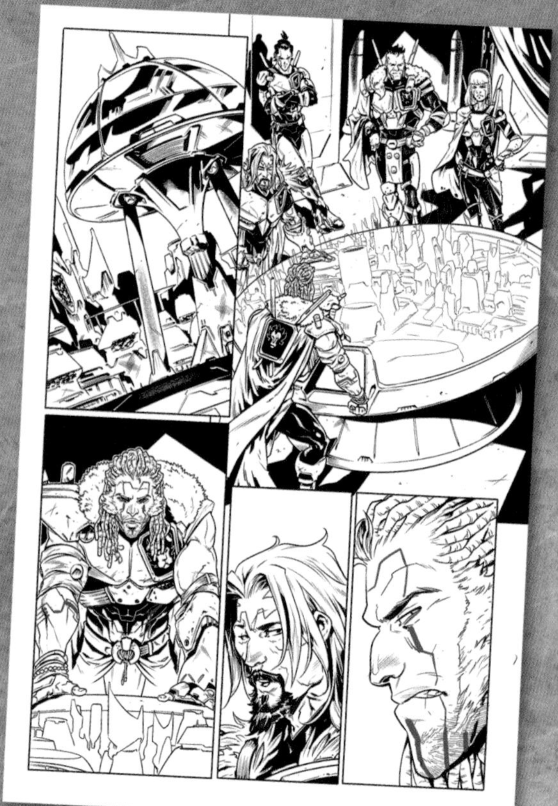

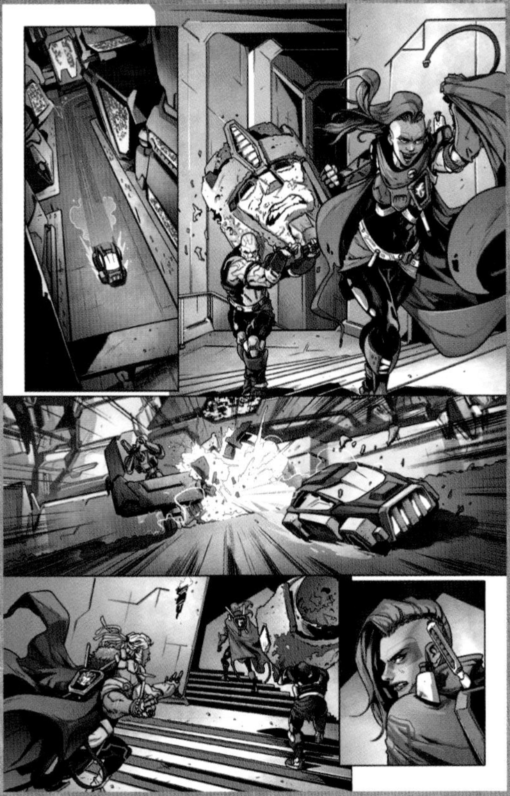

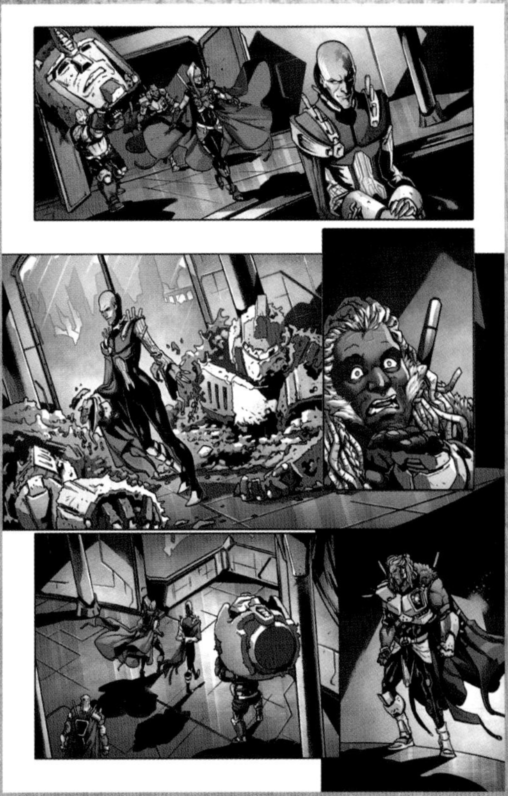

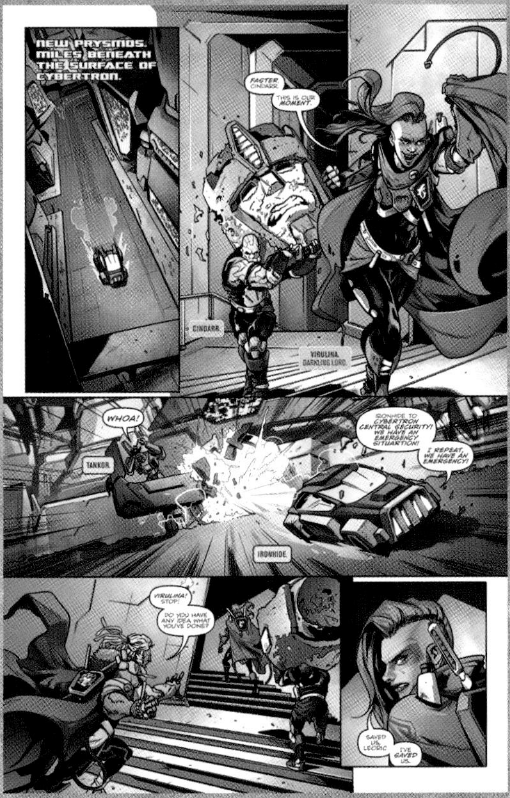
NEW PRYSMOS. MILES BENEATH THE SURFACE OF CYBERTRON.
FASTER, CINDARR.
THIS IS OUR MOMENT.
CINDARR.
VIRULINA. DARKLING LORD.
WHOA!
TANKOR.
IRONHIDE TO CYBERTRON CENTRAL SECURITY! WE HAVE AN EMERGENCY SITUARTION!
I REPEAT, WE HAVE AN EMERGENCY!
IRONHIDE.
VIRULINA! STOP!
DO YOU HAVE ANY IDEA WHAT YOU'VE DONE?
SAVED US, LEORIC.
I'VE SAVED US.

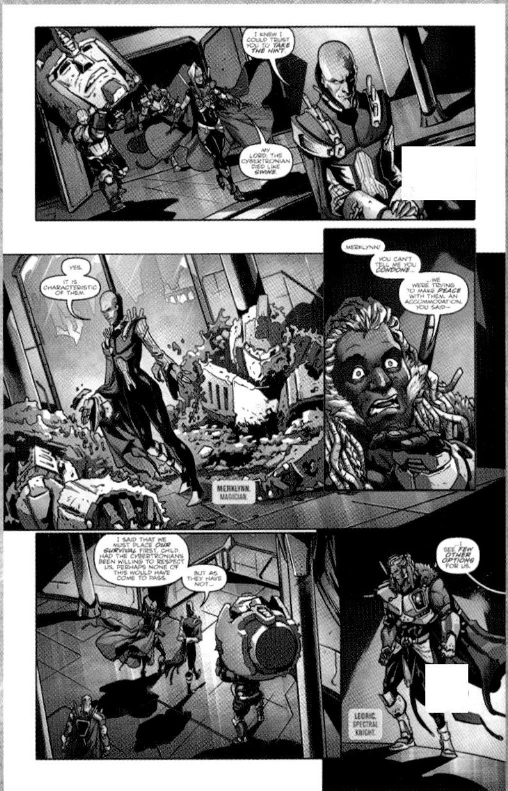
I KNEW I COULD TRUST YOU TO TAKE THE HINT.
MY LORD, THE CYBERTRONIAN DIED LIKE SWINE.
YES.
IT IS CHARACTERISTIC OF THEM.
MERKLYNN!
YOU CAN'T TELL ME YOU CONDONE...
...WE WERE TRYING TO MAKE PEACE WITH THEM. AN ACCOMMODATION. YOU SAID--
MERKLYNN. MAGICIAN.
I SAID THAT WE MUST PLACE OUR SURVIVAL FIRST, CHILD. HAD THE CYBERTRONIANS BEEN WILLING TO RESPECT US, PERHAPS NONE OF THIS WOULD HAVE COME TO PASS.
BUT AS THEY HAVE NOT...
I SEE FEW OTHER OPTIONS FOR US.
LEORIC. SPECTRAL KNIGHT.

LEORIC

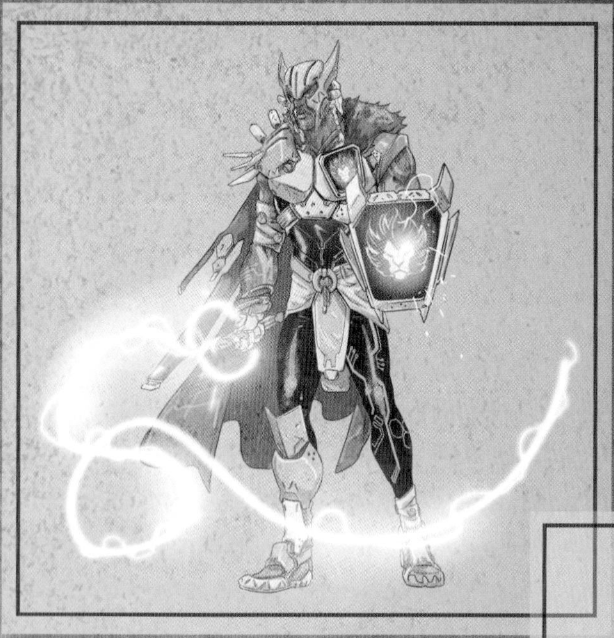

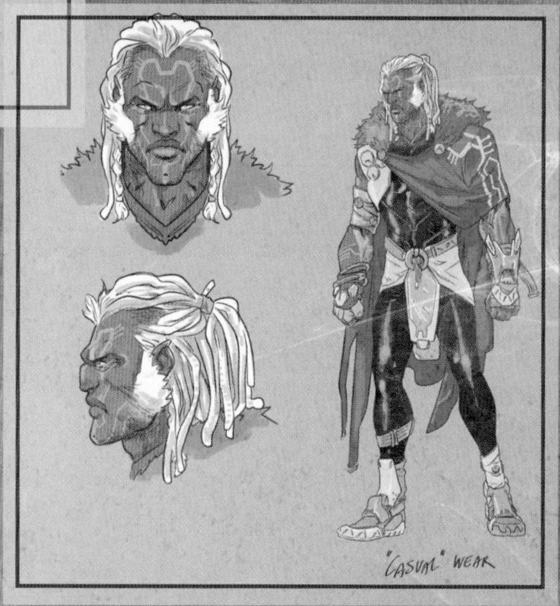
"CASUAL" WEAR

LEORIC BEAST

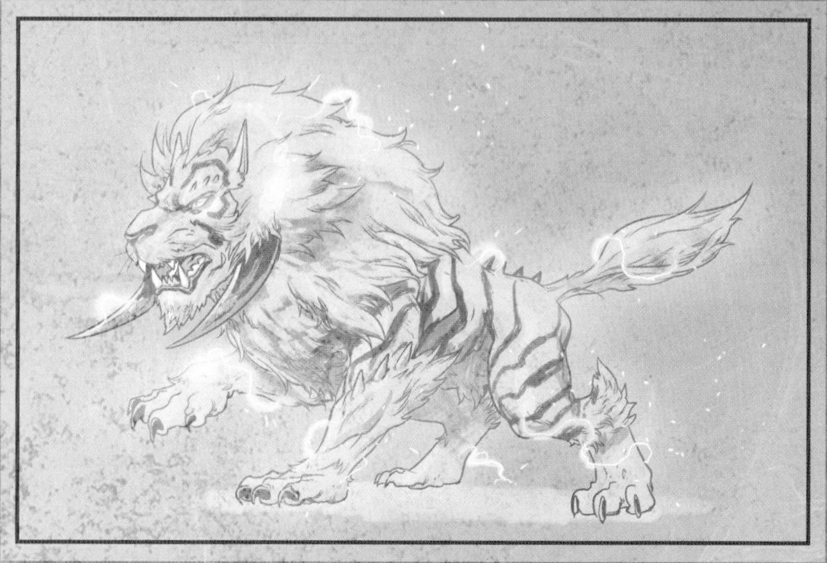

WITTERQUICK

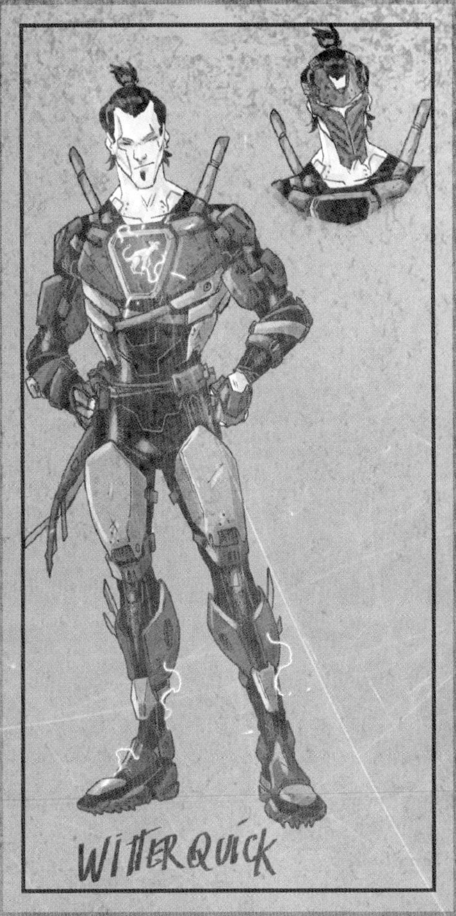
WITTERQUICK

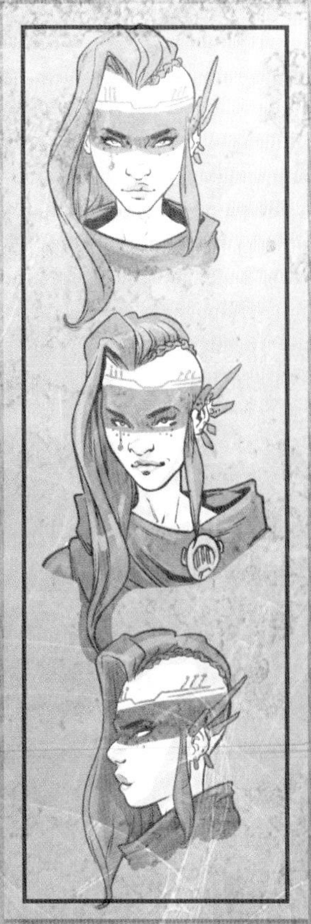

VIRULINA

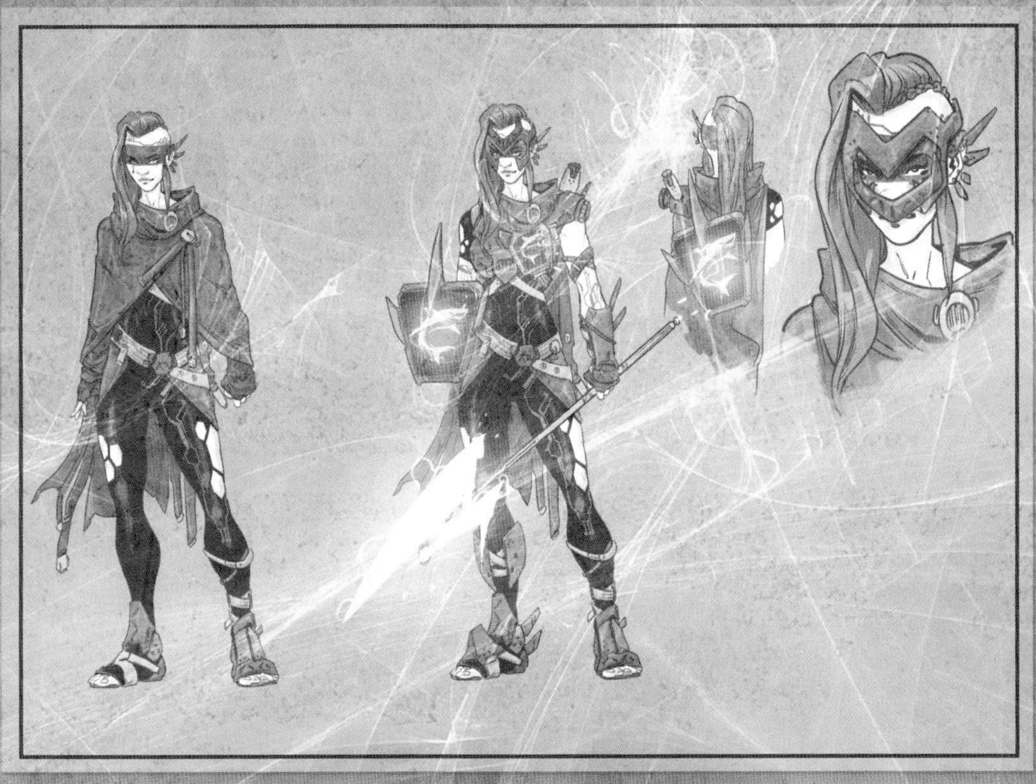

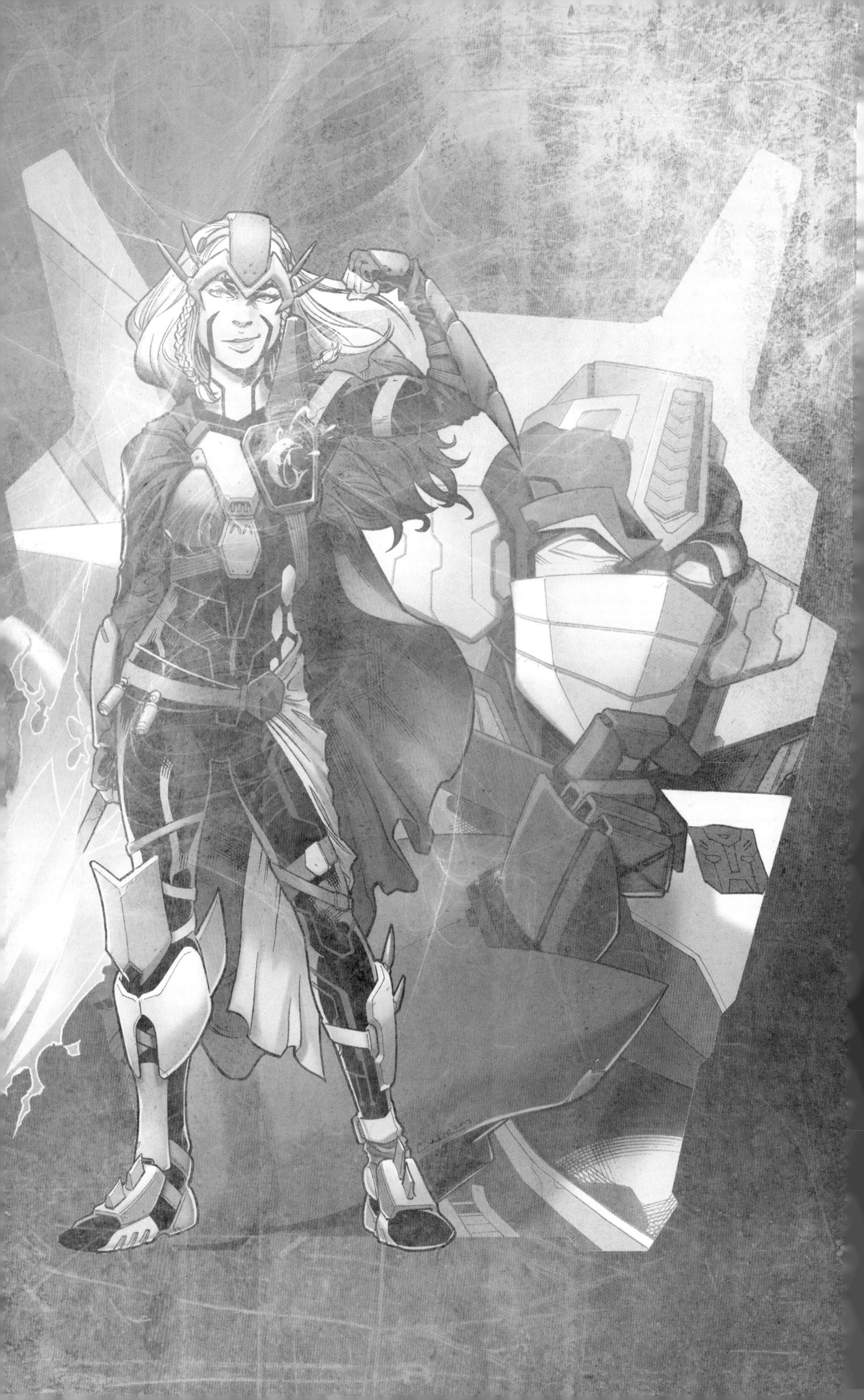